# THE TAVISTOCK LEARNING GROUP

# THE TAVISTOCK LEARNING GROUP

## Exploration Outside the Traditional Frame

*Clive Hazell and Mark Kiel*

**KARNAC**

First published in 2017 by
Karnac Books Ltd
118 Finchley Road
London NW3 5HT

British Library Cataloguing in Publication Data

A C.I.P. for this book is available from the British Library

ISBN-13: 978-1-78220-415-2

Typeset by V Publishing Solutions Pvt Ltd., Chennai, India


www.karnacbooks.com

# CONTENTS

# ACKNOWLEDGEMENTS

*Clive Hazell*

My adherence to social network theory leads me to the conclusion that many thousands of people are involved in the production of this text. Since it is impossible to acknowledge them all, I select some that are prominent. The usual disclaimer, that I alone am responsible for the pages I have written, holds. Dr. Piers Blaikie alerted me to the application of general system theory to social science in 1966. Judith Doss first encouraged me to attend a series of Encounter Groups in 1972. Shortly after, Dr. Daniel Scheinfeld showed how these ideas could be applied to families and cultural systems. Dr. Solomon Cytrynbaum first introduced me to Tavistock groups in 1978 and continued my education for decades after that. Dr. Robert Lipgar has always been a generous mentor and has shown me how to carry out empirical research in this troublous terrain. Dr. Margaret Warner, in her leadership of experiential group and community events that brought together multiple frameworks has stimulated in me decades of thinking across paradigms. Dr. Leonard Hochmann taught me for over a decade on the intricate relationships that exist between mind and body, especially as it relates to early childhood development. Dr. Diana Semmelhack has been a colleague and inspiration for two decades. Following her lead, I have participated in long term research showing how the Tavistock approach can be applied in group psychotherapy with patients carrying diagnoses of severe mental illness. More recently, Dr. Joseph Suglia has patiently and kindly alerted me to the significance of literary theory in the understanding of groups. There has been a steady groundswell of support from the A. K. Rice Institute for the Study of Social Systems and the Chicago Center for the Study of Groups and Organizations which provided sounding boards for us as we developed these ideas.

Of course, I must thank my partner in this venture, Mark. This adventure, intellectual, emotional, and spiritual would not have been possible without our working together. I have a lifelong gratitude for this.

Finally, I must thank my wife, children, and family, for, though I did try to fit the writing of this book into the comings and goings about me so it would not be noticed, my time and attention were compromised and I was not as "present" as I otherwise would have been. In addition, without the closeness, warmth, support, and positive challenges they give so unstintingly, none of this would have happened.

Again, while we owe a debt of gratitude to these individuals and organizations, what we have written here expresses only our views.

# ACKNOWLEDGEMENTS

*Mark Kiel*

I echo Clive's sentiments that with an acknowledgement and true respect of social systems theory, it is impossible to recognize all the contributions that made this text possible.

That said, I would like to identify those who have most directly supported this project:

I want to thank the groups, those I have been a member of and those I have had the privilege to observe or serve as a consultant to. You have taught me so very much.

I want to thank the mentors and supporters that have backed my development and learning in these endeavors, including Dr. Solomon Cytrynbaum, Ms. Charla Hayden, Dr. Robert Lipgar, Dr. Jeffrey Roth, Dr. Annemarie Slobig, Dr. Jack Saporta, and Dr. Margaret Warner.

I want to thank the A.K. Rice Institute for the Study of Social Systems and the Chicago Center for the Study of Groups and Organizations for the consistent support of my ideas and initiatives.

I want to thank Dr. Clive Hazell. Words cannot express my gratitude.

I want to thank my wife—I didn't know it could be this good. Your support and patience made this possible.

Again, while we owe a debt of gratitude to these individuals and organizations, what we have written here expresses only our views.

# ABOUT THE AUTHORS

**Clive Hazell** attended the Gilberd School, Colchester, England, and received a BA in Geography from Reading University, Berkshire and a Masters in Geography from Northwestern University, Evanston, Illinois. He worked on projects aimed at bringing about school change at the Institute for Juvenile Research, Chicago. These were funded by the U.S. Office of Education and the Ford Foundation. He graduated with a doctoral degree in Counseling Psychology from Northwestern University in 1982 and has had a private practice in Chicago since that date. He has attended and consulted at Tavistock groups since 1978 and has published several books and papers on this and other topics. Recent books address the therapeutic impact of Tavistock groups with patients carrying diagnoses of severe mental illness.

**Dr. Mark Kiel** is a clinical psychologist and group psychotherapist, and is board certified in Organizational and Business Psychology. He is the Vice-President/President Elect of the Chicago Center for the Study of Group and Organizations (CCSGO). Over the last decade, Dr. Kiel coordinated a group-based Personal and Professional Development program as part of the curriculum of clinical psychology, and teaches courses in group dynamics, psychoanalytic theory and practice, and

xi

organizational consultation. He is active in Group Relations Conferences serving as a director and consultant with particular interest in Large Study Groups, Institutional Systems Events, and post-conference application.

# PREFACE

Our intention in this book is to relate traditional group relations concepts with models, theories or aspects of other paradigms that are not usually considered or applied to the "Tavistock" model. It is our experience that most group relations work in the "Tavistock" tradition relies upon the theories of A.K. Rice (2013), Wilfred Bion (1961), and Melanie Klein (1975). In addition, there seems to be considerable emphasis, in practice, upon what might be termed a "phenomenological affective" approach where individuals share their emotional experiences and fantasies and the group members and consultants attempt to make sense of these in an "experience near" fashion from a "group-as-a-whole" perspective. This last approach will make, to a varying degree, use of the aforementioned three theorists. This tack is clearly of great utility and fertility as documented elsewhere, for example, by Semmelhack et al. (2013).

However, we believe there is much to be gained by explicitly applying as yet un- or under-used explanatory templates in attempting to understand the wide and diverse range of unconscious dynamics impacting and influencing social systems. At the very outset, we notice few references to the origins of systems theory itself and to other systems-based theories, such as Piaget and Inhelder (1969). Such an expanded integration should enable new perceptions and practical suggestions, as well as a wider field of possible application and theorizing. It should also promote engagement with neighboring disciplines such as philosophy, geography, decision-making, management, architecture, cultural studies, anthropology, literary theory, and the study of socio-technical systems.

Thus, this text has chapters linking group relations work with some of the more "academic" theories on group dynamics (Chapters One to Three). Chapter Four demonstrates ways in which existential ideas can throw light upon group dynamics from a different angle and Chapter Six reexamines the processes of formulating interpretations. Chapters Eight and Nine attempt to integrate recent thinking on trauma and the role of bodily processes to group-as-a-whole dynamics, while literary theory is applied to the processes of anti-work in Chapter Seven and community in Chapter Ten. Lacanian ideas are dispersed throughout the text and the Lacanian discourses are explicitly applied to unconscious group dynamics in Chapter Five. The ideas of Rice, Bion, and Klein are deployed throughout the work.

The book is also replete with examples from a variety of group and conference contexts in an attempt to further illustrate how the ideas presented in the text appear and can be applied. These examples are used with permission of the participants or have been disguised so as to preserve anonymity.

# CHAPTER ONE

# On learning groups

*Mark Kiel*

The impetus for this book is that the co-author and I are Tavistock group enthusiasts. We teach, consult, and spend a great deal of time thinking about these kinds of groups. Over the past fifteen years, we settled into a pattern of running Tavistock groups and then processing the events that transpired. That left an impression on us. Letting a significant amount of time pass between the groups' events and the discussion of them seems to have afforded us both a certain intellectual distance and flexibility. Over the years, we further fell into an informal habit of spending our time less processing our subjective experiences and more time offering very specific working hypotheses about what the theoretical and applied learning of a given group or group interaction might belie. We tended to focus on the extremes— groups that went especially well, groups that went especially poorly, and groups that performed especially curiously. Our "working models" of these notable events made their way into the courses we taught, our future group work and permeated our psychology world views. I took to writing shorts essays for my classes about the phenomenon in question and attaching vignettes about group interactions that seemed especially illustrative. Clive had done similar work previously in a more formal manner, culminating in a number of books on topics ranging from *Imaginary Groups* (2005), to *Alterity* (2009), to *The Experience of Emptiness* (2003). It is the intention of this effort to share some of our thoughts on these Tavistock-related sub-topics: at times revisiting established ideas, at times partnering the Tavistock model with other aspects of psychology or social science, and to along the way offer vignettes that we believe captured these conceptual ideas.

### Thinking from a Tavistock paradigm

Although it is the working assumption of this book that the reader is relatively well-versed in Tavistock/Group relations theory, a few key

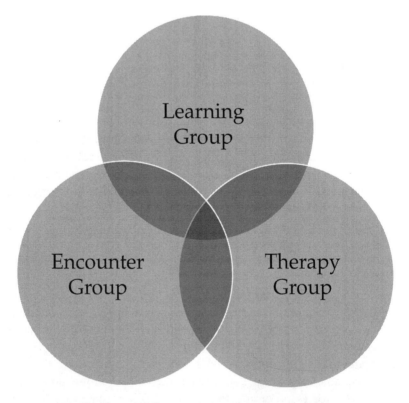

Figure 1. Similarity and difference in group task and practices.
*Note*: The task differentiates the groups, not necessarily the structure, application or technique. As noted below, this makes an experiential learning group both difficult to navigate and especially effective at "deep learning" (Semmelhack, Ende, & Hazell, 2013), and participant-specific insight.

reminders about fundamental concepts of the work are appropriate to start the frame, and to serve as launching points for the chapters to follow.

To start, Tavistock learning groups are not group psychotherapy, are not structured in a traditional fashion nor are they facilitator-led endeavors. The goal is not to impart a fund of knowledge like a lecture or didactic class. Rather, learning groups focus on the exploration or discovery of psychosocial knowledge by doing and experiencing. Whereas there is a wide breadth of potential learnings in the personal and professional domains that may occur, specific learning outcomes are not a task or goal in a formal or informal sense. Yet, as an experiential group enterprise, learning groups do have logistical and theoretical overlap with encounter groups, training groups, or psychotherapy groups—and it is possible for a participant to have an experience like one might from these other forms of group, as a by-product of their primary task. A visual may help at this point.

## A "hatred of learning"?

The theoretical founder of this type of group work, Wilfred Bion stated "… There is a hatred of having to learn by experience at all …" (Bion, 1961). This quote is oftentimes misunderstood or confusing, particularly to people who have not had previous experiences with experiential learning formats.

First, implied in the quote is the premise that there are multiple ways to learn. Bion was contrasting two specific aspects: learning through explanation and learning through experience. His career as a psychoanalyst and consultant to groups led him to conclude that people tend to like to learn by explanation. It tends to be less taxing, less anxiety-provoking, and quicker. The drawback is that it also tends to be less personally meaningful and at times, less relevant. Less relevant insofar as learning by explanation was "other-led" and may not even focus on or attend to the most important dimensions of the learner. To go a step further, Bion was initially surprised at the anger, angst, and hostility group members expressed when they were told they could learn what, how, and at what rate they wanted to do—without direct explanation from the formal leader of the group. In these learning groups, Bion believed his role was primarily to give a frame for learning to occur, and to consult to irrational, covert, and unconscious dynamics that prevented or undermined learning opportunities and group development. The role was not to lead, teach, guide, or structure in the typical sense of these terms. When he adopted this stance, and authorized the members to take up their self-authorization to work and learn in a manner, rate, and focus that was in line with the learning task and their subjective experience, they reacted in a manner that was, psychologically, hateful. Hateful in that they attacked the consultant, the task of the group and boundaries of the group in symbolic ways in attempts to seize the anxiety brought on by having to learn by doing, exploration, and experience (Bion, 1961). This concept is echoed and modified by De Mare (2011) with his concept of koinonia, or the state of impersonal fellowship that results from a large group's initial frustrations and expressions of hate.

A related set of concepts that may further help clarify this notion of "hatred of learning" is the notion of links. Bion asserted there were three primary ways the self can connect to objects. He called these connections "links" and said they were of three qualities, (L)ove, (H)ate, and (K)nowledge. These three categories may appear at first take to be oversimplified, but they are theoretically indicated from an object relational point of view. Bion, and other object relationally informed psychoanalysts assert that early in life, infants are only capable of simplified thinking (Bion, 1959). They "love" things—insofar as they have strong emotional ties to people that are idealizing in nature, and "hate" things—insofar as they have strong emotional ties to people that are antagonistic in nature. This dichotomy results in the defense of splitting. It is not until later in development individuals can see other people in their complexity, wholeness or unity. This last statement needs at least two caveats. The first is, no matter how much a person develops psychologically, they never lose the "Love/Hate" foundation of early psychical life—it is analogous to the "old brain," we may develop or add additional psychological apparati (like the "mid-brain" or "new brain"), but under it all, still serving basic functions is the old brain. The second caveat is that groups, by their nature, regress members to this "psychologically primitive" Love/Hate functioning. There are several reasons for this. A few examples:

- The cognitive: when you enter a group both explicit and implicit categorization begins (e.g., like me, not like me; familiar versus the novel, potentially helpful or potentially dangerous), in essence are you potentially "good" or "bad"—and this is analogous to Love and Hate.

- The emotional: groups are complex places where intense feelings are communicated consciously and unconsciously. If the feeling received is not one a member was anticipating or solicited, it can be experienced as violating and result in a defensive stance (and again drawing the members to identify where these unwanted experiencing are emanating from …). Defensive stances and searches for the cause of unwanted or unexpected feelings thus engenders more oppositionality.
- The perceptual: in a group of more than twelve members, people can no longer view the whole group in their perceptual field—someone and something is always going on that you are outside of sight. This results in a subtle shift to the paranoid and vigilant.
- The sociological: joining a group means giving up part of your autonomy or individualness—it's the price people pay to be part of a group (and usually, the bigger the group the more you have to give up …). Giving up aspects of yourself and autonomy is usually anxiety-provoking and we "down shift" psychologically to the splitting of Good/Bad or Love/Hate to cope in the short term.

What is missing from this discussion so far is the Knowledge Link (K-link). K-links are the capacity to contemplate, to understand complexity, to comprehend abstractly, and to think symbolically. K-links afford the capacity to make connections. Perhaps this is where the technical explanation of this introduction has run its course and some applied examples can be of use.

## "Assassins" and the importance of metaphor

I was giving a lecture about Tavistock principles and when I asked if there were any questions, one of the participants asked, "Is it true you called your group members 'assassins'?" I could think of several instances where I had consulted to a group and had characterized the group as a band of murderers, or saboteurs or polite assassins. Not sure what was all implied in the question, I responded honestly, "sure." The participant then asked why I would do such a thing. That second question was the key in understanding an important concept.

It is a premise of intrapsychic functioning that people first imagine possibilities—what are called "phantasies." Then people express those phantasies metaphorically. Finally they can act on those phantasies literally. Take an example like genocide. First a murderous impulse is imagined and is held on the "inside." Then it takes metaphoric expression, at first subtle then ranging to the more overt—such as shifting from comments to propaganda to marginalization to discrimination and on to hate crimes. As the various incarnations become more overt, the leap to the next step in the spiral is more possible. The psychoanalytic "intervention" to this cascade is abstract thought and interpretation. There must be openness to the symbolism in the second stage of events— between when the phantasy is internal and before the behaviors are acted on. That second stage is when the phantasy is first expressed in an indirect way, but which is a harbinger of things to come.

Impulse/Phantasy → Symbolic expression → Overt behavior
(On a continuum)

A Tavistock learning group, which by design removes the everyday distractions that obfuscate these metaphoric expressions, methodically seeks to identity and overtly comment on them. The intention of the method and frame is to make these metaphoric expressions "seen" and "understood" for what they could possibly represent, so they can then be worked with in a more conscious manner. Without the development of these K-links, there is great potential for unconscious, repetitive or escalating actions and behaviors.

Or said another way, it can be more helpful for a group to directly consider the possibility they are expressing aggressive phantasies than to wait and deal with the aftermath once an assassination of some sort has happened.

## Whistle-blowers, K-links, and scapegoats

The example above portrays K-links in some sense as a "solution" to maladaptive functioning. In that sense, the example only demonstrates one aspect of a complex concept. K-links oftentimes evoke ambivalent, poignant or painful feelings. This is akin to Melanie Klein's concept of the Depressive Anxiety—insofar as seeing something in its "wholeness" can have a dysphoric and un-quieting effect on the person having the revelatory experience.

A good example of this came up when I was attending a lecture about the phenomena of "whistle-blowing" from a Tavistock perspective.

A whistle-blower is a person who raises a concern about wrongdoing occurring in an organization or group. Dr. C. Fred Alford (2002), a foremost expert on whistle-blowing made the thesis that the whistle-blower is the first member of a group to imagine a possibility, conceptualize an issue, and then give voice to it. Take for example the employee that realizes her company is illegally dumping toxic waste in a river that passes by a school. The whistle-blower makes a K-link (she can imagine children playing in the waste and the effects that it may have on them) and then voices that link to others (which makes it harder for the rest of the group to deny, distort, or avoid). And how is the "keeper" of the K-link dealt with? The vast majority of whistle-blowers are shunned or ostracized by the groups they are part of for their thoughts and actions.

The Tavistock perspective, also known as Group-As-A-Whole analysis, is often referred to as the analysis of scapegoating, as it seeks to understand how members of a group are activated to perform a function on behalf of the group and then are discarded, blamed, or rejected for these actions. This is often because the scapegoat is unaware of how they are being unconsciously manipulated by the group. The example of the whistle-blower shows the other aspect to scapegoating. People can be scapegoated as easily and efficiently for what they know, as for what they don't know. For what they can understand, as easily as for what they don't understand.

This process is not exclusive to work settings and whistle-blowing activities. It happens in many instances, and can be highlighted in a Tavistock learning group. Consultants are often hated or attacked for looking for possible K-links, symbolic thought or early metaphoric expressions by the group. The first of the members to join the consultants or the Tavistock methodology are often subtly (and sometimes overtly) shunned or ostracized for "disrupting the status quo."

There are also pressures and dilemmas for the last group members to acknowledge or accept possible K-links. These members may experience a range of difficult roles and projections, from being "ignorant hold outs" in the eyes of the group, to repositories for resistance, to feeling shame for being so slow to accept new insights, to being noble for holding on to their conscious experience or "idealistic" convictions. That said, if the learning group is truly a "working group" and K-links are being made, the group will likely come to understand and integrate how these members are holding on to a very important aspect of the group's life.

## Hell and ignorance

The last example of this section exploring the "Hatred of learning" comes from a group relations conference. The conference was underway and the difficult task of learning from experience had started. A relatively novice consultant in training entered the staffroom and as the staff work began, essentially asked if the work was unnecessarily sadistic in nature. She explained she had a high degree of sympathy and empathy for the members who were struggling with the intensity of the experience and with the oftentimes anxiety-provoking nature of the Tavistock methodology. She implied that learning from experience was difficult enough, and added that when she was honest with herself, she thought the laissez faire but intense Tavistock model often made it even more difficult. She then voiced her fear clearly and succinctly. She said she knew learning from experience could be very difficult, but added that she wondered if the Tavistock method made it "downright hellish."

The response from the director of the conference was bold, and I believe worth considering here. The director replied, "We are not making it hellish, we are giving them the opportunity to see clearly the hell they are already in." A "wiser, but sadder" statement if I have ever heard one.

That said, the response has several dimensions to it. First, it suggests the baseline of human functioning is a difficult if not precarious one. To genuinely live, work, play, and interact is a complex and daunting endeavor. Second, it suggests there are methods that can bring this struggle to an overt and conscious level. Third, it is implied that it is better to consciously deal with those painful but very real dimensions then to ignore them or minimize them.

This perspective on the human psychological condition, the Tavistock methodology, and the requirements for experiential learning are often reacted to in an unfavorable light. All the focus on the irrational, unconscious, and covert barriers and obstacles to human and group development is unnecessarily pessimistic, skeptical, or even sadistic. When employed incorrectly, that may be true. However, the model also fosters a number of potentially empowering dynamics. It does not enable fragility. It assumes people can and will learn from their experience. It directly deals with difficult and profound issues. It offers the opportunity for members to pursue their experience in a manner that balances authenticity and responsibility. It affords the possibility that profound learnings happen in the "learning space" of the group and can be translated to the many other groups people find themselves (family groups, work groups, social groups, etc.). Those learnings can make a tangible and significant difference in the psychosocial functioning of the individual person and the groups they live amongst (Semmelhack, Ende, & Hazell, 2013). Melanie Klein's model of development posits that intense, wonderful, and positive experiences are very possible. For instance, she wrote extensively on the topics of gratitude, devotion, and compassion (Klein, 1975). However, she suggested these altruistic and enjoyable feelings are only possible in a genuine fashion if first the psychotic and part-object world of the paranoid-schizoid position is navigated first, followed by the poignant and complex whole-object world of the depressive position. The Tavistock methodology and theory follows this development trajectory as well.

Or said another way, the "hellish" aspects of our underdeveloped intrapsychic and social worlds must be examined and tamed prior to achieving and functioning in a complex, conscious, and hermeneutically engaged manner.

## Expanding the Tavistock paradigm by addition

Now that a bit of review of traditional Tavistock theory and terminology is underway, it is time to focus the content of the book as well as the themes of the chapters. Obviously, there are many topics in the social sciences that could be partnered with Tavistock group dynamics to generate novel areas for exploration. We think this is especially important to write about as aspects of group relations theory and practice have over time, become something of a "closed system." This is not to deride or overlook innovations in this subfield, but rather to promote the notion that such a heuristically rich model should be, and is capable of expansion, evolution, and growth. Indeed, if the Tavistock model is as important and effective for understanding psychosocial phenomena as many of us think it is, then surely such a model can be paired with other such "tools" and paradigms to investigate, understand, and expand potential learnings. To that end, this book is an overt effort to be conceptually, intellectually, and theoretically open, curious, and expansive. In the chapters to follow we will explicitly focus on the following content areas:

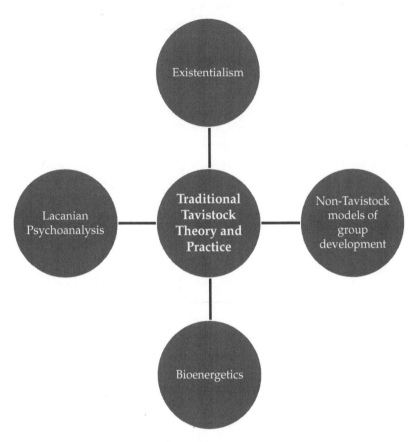

Figure 2.  Specific content topics of this book.

As will be presented, we believe these sub-fields of psychology are especially helpful in having a deeper and more expansive conceptual framework for doing Tavistock group work. That said, this book is also constructed around a conceptual relation between Tavistock theory and application and four concepts we assert are fundamentally related to the foundation of group relations work, but that needs further articulation and explanation.

Please note that whereas many chapters are structured around specific content areas (Figure 1), the conceptual topics (Figure 2) are more fluid and bend from one chapter to the next. In this sense, the full arc of the book is an effort to partner traditional Tavistock concepts with non-Tavistock topics and themes to expand understanding. However, these reconfigurations often result in new questions or complexities,

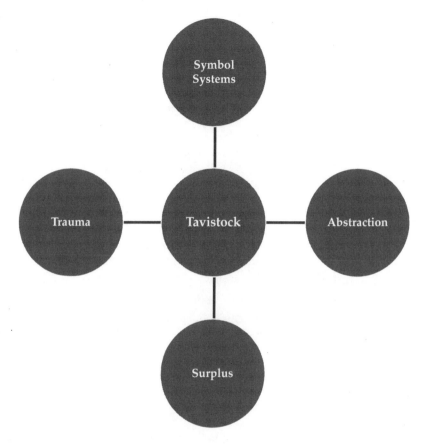

Figure 3. Thematic topics of this book.

which the following chapter, in turn, attempts to further explore. Thus, the individual chapters can be read as discrete sections, but for a fuller conceptual understanding the book is best examined as a whole.

Now, as both examples of revisiting well-worn areas of Tavistock theory and to also offer an additional hypotheses that expounds on the complexity of these phenomena, the following will be considered:

- The perception of scarcity.
- The perception of lawfulness.
- The Tavistock learning group: a vortical environment.

As mentioned previously, members in Tavistock groups are not told what to learn, at what rate to learn, or how to learn—rather they are given a social space and are resourced with consultants and fellow members, in which to learn. Couple that template with first, the interpersonal flat stance most Tavistock consultants assume and second, the psychological focus on process over content, and members arrive at a number of frequent member refrains:

- We have no task.
- Nothing is going on.
- We are impoverished.
- There is no purpose to be found here.

Whereas some of these matters are touched on in other chapters, here these dynamics are looked at from a lens of surplus and scarcity.

Much of economic theory is based on a principle of supply and demand, with the undergirding principle that with more scarcity comes more demand. The work of Karl Polanyi (1974) suggested a significant alternative to this traditional view. Polanyi was an economic historian who asserted that perhaps surplus, not scarcity, was the defining feature of modern economies and social systems. He asserted that in "nonmarket societies" the economy cannot be distinguished by reference to an interrelated flow of rational calculations. Instead, the historian or anthropologist must start from the material objects which serve to satisfy wants, and follow their movements to see what operational patterns and groupings emerge. The key point is that choice does not presuppose insufficiency of means, that is, "scarce" resources. Rather the opposite: if means are less "scarce," the more and harder choices we are forced to make (Polanyi, 1974). Said another way:

> As long as social organization runs in its ruts, no individual economic motives need come into play; no shirking of personal effort need be feared ... In such a community the idea of profit is barred; higgling and haggling is decried; giving freely is acclaimed as a virtue; the supposed propensity to barter, truck and exchange does not appear. The economic system is, in effect, a mere function of social organization. (Polanyi, 1957, p. 49)

What does this short diatribe on economics and production have to do with learning groups? As was pointed out in the introduction, learning groups in the Tavistock tradition have a lot more going on in the social space of the group than is the focus of the primary task. As Polanyi suggests, the psychological dimensions of purpose and relatedness are more anxiety-provoking when there is a surplus in a social system where literal production is not a demand. A genuine scarcity of resources is not nearly as much of a problem as having a rich potential reserve. Polanyi asserts a social system will go so far as to systematically destroy surplus rather than have to deal with the issues it elicits (he cites war and imprisonment as mechanisms at a societal level). The learning group derivative of this dynamic should be evidencing itself. When a learning group encounters the rich potential of group life, the diversity and depth of members, and the help and interpretations of trained consultants, the group experiences "surplus-anxiety." The group then tends to unconsciously, but systematically undo, destroy, or deny the surplus rather than acknowledge and utilize it. Defensively speaking, this results in a reaction formation as an experience of emptiness, meaninglessness or impoverishment. However, as will be addressed in the chapter on existentialism and the learning group, this impact may go beyond defensive reactions, it can lead to a collapse of meaning and the capacity for meaning-making.

This concept is also echoed by another economist, George Bataille (1949):

> Changing from the perspectives of restrictive economy to those of general economy actually accomplishes a Copernican transformation: a reversal of thinking—and of ethics. If a part of wealth (subject to a rough estimate) is doomed to destruction or at least to unproductive use without any possible profit, it is logical, even inescapable, to surrender commodities without return. (Bataille, 1949, pp. 25–26)

Regarding the next figure, note how only part of the represented group space is the primary task, and note how a group member or consultant could be confused or at a difference of opinion regarding activity in the green of purple zones of the group space and task. The hypothesis posited here is that members tend to deal with this complexity of choice and surplus of resources by denying the potential and collapsing it psychologically to a point where they are dealing with a seemingly more acceptable set of problems, withholding by the consultants, emptiness of the space, or a lack of definition in task.

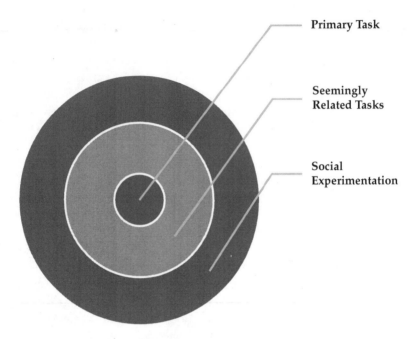

Figure 4. Range of related tasks and social dynamics possibilities in a learning group.

## Variation on a theme: potential and reality

Just as groups and group members must manage the dynamics of surplus and scarcity, in a similar vein, they must manage the dynamics of potential and reality demands. As mentioned above, the opportunities learning groups afford members are especially rich and can strike at the quick of our social and relational nature. In a Winnicottian sense (1965), this "potential space" (1965) generated by group life offers a seemingly unlimited number of learning possibilities. This type of social space is uniquely designed to offer interactions that when managed in a "good enough" (1965) manner, can offer opportunities for the psychoanalytic concepts of spontaneity, work, and play—key tenets for growth, development, and psychological sophistication—be it for individuals or groups. The importance of this potential space is referenced throughout this book in various fashions and incarnations.

On the other hand though, groups do harm. They remind us of the harm we have received. They strike at the vulnerable quick of our social and relational needs. It can be argued this too has to do with the balance of surplus and scarcity, potential and reality. At this intersection is the notion of trauma when considering amount. As Leonard Shengold stated, trauma is the result of "Too much too muchness" or "too much not enoughness" (1975). (This will be further discussed in Eight, The impact of trauma on the learning group and will be re-addressed from a different perspective in Chapter Nine, The body and the group and Chapter Ten, The large group community and therapeutic potential). Either way, "amount," and the perception and experience of it, is a critical feature to the experience of life in a social system and organizes much of the group members' and consultants time. However, following this line of reasoning it can be posited that understanding these dimensions of surplus and scarcity is at the very center of understanding trauma as well.

Lastly, and purposefully placed at the end of this discussion, lies reality demands. I say purposefully because many essays on these topics start with this consideration—but as the Tavistock method so aptly teaches, one may learn more from starting with psychological, systemic, and symbolic matters first.

It is said that humanity has experienced three great insults since the Enlightenment. First, is that earth is not the center of the universe (in fact, astro-physically speaking the earth is pretty much off in a corner somewhere …). Second, humans are animals descended from apes (in a much less direct or pristine form from what many consider The Divine). Well, at least one could argue that humans transcend these base animal instincts and reach lofty and pure intellectual heights. (Insult number three.) Freud asserted humans do not control their own base nature, intellect, or even behaviors! In fact, the structures of the mind are forged under a hidden agenda which people are often unaware of and are often perturbed to consider—the role of the unconscious. Finally, the Tavistock model needs to be considered as a fourth insult. It is not only one's personal unconscious that is significantly influencing them; it is the unconscious dynamics of others. This is a type of reality demand this model identifies and brings front and center to learning group members. It is very destabilizing and distressing—both when first glimpsed because of its novel and provocative possibilities and when witnessed over time, because of its insidious, persistent, and elusive nature. This reality demand also leads to another common perception and set of reactions.

## The perception of lawfulness

When it comes to the matters of lawfulness, intentionality and order in systems' behaviors there are several schools of thought. In general, let us start by saying, most observers of groups, systems, and social phenomena agree that there appears to be a logic or identifiable mechanisms that govern collectives' behaviors. For example, imagine groups where, without conscious planning:

- All the men sit on one side of the circle and all the women sit on the other side.
- The three members most resistant to engage with the group show up wearing red.
- The groups' three consultants all become confused or forget about the ending time of the group and wind up ending the group fifteen minutes early.
- Two members have similar dream material from the night before.
- All the people of color are late for a given group.

A more complicated and specific case example can be offered later, but hopefully these superficial examples give the reader an idea of basic manifestations. The Tavistock practitioner assumed there is an unconscious order, meaning or purpose to events like these. Furthermore, understanding such unconscious expressions is key for the development of insight and the ability to do complex work. However, such assertions are often met with a number of frequent member refrains:

- You are making connections where none exist.
- You are trying to make meaning out of coincidences.
- Things are just random.
- Not everything means something.

Theoretically, comments like these are grounded in models that suggest the appearance of conscious or unconscious coordination of activities is just that, an appearance. These schools of thought generally focus on the existence of the individual as a strict construct (orthodox humanism) or include paradigms that deny meaning making at all (like nihilistic philosophies).

But there are also several models from different eras of thought that suggest there is a principal of lawfulness at work. Consider:

- The classical psychoanalytic tenet that if the Ego is not omnipotent, it should at least be credited with a far greater capacity to both orchestrate and undermine actions then is regularly considered. This leads to orchestrated activities that people have little or no awareness of (Freud, 1901).
- Jung posits the term "collective unconscious" to represent a different form of unconscious activity common to humankind as a whole and originating in the inherited structure of the brain. It is distinct from the personal unconscious, which arises from the experience of the individual. His term for unconsciously "coordinated" action is synchronicity (Jung, 1977).
- The British Object Relationists offer an explanation: shared introjects by all members of a group afford the creation of a group mentality that influences, if not governs, group life and all those who participate in it (Bion, 1961).
- Socio-technical systems theory draws a parallel between physical systems (an eco-system or a molecule for instance) and a social system. In both examples, impacted or effecting one part of the system radiates out and impacts all parts of the system. This mechanism wears away the assertion "I" and "other" can remain unrelated (Gould, 2006).
- Advances in the field of social psychology and sociology demonstrate both the impact of the group on the individual (much less palatable than the more popular understandings of how an individual impacts the group ...) and how collectives oftentimes work at cross purposes compared to the conscious intentionality of the members that make it up (Trist & Bamforth, 1951).
- Chaos theory suggests deterministic systems have behaviors that can in principle be predicted. This theory suggests "chaotic systems" are predictable for a while and then *appear* to become random. The amount of time for which the behavior of a chaotic system can be effectively predicted depends on three things: How much uncertainty observers are willing to tolerate in a forecast; how accurately metric and methods are able to measure a current state; and a time-scale depending on the dynamics of the system (Gleick, 1987). In

essence, perceived randomness is a failure of data, instrumentation, and to a degree, expectation. In this model, social systems are analogous to weather patterns or the stock market. Phenomena are not "random," but that term is used in favor over "I can't understand all the variables nor can I handle my limits of knowledge ..."

Whereas one may say, "look at these six models cited above, their mechanisms are so different, this must demonstrate some form of contradiction or unreliability." I suggest they offer a different type of reliability. Using different premises they all arrive at a similar conclusion: collectives follow additional rules than individuals, and those rules have a lawful mechanism that can be used in the service of understanding. I would like to add one more consideration: Emergence theory.

Emergence theory is a multi or poly-theoretical and scientific model that spans multiple disciplines beyond social systems. In short, "emergence" is conceived as a process whereby larger entities, patterns, and regularities arise through interactions among smaller or simpler entities that themselves do not exhibit such properties (Johnson, 2001). An example to consider in detail is an ant colony. The queen does not give direct orders and does not tell the ants what to do. Instead, each ant reacts to stimuli in the form of chemical scent from larvae, other ants, intruders, food, and buildup of waste, and leaves behind a chemical trail, which, in turn, provides a stimulus to other ants. Here each ant is an autonomous unit that reacts depending only on its local environment and the genetically encoded rules for its variety of ant. Despite the lack of centralized decision-making, ant colonies exhibit complex behavior and have even been able to demonstrate the ability to solve geometric problems! (For example, colonies routinely find the maximum distance from all colony entrances to dispose of dead bodies) (Johnson, 2001).

Are we ants? (Spoiler: Yes)

What is more likely—There are no such things as collectives, social systems or group logics that assert order over those that make them up, or that like the ant example above, humans respond to stimuli (in this case, overt and covert interpersonal communications instead of chemical trails) and despite the lack of formal, top down leadership, begin to exhibit complex social behaviors? It most surely is the latter, and the Tavistock method is a unique and particularly effective means to decode these processes and inform other possible courses of action than the passively emerging options that are as often anti-social as they are pro-social. Which leads to the last of these related topics.

### The Tavistock learning group: a vortical environment

In 1965, Emery and Trist presented a simple but exceedingly helpful frame for considering system dynamics. For the sake of brevity, here is the key concept presented in table form.

These are the four so-called organizational textures of social systems. The authors assert that fields I–III (Placid clustered I, Random placid II, and Disturbed reactive III) were well researched concepts. Their primary focus of the model was on exploring systems in the "Turbulent field"—or as they stated, "What becomes precarious under type IV [Turbulent] conditions is how organizational stability can be achieved. In these environments individual organizations, however large, cannot expect to adapt successfully simply through their own direct actions ..." (Emery & Trist, 1965, p. 13). Turbulent fields are characterized by high uncertainty, group think, coping skills masquerading as social values and artificial, sometimes arbitrary rules of order used to diffuse feelings of anxiety and uncertainty (Emery & Trist, 1965). Sound familiar yet?

Emery and Trist go on to ponder a possible V field, a highly turbulent-like texture without adaptive properties, characterized by self-sabotage

|  | Low dynamism | High dynamism |
|---|---|---|
| High complexity | Placid clustered | Turbulent |
| Low complexity | Random placid | Disturbed reactive |

Figure 5. Emery and Trist's four kinds of organization–environment relationships.
*Source*: Emery and Trist (1965).

and self-defeating impulses. Oðuz Babüroðlu (1988) went on to name this the vortical environment stating,

> When the system is sealed off from the environment so much so that transactional interdependencies are almost non-existent, and the system's parts have effectively immobilized each other, the causal texture of the environment can no longer be considered turbulent. At this juncture, the causal texture has effectively become vortical. (Babüroðlu, 1988, p. 17)

Expounding he added, "... vortical, suggesting that the environment takes on some of the properties of a vortex or a whirlpool so that it may have the capacity to swallow up or engulf anything that approaches it" (Babüroðlu, 1988, p. 1).

Rather than a grid format, Babüroðlu presents the fields in the following manner where L indicates some potentially lawful connection and the suffix 1 refers to the organization and the suffix 2 to the environment:

Placid, random        L11
Placid, clustered     L11 L12
Disturbed, reactive   L11 L12 L21
Turbulent             L11 L12 L21 L22
Vortical              L11 L12 L21 L22

The frame of a learning group offers a forum capable of high complexity and high levels of dynamism, and thus the potential for turbulence as defined by Emery and Trist. When the trappings of typical and familiar organizational structures are removed by the Tavistock method—as are tangible throughputs like the generation of agreed upon work products most people are familiar with—monothematic dogmatism, polarization, and stalemate, or the "second order maladaptive responses to turbulence" begin to operate according to Babüroðlu. A group's implementation or adoption of these maladaptive responses, in turn generate a vortical environment.

If you are like me, you may be saying to yourself at an intellectual level "That's fascinating ..." but at an emotional level are experiencing something close to abject fear at the thought of willingly participating in such an experience. This combination of fascination and fear may be a signpost suggesting that this is a good place to end the introduction to this book.

Life is filled with complex and dynamic circumstances. To rephrase Kierkegaard, to live is to experience turbulence (Kierkegaard, 1843a). Indeed much, if not all satisfaction and misery in life is directly correlated to the ability to manage "turbulent" groups (and indeed at larger levels, turbulent organizations, nations, and even societies). Any given family one is born into, any institution one works at, or any social system one interacts with has the potential, if not likelihood, to be a turbulent or even vortical environment at some time in its functioning—this is an emotional, pragmatic, interpersonal, and transactional reality. In the chapters that follow are partial explanations, hypotheses, considerations, and models for navigating such circumstances and environments—first in the setting of Tavistock learning groups and later in so-called "real world" settings. We argue that if such group experiences are part of life, one may as well become skilled and informed about navigating such realities. The Tavistock model is an ideal compass. The learning group an essential tool.

# CHAPTER TWO

# The Hill interaction matrix: a modification and elaboration

*Clive Hazell*

Semmelhack, Hazell, and Ende (2013) present seventeen years of quasi experimental studies that demonstrate the therapeutic effectiveness of Tavistock style groups with those diagnosed with severe mental illness. In these studies, significant improvements in anxiety, depression, coping, and group cohesion were found in members of Tavistock style groups. In addition, Semmelhack, Ende, Freeman, and Hazell (2015, pp. 187–211) describe in more detail the dynamics that took place in these groups. In this section, it is our aim to further explain the reasons why the Tavistock group can promote such growth. Such an explanation seems apposite because the Tavistock group is not intended to provide therapeutic benefit and groups in this tradition are usually regarded as not having especial therapeutic potency. Hill, for example (1965) ranks the "group/confrontive" intervention as eighth on a one to sixteen scale of therapeutic effectiveness. The above-cited studies by Semmelhack Hazell, and Ende (2013) call this rating into question. In this section we will attempt to show why the Tavistock style group has such effectiveness. We will do so by using Hill's three vectors of therapeutic action (1965), namely: member centeredness, interpersonal threat, and therapist role taking in addition to positing several other dynamisms that could have therapeutic impact.

Hill (1965) provides a matrix that provides a descriptive map of group and individual dynamics (see Figure 6). The chart has, on its horizontal axis, four categories of "content", namely what is being covered in the interaction. Thus the group or pair may be talking about a "topic" (for example, the weather or vacation spots), the "group" (e.g., the composition or mood of the group), "personal" concerns (e.g., how one is feeling today, or one's personal history) or "relationship" issues (e.g., how one might feel about another member or how one has a different attitude from another).

On the vertical axis we find five categories that delineate the "work style", that is, the way in which the content is being processed. Thus, the style might be "responsive." In this style members only react to direct questions or instructions, usually from someone in a leadership role. Thus, reading across the matrix members might respond in a structured way to specific questions or directives having to do with a "topic", the "group", something "personal" or a "relationship." The responsive style has been found by Hill to have negligible therapeutic benefit. It is thus not included in his ranking of the cells.

The "conventional" work/style category refers to interactions that are everyday topics that involve little or no risk. Thus, for example, cross hatching with the content categories we might see a conventional discussion of a topic (e.g., the local sports team), of the group (e.g., how everyone is stressed by mid-term exams), of something personal (e.g., one's exercise habits) or of a relationship (e.g., how two members are both Pisces).

The "assertive" is associated with attempts at differentiation of oneself or the group from others. Thus, at the intersection of "assertive/topic" we would find attempts to change the topic of the content or to separate oneself from the prevailing opinion in an almost rebellious fashion. The assertive/group intersection would include attempts by the group to establish its own unique identity, separate from other groups, perhaps through some ideology or by giving itself a label or expounding upon its unique history and development. At the personal/assertive intersection we would see an individual attempt in a personal way, perhaps by sharing a hitherto unknown part of themselves or their history to the group, thus creating for themselves a separate identity in the group. At the assertive/relationship intersection we would find a couple or a subgroup discussing the differences their relationship had from others around them.

Only the last two rows (speculative and confrontive) have been found by Hill to have psychotherapeutic benefit.

The "speculative" category describes interactions which have the stereotyped characteristics of psychotherapy but fall short of the authentic contact involved in this. Thus we see it as a form of "pseudo-psychotherapy." In this we see well-intentioned but usually unsuccessful attempts on the part of individuals, groups, and pairs to help or "cure" others through interventions that often have a clichéd feel to them. Sometimes this would be in the content of a topic, such as how to cure the world's ills. Sometimes it will refer to the group in identifying and solving the problems of "intimacy" in the group. Sometimes an individual might present themselves as a "patient" for the group to cure (the speculative/personal intersection) and sometimes a couple might call upon the group for an intervention (the speculative/relationship intersection).

The final row of the matrix, "confrontive" receives the highest rankings in terms of therapeutic effectiveness. The confrontive work style involves sharing one's authentic impressions, thoughts, feelings, and ideas on a topic, on the group, about one's own person or about a relationship. The confrontive dynamic is non aggressive, dialogical, unconventional, and usually involves spontaneity. It is usually associated with the anxiety of taking a risk of a new behavior, either on the part of the individual or of the group.

Hill goes on to rank the therapeutic effectiveness of these cells and these are given on the table in numbers in parentheses. As we can see, the confrontive/relationship cell is ranked highest at sixteen, while the confrontive/group cell is ranked at eight. The reports of Semmelhack and colleagues (2013, 2015) would seem to challenge such a low rating.

The remainder of this paper will present some ideas on how and why the Tavistock group may indeed generate more therapeutic impact than that argued by Hill's ranking. We will do so by showing that the Tavistock style group in fact mobilizes the three vectors of therapeutic potency described by Hill (member centeredness, interpersonal threat, and therapist role taking) and five additional factors that also have therapeutic impact.

The Tavistock approach is a psychodynamic approach insofar as it aims at uncovering group dynamics that are not usually part of members' awareness. The consultant, for example may point out that the group seems to be involved in processes that are not immediately obvious

| | Non-member Centered | | Member-Centered | |
|---|---|---|---|---|
| Content ⟶<br><br>Work Style ↓ | I<br>Topic | II<br>Group | III<br>Personal | IV<br>Relationship |
| A<br>Responsive | IA | IIA | IIIA | IVA |
| B<br>Conventional | IB<br>(1) | IIB<br>(2) | IIIB<br>(9) | IVB<br>(10) |
| C<br>Assertive | IC<br>(3) | IIC<br>(4) | IIIC<br>(11) | IVC<br>(12) |
| D<br>Speculative | ID<br>(5) | IID<br>(6) | IIID<br>(13) | IVD<br>(14) |
| E<br>Confrontive | IE<br>(7) | IIE<br>(8) | IIIE<br>(15) | IVE<br>(16) |

Pre-work (spanning rows A–C), Work (spanning rows D–E)

Figure 6. Hill interaction matrix.

to group members, such as covert competitiveness, scapegoating, splitting, unacknowledged hostility or eroticism. Consultations may be "pitched" at various levels of unconscious process; sometimes focusing on relatively available but unacknowledged "hidden agendas," sometimes focusing on defenses. At other times, the consultations may be quite "deep" and aim at hypothesized "primitive drives and their derivatives." In the end, however, the focus is on an increased attention paid to unconscious processes as they occur in the here and now. We argue that this factor, let us call it, "encounter with unconscious dynamics," is what in part accounts for the therapeutic benefit found by Semmelhack and colleagues (2013, 2015), and also calls for a higher rating of therapeutic benefit found in cell IIE of the Hill interaction matrix. The therapeutic potency of the encounter with unconscious dynamics works through eight pathways. First through third, it includes in its process all of the three factors posited by Hill to be of therapeutic benefit, that is, it involves member-centeredness, interpersonal threat, and therapist–patient role taking. Fourth, the encounter with unconscious dynamics is therapeutic in and of itself. Fifth, from an object relations perspective, Tavistock group as a whole work results in the development of a "group object" in the minds of members. This formation has potent therapeutic benefit. This establishment of a containing group object also establishes a psychosocial matrix which induces the activation of Hill's three factors that is; it creates a psychological safety that enables member centeredness, risk taking, and patient-therapist role taking. Sixth, the psycho-educational components of the Tavistock group (for example, learning about authority, roles, boundaries, tasks, and their inter-relationships) have enormous therapeutic impact. Seventh, the regression that frequently occurs in Tavistock groups provides ample opportunity for participants to rework earlier developmental impasses (for example, separation–individuation, oedipal, identity) in a more supportive psychosocial matrix. Eighth, the Tavistock experience results in a deeper sense of group cohesion (Semmelhack, Hazell, & Ende, 2013) and this has therapeutic benefit while also meeting the deep need in humans to belong to a "community" (Nancy, 1991).

Even though these individual issues are not the primary focus of the consultations, which are pitched towards the group as a whole, the individual growth is likely to happen nonetheless. Tavistock includes member centeredness, interpersonal threat, and therapist–patient role taking.

The first three items are taken directly from the dimensions that are hypothesized by Hill (1965) to have therapeutic potency.

Member centeredness: The Tavistock approach is a here and now approach. Its explicit aim is to examine the group dynamics in the here and now. Groups, when they first assemble, will typically talk about things like the weather, their vacations, their bosses or teachers, all typically unrelated to the here and now process. A fairly common consultation to these dynamics involves treating them as a "derivative" as a disguised, encoded communication about the here and now of the group. Thus, if members are talking about dangerous neighborhoods they had to go through to get to the group a consultant might offer the idea that this is a disguised and careful way of talking about the perceived risks of being in this room with this group. This is clearly member centered. Certainly it is not aimed at an individual member (unless the group is using a particular member to lead such a discussion) but it certainly is focused on the members as a group and their activities as a group.

Interpersonal threat: Group dynamics are extremely powerful energy systems. Working with a group is analogous to working with a sixteen wheeler truck, while working with an individual is analogous to working with an ultralight airplane. Confronting a group on its behavior is usually experienced as extremely risky. Bion (1961) posits that humans have a profoundly ambivalent attitude towards group membership. We are perhaps uncomfortable with our groupishness because groups, although essential, are also very dangerous places. Groups can kill you, both physically and psychosocially. One must be careful. Thus to stand up and comment on a group dynamic, especially when one is not protected by role, authority, status or a backing from a subgroup requires enormous courage. While it is of enormous therapeutic benefit to be able to confront another individual on their behavior and its impacts, it is of equal benefit to be able to do this (with the correct timing, tact and nuance) with a group, such as a family, department or community. The Tavistock experience enables this and provides ample opportunities to practice this.

Therapist–patient role taking: In positing this dimension, Hill focuses on the therapeutic impact of patients helping each other and moving away from the assumption that it is the therapist and only the therapist that has any resources or usefulness. Many Tavistock-style consultations work exactly along these lines insofar as they confront and expose such "dependency assumptions" in the group. The group is essentially leaderless on day one and typically seeks guidance from the consultant who, for better or worse, is there only to consult. Thus groups will typically attempt multiple ways to engage the consultant as an "oracle" or magical leader and will thwart and undermine attempts at leadership from amongst the membership. When these dynamics are exposed and members start to exercise leadership and, as part of this leadership start to make consultations themselves, this is indeed a complex experience. It is also an experience that involves therapist-patient role taking, not only on a one-to-one relationship, but also on a one-to-the-group relationship. In many ways this is far more complex, taxing, and rewarding. The transferable skills are enormous.

It is important to note that while these therapeutic aims are achieved that they are achieved without "desire, memory or understanding" (Bion, 1978, p. 41). The consultant simply consults. He does not facilitate or guide, cajole, praise, guide or criticize. As Bion remarks, the mind feeds on truth. The group perhaps feeds on the "truth" of the consultations. Attempts to rush the process through guidance will undermine the opportunities for learning.

## The encounter with unconscious dynamics is therapeutic in and of itself

We believe this qualifies as a fourth dimension to be included in the Hill interaction matrix as a means of determining the therapeutic benefit of a group interaction. Cells on the matrix that are rated as higher in therapeutic benefit will also involve a greater degree of encounter with the unconscious, not only of individuals, but also of the group-as-a-whole. Once this dimension is included, then the rating of cell IIE will rise.

Volumes have been written on the potential therapeutic benefit of opening one's awareness to unconscious dynamics. It is an issue that can be addressed on multiple levels. One hypothesis I have forwarded (Hazell, 2003) is that humans come equipped with a "hermeneutic function" (not unlike Klein's "epistemophilic instinct" or Bion's "curiosity"). The deployment, activation, and consummation of this drive is as vital to the sense of well-being as any of the other drives psychologists have posited. Mental health problems can be understood at least in part as resulting from the derailing of this important drive—the drive to assign meanings to things. In everyday parlance it shows up as looking at things from another perspective, thinking about thinking, wondering what things might symbolize, coming up with different meanings or interpretations or readings of events and so on. Such activities destabilize our cognitions, our world view and our view of ourselves but it is just such accommodations (Piaget & Inhelder, 1969) that open up new behavioral, sensory and perceptual horizons.

The Tavistock group provides a saturation in such interpretive activity. Destabilizing at first, it soon becomes stimulating and perhaps even fun. However, venturing into the unconscious is not a walk down a daisy-lined pathway and individuals and groups perhaps are bound to go through some tense moments. These tensions, however are for the most part contained by the attentiveness to the group and its boundaries and the empathic attunement of the consultations which help bind in the anxiety and create an *esprit de corps* which enables consolidation and further exploration.

*Group-as-a-whole work results in the formation of a "group*
*object" that can have therapeutic impact*

Following roughly the thinking of Fairbairn (1952) I think there are two types of internalized objects: *introjects* which are semi-autonomous to autonomous nuclei that result from trauma and *memory objects* which are semi-autonomous integrated foci that are integrated into the mind under normal operating conditions. It is largely the former that present the individual with difficulty since the latter are open systems and are thus in communication with the rest of the personality and are thus amenable to change. Therapy can thus be regarded as involving the creation in the mind of the client of a memory object that sets about coordinating the other internalized objects in their mind. The new memory object is created via the interpersonal relationship of the therapist and client.

In a group situation the same thing can be said to occur except that it is not only individuals that are internalized, it is the group as a whole. I am hypothesizing here the notion of a group object and, by extension, an institutional or organizational object. These too can fall into the category of introject (insofar as they are internalized under conditions of trauma) or memory objects, insofar as they are internalized under conditions that are contained and manageable.

The group as a whole experience (again, cell IIE of Hill's matrix) will usually lead to the creation of a beneficent, calming internalized group memory object. The sequence of the group is roughly that described by Hazell (2005) and results in the formation of a container/contained situation so evocatively described by Bion (1978).

On the one hand, the group when it is a working group, becomes rather like a dialysis machine for a kidney patient insofar as the individual member (or subgroup) will unconsciously projectively identify unwanted mental contents into the group. These are then worked through (in the early stages with the assistance of consultations, in the later stages without such help) analyzed, digested and spoken about in such a manner that the individual member can reassimilate these troublesome ideas and integrate them into their mentality. Rosenfeld (1985, 1987) shows us that this is not always so easy, but once this flow has started, the group itself becomes cathected as an internalized object and starts to gain an influence in the individual's internal matrix of objects. The internal political ecology of the objects starts to shift and the individual's behavior starts to change. Klein and Bion theorize that this flow of overwhelming ideas from baby into mother and back from mother into baby after the mother has metabolized these thoughts into something digestible is the root of mental well-being, the root of inter-personal connectedness, calmness, and relative integration. The mother is in a receptive state of mind called "reverie" and, insofar as she is not simply expelling violently the baby's unwanted contents back into the baby who, in turn, becomes overwhelmed, she is being "continent" and not "incontinent." Groups can develop to the point where the group as a whole is in a state of reverie and continence. Such a group is extremely useful psychologically. Such a group will be internalized, much as a continent mother is internalized as a memory object, and this will be to the therapeutic benefit of the members.

## The psycho-educational components of group-as-a-whole work have potent therapeutic impacts

Tavistock groups are usually established for psycho-educational pur-poses. The aim frequently involves participants learning about aspects of "group dynamics" through experience and much thinking and work has been achieved in this arena (Colman & Geller, 1985). The list of con-cepts to be learned and to be learned through lived experience is quite long and we shall not go into them in great detail here as they are han-dled very adequately elsewhere.

If we posit that the human animal is a group animal (albeit in conflict with its own groupishness) then successful adaptation to life would seem to rest on the individual's capacity to conceptualize, join, partici-pate in, leave, and rejoin groups. In modern societies these processes will occur simultaneously for the individual and asynchronously; that is, one will usually find oneself a member of multiple groups at the same time and at different phases of the joining, participating, leaving, rejoin-ing cycle in different groups at the same time. So much is "common sense," everybody "knows" that on some level or another. However the lived process is extremely complex, dizzying even. Group-as-a-whole work provides experiences where one may go through a cycle (or two or more) of this process with the addition of the consultant's voice and a culture of observing the group. This can provide participants with a useful set of perspectives on the ways in which humans (including themselves) participate in these complex and powerful assemblages.

Typically, members will learn a thing or two about the following (a sampling):

- Fantasies: How dynamics in groups can often be irrational and driven by fantasies, both conscious and unconscious.
- Authority: How issues of authority are handled in groups and ways in which it is established and lost.
- Boundaries: The ways in which individuals and groups struggle to form boundaries and how these boundaries relate to fantasies, authority, task, and role.
- Affectivity: How feelings ebb and flow in groups; how certain groups or individuals can be loaded with feelings for the group.
- Task: How groups typically have very ambivalent attitudes towards the tasks of the group and how groups often end up not accomplishing their tasks or even completing tasks that are the exact opposite of their stated one!
- Leadership: Learning about the trials and tribulations of the leader/ follower dynamic especially how it is often saturated with fantasies that render it extremely challenging.
- Basic assumption life: Learning of the deep unconscious process operating in groups—of dependency, fight and flight, pairing and oneness, for example. Learning how to observe these in groups, observe their impact and one's role in their unfolding.
- Scapegoating/repository: Learning the dynamics of repository which operate through the defense mechanism of projective identification (Grotstein, 1977). Observing how individuals in the group are targeted with troubling thoughts, feelings, and fantasies and the ways in which these can drive a person crazy.
- Application: Taking part in learning exercises where one can take some of these learnings and apply them to other situations and examine their utility.

All these learnings, and others, may be usefully regarded as adaptive. They provide the participant with a more complex mental map of themselves in relation to groups. Such an enhanced mental map may be called, without too much of a stretch, ego strength or perhaps, coping skills. It will certainly involve some sort of self-awareness or self-monitoring. These processes may account for the therapeutic impact of group-as-a-whole work.

The normative regression that occurs in Tavistock groups can provide opportunities for the safe reworking of developmental impasses: The phenomenon of the regressive tug experienced in groups has been remarked upon by a long series of writers in this field, dating back to LeBon (2002) and Freud (1921). Bion (1961) provides a categorization of the forms this regression might take, namely in the form of "basic assumption groups": dependency, fight–flight, and pairing. Others have added to this list, notably Hopper (2003) with basic assumptions "massification and aggregation." These forms of regression are often remarked upon by consultants and groups consequently, to a greater or lesser extent, confront and work through these issues. As the group as a whole works through these powerfully charged states, there will often emerge "leaders" or "central persons" to use Redl's felicitous term (Redl, 1967) who occupy much of the group's attention. These individuals and the other members of the group, who are participants in the work and called upon to examine their participation in these usually unacknowledged dynamics, will frequently go through transformation at the individual level. Such transformation is not the stated explicit aim of a group dynamics format, but we argue that it will occur all the same. This fact can help account for the significant therapeutic effects found by Semmelhack and colleagues (2013, 2015) and for the experiences of deep and long lasting self-transformation often reported by individuals who have participated in Tavistock-type groups.

For example, individuals caught up in groups wrestling with issues of basic assumption dependency will often work through issues that might be referred to as orality, differentiation, fusion, and enmeshment. Groups caught up in basic assumption fight/flight will often cause members to work through issues of trust, belongingness, paranoia, persecutory anxiety, and boundary management. Groups working through issues related to basic assumption pairing will engender in participants the examination of oedipal issues—rivalry, jealousy, envy, voyeurism, exhibitionism, castration, and sexuality—all the issues related to love triangles and "babies" of all sorts. Finally groups involved in the basic assumptions posited by Hopper (2003), namely massification and aggregation, will perhaps be nudged into the examination of personal adjustments to trauma and its *sequelae*.

Again the consultations are pitched at the level of the group-as-a-whole but to the extent they are on target and picked up on by the group, a culture of examination is created in the group which stimulates the examination and re-experiencing by individuals of earlier developmental impasses. The matrix of deep safety proved by the group-as-a-whole environment (Hazell, 2005) enables the individual to metabolize these experiences in a supportive social context.

## Belonging, cohesion, and community

Following Nancy (1991) we hypothesize that there is a drive in humans to be a part of a community. We also hypothesize that just as symptoms may emerge when the other drives are frustrated (for example sex, aggression, and Klein's "epistemophilic instinct") so may they emerge when the "drive to be a part of" is frustrated. The Tavistock style group has been shown to have significant impact on the sense of cohesion (Czochara, Semmelhack, & Hazell, 2016; Semmelhack, Hazell, & Ende, 2013) and this may correspond to the satisfaction of the drive to affiliate in a group or a community. In addition, Yalom and Lescz (2005) argue that the sense of cohesion is one of the therapeutically potent factors in group psychotherapy. The Tavistock group, for all of its anxiety-producing reputation does, since the interventions are pitched at the group-as-a-whole level and since there is a vigorous interpretation of scapegoating through the mechanism of projective identification, seem to result in increases in realistic cohesion rather than the "magical" or identificatory cohesion one finds in basic assumption fight or flight or basic assumption oneness, for example.

We may now have a theoretical framework for explaining the therapeutic impacts of group-as-a-whole work found by Semmelhack and colleagues (2013, 2015). We also would seem to have a claim to re-evaluating the ranking of therapeutic impacts provided in the Hill interaction matrix (1965).

Again, the Tavistock group is not intended to be a therapeutic modality. It is delivered as a means of understanding group dynamics. Its therapeutic benefits seem to be a by-product of this work, much as sawdust is a by-product of a lumberyard. One is reminded of the hypothesis offered by Lecky (1969) that one should attempt to achieve happiness not directly but indirectly through work. Happiness is, he argues, a by-product of work. Perhaps the reduction in anxiety and depression and improvements in cohesion and coping skills found by Semmelhack, Hazell, and Ende (2013) is an example of just such a mechanism. It is also perhaps an illustration of the efficacy of approaching analysis without "desire, memory or understanding" as Bion suggests (1978). If we pursue happiness directly we operate under the aegis of the pleasure principle, not the reality principle. This is not generally a good operating principle since in the end, reality always wins. Perhaps it is better to pursue the work of understanding the group in the here and now under the aegis of the reality principle and let the pleasure, or at least, reduction in pain, emerge as a by-product.

Additionally, we are lead to reconceptualize the Tavistock group when we cross reference with the "models of the mind" approach forwarded by Gedo and Goldberg (1976). In this they forward the idea that the type of therapy offered should be calibrated according to the developmental impasse the individual is suffering from. Thus for example, if the individual is suffering from a traumatic state (mode I) and is overwhelmed, the intervention should be that of *pacification*. If the individual is suffering from psychotic disintegration (mode II), then the modality used should focus on *unification* of self and object representations. If the individual has narcissistic issues (mode III) then the modality should involve a focus on *optimal disillusionment*. If the individual is suffering from a "neurotic character disorder" (mode IV) then the intervention should be pitched towards *interpretation* and finally, if the individual is operating at "expectable adult functioning" (mode V), the approach should involve *introspection* (Gedo & Goldberg, 1976, pp. 153–168). Given that the Tavistock style group has a positive therapeutic impact on the "severely mentally ill" who arguably included persons operating in modes I, II, and III and since it could be argued that individuals in mode IV and V also benefit from Tavistock style groups in ways that could be deemed psychotherapeutic, we are drawn to the conclusion that the Tavistock style group is not just an interpretive device. Nor is it just a device for introspection. It also is, strange as this may sound, a means of providing optimal disillusionment, unification, and pacification. This last is doubly significant because it flies in the face of the stereotype of the Tavistock style group as a harsh, unempathic environment suited only for those with "nerves of steel."

# CHAPTER THREE

# Gibb's trust model: a modification and elaboration

*Mark Kiel*

In 1964 Jack Gibb presented an elegant and generative model of group development using the concept of trust formation as an explanatory cornerstone.

In short, the model was as follows:

Stage I:   Who am I? (A concern about acceptance, membership or inclusion)

Stage II:   Who are you? (A concern about information-flow and decisions)

Stage III:   What are we here for? (A concern about tasks and aims)

Stage IV:   How are we going to do it? (A concern about control and organization)

Gibb claimed that at the beginning of a new group these questions have to be addressed and dealt with before any realistic work can be done by the group.

Gibb's model is also useful as a tool for helping to understand what is blocking a group's progress.

Stage:
> Unresolved:
> Resolved:

**I.** Acceptance
> Fear, distrust
> Acceptance, trust

**II.** Information
> Hidden feelings, caution
> Spontaneity, sharing

**III.** Aims
> Competition, apathy
> Creative work and play

**IV.** Control
> Dependency, power struggles
> Role distribution.

The key to this matrix is that if a group is having difficulty at one of these levels, then the cause will be found on the level before it. Thus, before the group can effectively move on, it needs to go back and resolve or work on the previous level's task.

This model is helpful, parsimonious, and has heuristic value. Regarding this last point, the following additions and modifications to the model open additional avenues of consideration when complimented by Tavistock theory:

## Tavistock/group-as-a-whole considerations

Stage I: Who am I-in-this-group?
Stage II: Who are you-in-this-group?
Stage III: What are the formal and informal tasks?
Stage IV: Who are we?
Stage V: How are we going to perform the task?

## Stage I revisited

Gibb states that members of a group ask questions like "Am I in the right group?" "What do I do to be accepted as a member?" and "Who am I here in this group, at this moment?" From a Tavistock informed point of view, the last question is the most salient. Group-as-a-whole theoreticians do not support the "myth of individuality"—the notion that people exist, function or are uninfluenced by the groups and systems they are part of. To that end, there is no absolute "I"—only an "I-in-the-life-of-this-group" (or even more particularly, "I-as-part-of-this-group.") This does not mean a member won't contemplate or struggle with the first two questions posed in this paragraph. Rather, they will ultimately get to the question of "Who-am-I-in-the-life-of-this-group?" To further complicate this concern, this question will be revisited at two other stages in the development of the group life: at stage IV—when the question is posed "who are we?" (and as part of the group, therefore the "individual's identity" may be reconsidered), and at stage V—when role distribution is assigned or accepted at the group level.

## Stage II revisited

Gibb states that members of a group ask questions like "What do we have to know about each other in order to be able to trust each other enough to work together?" Or follow a logic such as "If no one in this group will give me any information about who they are or what they are feeling, then I'm going to be cautious about telling them anything about me and how I am feeling. There won't be much trust developed, and the group will sit and do nothing, or make petty decisions on a superficial level about things that don't matter much." Again, at an overt level of analysis, this concern and this logic are spot on and readably applicable. But, Tavistock theoreticians focus their attention on irrational, covert, and unconscious barriers that impede or impair group functioning. Thus, the question "Who are you?" is more complex than just the data sharing and risk taking Gibb initially offers. "Who are you" invokes the issues of coming in contact with "the other." The technical term for this is alterity—the experience of other-ness. Having an alteric experience is very complex, oftentimes traumatic, and potentially incredibly enlightening (Hazell, 2009). In a very simplified scope, coming in contact with "an other" in a meaningful context like a group invokes issues of diversity, difference, conflict, same-ness, phenomena like "the looking glass self" and a continuum of psychological "closeness/distance" ranging from:

Fusion ↔ Separation ↔ Individuation ↔ Interdependence ↔ Detachment

From a group-as-a-whole perspective, as a member finds important parts of themselves in the experience of others, this stage is incredibly important to navigate—both at Gibb's conscious level, and at a Tavistock unconscious level.

## Stage III revisited

Gibb states that members of a group ask questions like "Are we all working on the same thing?" "Do we think it's worth doing anyway?" "Are we all committed to it, and willing to give it our backing?" Again, these questions are spot on and necessary to be answered for group process. Tavistock theory focuses a significant amount of its model on the question of task—in fact, it often starts with this issue, leaping over the two previous stages identified by Gibb. The Tavistock logic being in large part, if you identify and partner with the "here and now" task of participating and observing the here and now as it happens, stage I and II questions will be explored and meaningfully answered in time. Some of the differences between the models are accentuated by Gibbs' model bending toward "work groups" and goal directed through puts and the Tavistock model bending toward learning group formats and process directed through puts. However, both models are in agreement that the capacity and demonstration of creative work and play are the hallmarks of successfully navigating this stage. The only Tavistock considerations to be added is that informal tasks and aims that are close approximations of the formal task(s) of the group are closely scrutinized, as they may be the symbolic first steps in adopting anti-work or irrational work stances. Second is the issue of non-active members. Groups can accomplish "work" without having all members "on board" or equally dedicated to the task. However, in group-as-a-whole theory, these members may be performing a critical and significant repository function that would need ongoing examination for the creation and maintenance of a sophisticated work group.

## Stage IV addition

This stage is a complete addition to Gibb's model. It is a key group "question" to be answered by both group members and group consultants in the Tavistock frame. At a group-as-a-whole level, the group—not the individual members—are the focus of inquiry. As Bion (1961) has pointed out, the first question one encounters when attempting to solve the problems of group psychotherapy is whether one aims at doing psychotherapy in the group or of the group. The former involves doing what is essentially individual therapy in a group of people while the latter involves working with the group as a whole—examining its dynamics, tensions, conflicts, defenses, and so on. In learning groups in the Tavistock tradition, sorting out the group's identity, the group's issues, and the group's conflicts is the mechanism by which other, very important tasks are connected too. For instance, by understanding the social system a group creates, and the psychodrama it enacts, it can begin to sort out issues that deeply affect members. Some of these issues include members' sense of belongingness, a sense of "collective self-esteem" (the self-esteem a person gains by being part of a group they feel good about), as well as things the personality, style, and norms of the group. Furthermore, understanding "who are we?" for an individual not only goes back to (re)inform stage I's question of "Who am I?" but can set the stage for deeply and meaningfully answering the question of stage V. Lastly, the conscious group identity and the latent identity at work but unarticulated are oftentimes different, if not outright contrary, unlike the example above.

## Stage V revisited

In this final stage, Gibb states that members of a group ask questions like "Who is in charge?" "What are the ways of doing things in this group?" and "How are we going to get ourselves organized?" As Yalom (2005) states, groups quickly become a microcosm for the group members' lives. They recreate their most ingrained relationships, transferences, habits, and psychosocial expectations in relatively short order. Tavistock theory goes a step further. It asserts that members not only do that, but because of irrational, emotional, and covert group processes, members oftentimes become exaggerations or caricature of those pre-existing tendencies through processes like role suction, repository functioning, and projective identifications. In a learning group in the Tavistock tradition, "Who is in charge?" is de-emphasized as self-authorization and other-authorization to do the work of learning becomes a collective endeavor. "How are we going to get ourselves organized" shifts to "How are we going to get ourselves organized given what has been learned about role tendencies and who we are as a group?" The answer to both versions of the question is "role distribution," but in the Tavistock informed learning group there is a caveat: "novel, flexible or adaptive role distribution." Indeed, if dynamics about the intersection of group demands and individual predispositions were learned, the outcome should be the taking up of expanded, changed or adaptive roles in a more-conscious, group-authorized manner. Formerly undiscovered aspects of the "I" and the "I-in-the-life-of-this-and-other-groups" can be enacted, utilized, and experimented with in the service of the ongoing task of learning, practicing, and navigating the world as what Bion called a universal condition: "The individual is a group animal at war, not with himself for being a group animal, but with himself for being a group animal and with those aspects of personality that constitute his 'groupishness'" (Bion, 1965, p. 131).

## The dual task: learning and working

The impetus for this chapter was work I did with an atypical group class. The structure and tasks of the class were as follows: The clinical psychology program I teach in requires a year-long process group for first year students. The class is called Personal and Professional Development (P&PD) and it is intended to give the clinicians in training both an opportunity to experience process based learning (as opposed to outcome based) as well as a forum to explore how students' personal characteristics may complement or contrast roles and tasks required of a clinician. These group experiences are run by a faculty member and two advanced students who serve as co-leaders. The advanced students have a course and group of their own too. In fact, the experience of the advanced students is threefold. First they gain experience running small study groups with an experienced group-trained faculty member. Second, they participate in another year-long group class entitled Advanced Group Leadership and Supervision. In the fall semester this class takes the form of a twelve-week process group that in many ways parallels the P&PD task. However, in the spring term the task pivots and they begin a duel task of remaining a learning group (observing and processing their group experience as it happens) but a work task is added. Thus, the third task begins as the advanced students plan and eventually conduct a weekend group retreat for all the P&PD small study units in the summer term. The retreat includes additional small study groups, a large study group where all members of the retreat participate and to a lesser extent, inter-group events. Thus, the "advanced group" were learners, "juniors" consultants, work creators, and managers.

Although I described this experience as atypical above, many group practitioners will be familiar with a management group, staff group or consulting team performing a dual task of learning and working as a common, if not difficult task. And I agree, that is not particularly unique. Rather there were two patterns that emerged that proved problematic. The first was longitudinal in nature. Year after year, despite changing structures, styles, faculty, and degree of institutional support—the advanced group students appeared to hold, receive or contain a disproportionate amount of emotional distress at the end of the yearlong program (compared to first year participants and faculty members). The second issue was a particular group who identified a processing problem very early in its group life and despite being an intelligent and motivated team, never overcame the problem in a manner that was sufficiently generative or insightful for the membership as a collective.

In hindsight, the group in question had structural and process struggles and successes in each of Gibbs' stages.

### Stage I

The structure of the course as well as the multiple tasks and roles the group members were thrust into immediately led to some conscious identity issues Gibbs' model may identify—were they first and foremost group members responsible for learning? Consultants responsible for the learning of others? Producers responsible for generating a product? Although the sorting out of these roles is definitely part of the work task, too much literal discussion of the topic is defensive. The discussion on dichotomous or uni-dimensional work roles obfuscated the point about Stage I discussed above: from a Tavistock paradigm, the fall task was to be open to the spontaneous learnings, behaviors, and productions of a group and the making of K-links to continue this process. The preoccupation with what the members' identity "should be" slowed down the exploration of what they were and what they might become. In this sense, there was resistance to considering the "I-as-part-of-this-group."

Indeed, early in the learning group portion of the fall semester one member was experiencing an emotional roller coaster while in the group and took on an "identified patient" quality for the group. Most of the other group members responded by either subtly shaking their heads in confusion or offered the most literal of solution focused strategies. A fairly routine consultation was made suggesting that perhaps the emotional member was acting "crazy" in large part because the majority of the group members were in active denial of the intensity and emotions present in the group. Within a few minutes a another member—quiet, articulate and without much expressed emotion in the group thus far—explained not only did she feel unable to authentically participate in the group, but that what the group members knew about her from outside of the group was actively impeding her ability to join and trust the group. As this member's anger got expressed both the "emotional member" appeared less activated, and the group began considering how their out-of-group relationships and identities may have a negative or dangerous implication for group participation. This, in turn, led to a different level of trust and acceptance in the group. Trust and acceptance are not an absolute, and there would be continued problems with each, but the quality and depth of the difficulties changed for the better.

| Stage I: | Unresolved: | Tavistock mechanism: | Resolved: |
|----------|-------------|----------------------|-----------|
| Acceptance | Fear, Distrust | Recognition of repository functioning | Acceptance, Trust |

## Stage II

Weeks later, while still in the learning group format, another exchange took place that heralded the start of the information sharing stage. One member who routinely brought up the topic of diversity was bringing the matter up again. This woman of color expounded on the importance of diversity and how this group struggled to work with it to a degree she thought would be helpful and productive. Another member, one with significant but less visually obvious diversity characteristics, departed from the content of the discussion and made a personal process observation saying that she experienced the woman of color as having a lot of power in the group. She went on to say that this power came in part from the woman's racial diversity, but that it frustrated her because this "special status" was used to call attention to others lack of participation, without equal expectations or participation from the woman of color. The woman of color had a combination of surprise and hesitancy on her face in reaction to the comment. After the pause she replied, "I feel the same way about you." Her comment had a curious tone to it, rather than a blaming or deflective quality. Now it was the other members chance to have a look of surprise and hesitancy. She, in turn, commented that she found the interaction weird and with a bit of prompting from the group to say more, said that she didn't like to admit it, but that the woman of color irritated her and there was something about her she did not like. The woman of color said that was how she felt about her as well—and that she too had a strange and awkward sense of their mutual disclosures. The group was then activated and did work around the parallels and mirroring dynamics between these two members. By the end of the session, both women expressed a relief having finally talked about the matter and as an aside, had slightly warmer feelings for each other. As will be evident in the stages that follow, although this appeared beneficial for the two members involved in the discussion, the inability for the group to do this type "information sharing" using projective identifications and other projective processes on an ongoing basis would impact in next stage and ultimately their ability to accomplish work tasks.

| Stage II: | Unresolved: | Tavistock mechanism: | Resolved: |
|---|---|---|---|
| Information | Hidden feelings, Caution, Capacity to use projective identifications | Spontaneity, Sharing | |

*Stage III*

Near the end of the learning group and bridging into their working group format, role lock became more and more prominent in the group's functioning. Near the end of the learning group, a male member of the group repeatedly invalidated a number of women in the group with dismissive comments with a patriarchal quality to them ("That's what happens when you do something dumb," "That's irrational, I can't understand you," or "I don't feel the same way, sorry …"). Despite being a smart and thoughtful man, while in the group, neither interpretations from the consultants nor feedback from fellow members appeared to impact this dynamic. When the work of planning the retreat began, the member who was given the task to register and prepare the participants for the weekend retreat started harboring phantasies that the membership did not like her. Over the course of the weeks leading up to the retreat this phantasy ranged from "I'm the withholding mother," to "they hate me," to an avoidance of interacting with the members at the retreat for fear of their reactions. Other examples include a quiet member growing quieter for longer stretches at a time, and positive "cheerleader" relentlessly pursuing unanimous consent from the group regarding decisions.

These were all signs in Gibb's model that the previous stage's tasks needed to be revisited and reworked. Unfortunately for the group, their consultants only saw the dynamics clearly in the later stages of their group's development.

| **Stage III:** | **Unresolved:** | **Tavistock mechanism:** | **Resolved:** |
|---|---|---|---|
| Aims | Competition, Apathy | Rejection of role suction | Creative work and play |

### Stage IV

One of the major events at the weekend retreat was a large group diversity event. The event was important as it was often one of the most impactful events over the weekend but also, given its nature, was a high risk/high reward enterprise depending on how it was facilitated and structured. Like most cohorts that designed and ran the retreat, there was a wish to design an event that maintained the tradition of the past contributions while also adding a novel influence that distinguished the event as their own. This dynamic was further exacerbated by a growing sense of a problematic group identity. Group themes had emerged from the group mentality, the difficulties in spontaneity and sharing at Stage II hampered the members' ability to share their multiple identities and dimensions as people within the group, and the resulting role lock stifled play (in the analytic sense) (ref) and the ability to do creative work the group was capable of. The role lock experienced by individual members also manifested at the group-as-a-whole identity.

About one month out from the retreat, during another discussion of the diversity event one member of the group articulated the answer to the question, who are we? While discussing their frustrations, the one member said, "How can we plan a decent diversity event, when we suck at diversity?" Now it was the impression of the consultants that they did not suck at diversity. They were individually committed to it and as a group had at times (although brief) evidenced the ability to do exploration and learning about a number of diversity matters including race, privilege, gender, out-grouping, and internalized "isms." That said, rather than a group identity that was spawned from the group-in-the-mind, interpreted and impacted via both consultation and play, and tested and employed against reality demands, this group adopted what Winnicott identifies as a "false self" (1965) or as posited here, a reactive group identity—a defensive imago fashioned from a group collusion to accept an identity of necessity. This is in contrast to performing the demanding and daunting work of repeatedly contributing to the group process until a more organic group identity emerges, not of necessity, but of authenticity and spontaneity.

It is easy to understand why work groups have difficulty at this stage. Time is limited, a work product needs to be generated, there is no guarantee that more contributions will result in immediate changes and the thought of going back to the tasks of previous stages can be impractical. This is what can be so helpful utilizing Gibbs model with a Tavistock lens—when employed correctly there is a greater chance of identifying in an actionable timeframe difficulties in group development instead of historical back-tracking after the fact, like is done here.

| Stage IV: | Unresolved: | Tavistock mechanism: | Resolved: |
|---|---|---|---|
| Identity | Reactive group identity | Group-in-the-mind analysis | Emergent group identity |

## Stage V

In the final weeks and days leading up to the retreat, work was accomplished but decision-making and group authorization of members was characterized by splits related to dependency and independency. For example, one member asserted the event he was facilitating was "fine" and neither sought nor was offered consultation or feedback. This was contrasted by another member who would not commit to an event format without unanimous consent and enthusiasm from the group. The consent was provided, but enthusiasm varied from member to member and so the decision remained unmade. The dependency and independency dynamics appeared to parallel dynamics between other-authorization and self-authorization. The lack of interdependence at the group level left members over-reliant on one method of authorization and their work styles followed suit. This became clear to the consulting team and in turn we pitched various consultations, suggestions, and feedback to the group focusing on group authorization and interdependence.

Many of these consultations were utilized by the group and by the time the retreat was in progress several members appeared to shed the role lock in the service of work. For example, the woman who harbored fears and phantasies of the membership requested a facilitation role for one event that allowed her to share her excitement and passion with the retreat participants and subsequently felt seen in a different light by them, wound up and providing an excellent introduction to a pivotal event. Quiet and withdrawn members re-engaged to a significant degree. The member dependent on the group's enthusiasm for decision-making made choices and then executed her tasks utilizing the members that shared her excitement and assigned realistic duties to those who did not.

This is not to say the struggles at stages II, III, and IV were made irrelevant—those unresolved aspects echoed throughout the retreat and even in post-retreat review sessions. One member summed it up well, she said she was proud of the job the group did but lamented the lost learning opportunities. Another member added that the retreat participants had an experience of personal and professional development, but that she as an advanced group student did not get as much personal development as she had hoped for due to how their group functioned. Another member shared that she now understood the difference between needing consensus and needing authorization to accomplish work, but it was not the lesson she had hoped to learn upon joining the group.

| Stage: | Unresolved: | Tavistock mechanism: | Resolved: |
|--------|-------------|----------------------|-----------|
| I. Acceptance | Fear, Distrust | Recognition of repository functioning | Acceptance, Trust |
| II. Information | Hidden feelings, Caution | Capacity to use projective identifications | Spontaneity, Sharing |

| III. Aims | Competition, Apathy | Rejection of role suction | Creative work and play |
| IV. Identity | Reactive group identity | Group-in-the-mind analysis | Emergent group identity |
| V. Collaboration | Dependency, Power Struggles | Authorization of Inter-Dependence | Role Distribution |

As is now illustrated, Gibb's model is modified in two important ways. The first is the specific inclusion of the "Who are we?" stage associated with group identity. When unresolved, this process leads to a group identity that is reactive, defensive, and in a sense, adopted by a group to ward off challenges and anxieties. When resolved, this process leads to a group identity that is organic, emergent, and in a sense, discovered by a group doing work. The primary mechanism for the development of an emergent group identity is the utilization of group-in-the-mind analysis to identify themes in the group mentality, while comparing and contrasting these to reality demands and group work performance data. Analysis without performance data or vice versa is a catalyst for reactive group identities as one capacity is privileged over the other. The second, broader, modification is the redefinition of trust. In Gibb's original model the concept of trust is primarily an interpersonal dynamic, with secondary task and role elements. In this modification, trust is primarily an object-relational dynamic achieved through group-as-a-whole mechanisms. Thus, objects (the group, group members, consultants, even the work product) become "trust-worthy" objects via the "Tavistock mechanisms" listed above. Good, or more specifically in this context, Trust-worthy objects, may not be interpersonally warm, engaging or empathic. Rather, they are consistent, contemplative, and authorizing—and these traits are uniquely suited for psychological trust, deep learning, and sophisticated work. As an extension of this process, Klein (1975) asserts that successful work of this trustworthy nature does tend to produce a variety of prosocial and rewarding feelings for individuals and groups including compassion, devotion, and gratitude. A key difference being that in the Kleinian conceptualization these are the result of successful trust and object relational work not a means or technique to achieve work stances as the interpersonal models suggest.

# CHAPTER FOUR

# Existentialism and the Tavistock learning group

*Mark Kiel*

The group-as-a-whole/Tavistock methodology is firmly rooted in psychoanalytic theory, especially the British School of Object Relations psychoanalysis of Klein (1975) and Bion (1961). Yet, as one of the primary theses of this book, the Tavistock model has heuristic value and power that transcends its psychoanalytic beginnings and current center. This extrapolation has previously included the topic of organizational transformation (Obholzer & Roberts, 1994), the study of multicultural dynamics (Hofstede, 2010), social psychology (Menzies-Lyth, 1960), and society/global phenomena (Volkan, 2014). This chapter seeks to demonstrate how the theory and practice of a Tavistock group has implications and applications for existential psychology and matters related to existence.

Existential psychology, like the study of existentialism in general, is broad and because of its connection to the philosophy of humanism, is hard to unify and define. That said there are several topics that fall within this category that readily apply to Tavistock work and concepts. They include:

Freedom and choice → Hatred of learning
Existential awareness → Social defenses

Death anxiety → Time boundaries
Authenticity → Self/other authorization
Connection and isolation → The "myth of individuality"
The denial of death → Psychotic anxieties

## *Freedom and choice*

A seemingly disproportionate amount of the literature on group dynamics focuses on the joining process and how to achieve a "working group" or "sophisticated group" (Hill, 1965). In essence, this is the process of meeting others and working with them on an agreed upon and rational task. Much of the literature, in fact a core tenet for consultants, is to consult to "unconscious, irrational, and covert barriers" to achieving group work. However, another defining tenet is that consultants do not tell group members "What to learn, how to learn or at what rate to learn." The consultants only offer a space and resources to learn, and it is up to the group members to decide if and how they want to take up the learning task. Note the first part—"if." It is by no means a given that members will take up this opportunity, even if they joined the group with the express interests of doing just that. Bion was so struck by this contrast—the conscious wish to learn and the unconscious avoidance of learning by experience, that he posited a "hatred of learning." Whereas Bion's psychoanalytic, affective, and unconscious explanations for this phenomenon remain valid and applicable; it is also readily arguable that the frame of the Tavistock learning group as well as the role and task of the consultants bring the issue of choice directly front and center to the members in a way that is not easily avoided. Indeed, the experience of this freedom can be experienced as affrontive—especially if members expect an experience of what Heidegger called "self-alienation"—being "at home" in the idle talk of "the they" (Heidegger, 2008).

An example: A weekly learning group had met about four times. Introductions, adjustment to the Tavistock frame, and some initial forays into the "here and now" had occurred over those meetings. The group members began interviewing each other. Their expressed logic was that if they "knew" each other more, they would feel more comfortable, and then they could move forward. I consulted that this was perhaps interpersonally true, but that at the same time it was a flight from the group experience—they wanted to be anywhere in the world, where they grew up, where they went to college, where they had taken vacations—anywhere but in that room. The majority of the members expressed a sentiment that I was a cold splash of water on what was otherwise a nice, little group process. After a few minutes of that, and a return to the "there and then" one member said something to the effect of, "I'm not sure I agree with the consultant completely. I don't want to be elsewhere ... I'm just not sure I want to be here." Several members asked what he meant by this. His reply, from an existential point of view, was his was trying to decide whether he wanted to live in or with this group. "I mean, what if I want to be here? What if I want to get real with you all? What if this becomes important? What then?"

What happened then was the group began a debate, whether they wanted to choose engagement, connection, and authenticity, with the very real possibility that they may encounter disappointment, isolation or inauthenticity. Over the next twenty weeks the group passively chose the latter. They chose a boring pseudo-life of small talk and the killing of time that was "safe" and "uneventful." In the last session, while an informal stocktaking was occurring, a member asked why the group had seemed so tedious. The man who had reframed my consultation way back in week four said, "I feel like I was cheated ... Or maybe I cheated you all ... Either way I didn't try. Not really. This is what you are left with when your fears outweigh your efforts ..."

Whereas a basic assumption: Dependence or a social defense of group avoidance can be posited in a circumstance like the above, so too should the existential matter of choice (at both an individual and group level). In Sartre's view, the recognition and acceptance of one's freedom and responsibility—and of the consequent experiences of anguish, forlornness, and despair—is "good faith." Furthermore, the refusal to recognize and accept the reality and consequences of human freedom and responsibility is "bad faith" or self-deception (Sartre, 1993). A person, or group, of good faith will thus take charge of its own existence, defining its meaning, value, and direction for themselves, and will act courageously and with a "tragic sense of life" (Unamuno, 2012) face the fact of his or her own ultimate finitude and contingency. After acting in bad faith for much of its life, the group above—as voiced by the man who felt cheated/a cheat—voiced the possibility and potentiality of the option of "good faith." Too late for the life cycle of that particular group, but not necessarily too late for the group members if that learning, and the hatred of that learning, could be held onto, made more conscious and imported into other choices, social dynamics and relational circumstances.

## Existential awareness

Arguably, one of the biggest differences between psychoanalytic theory and existential psychology theory is the nature of anxiety. In classical psychoanalysis the mechanism of anxiety works as such:

Drive → Anxiety → Defense mechanisms
(… and the over use of defenses becomes pathological)

In existentialism:

Existential awareness → Anxiety → Defense mechanisms
(… and the over use of defenses becomes pathological)

However, as my co-author so aptly points out, the hermeneutic function appears to be the bridge across this divide:

> … a function that critically and creatively generates meanings of events—that creates interpretations. In addition, it is posited that psychological well-being is compromised if this function's activity is hampered. Psychotherapy can be regarded as an activity that restores the fullest possible level of functioning of this hermeneutic function by exercising the play of interpretations and by uncovering the psychological phenomenon, such as trauma or family or societal culture that might inhibit the activity of the hermeneutic function. (Hazell, 2003, p. 229)

He goes on:

> To be mentally healthy is to have a flourishing F [hermeneutic] function. What would a flourishing F function look like? It would first of all be available to the individual (and to the group and society, but that is another set of arguments). The individual would be able to generate and enjoy new interpretations of old events. The F function should not generate a paralyzing anxiety of certainty,

but should lead to a generation of new meanings. The F function should be critical, that is, the new meanings are not just accepted wholesale but are subjected to rules of validation and exploration. The F function should be fluent, original and elaborate along the lines of Torrance's definition of creativity ... (Hazell, 2003, pp. 237–238)

Two points about this: one, be it impulse or awareness, the capacity for interpretation (The F function) is the method for taming and possibly using the dynamic in the service of consciousness or maybe even growth; and two ... what was that parenthetical comment about the "group and society"?

Bion (1961) makes an undeniable argument for the identification and explanation of the "social defense"—a defense a group uses to ward off the irrationality of endings. In fact he states, at a most basic level all groups seek to survive (sounding existential yet?) even at great costs of distortive psychological machinations (the so-called basic assumption functioning). Klein's focus on Thanatos—the death instinct—is one dynamic many existential psychologists believe is a direct acknowledgement of an existential awareness, not "just" an impulse (Yalom, 2005). Bion uses that as undergirding for his understanding of group life. And in doing so he identifies, consciously or unconsciously (pun intended), another mechanism:

Social dependence → Existential awareness → Anxiety → Social defenses
(... And the over use of defenses becomes pathological for the group, and eventually, but not necessarily immediately for any given group member!)

Bion (1961) stated we are "group animals at war with our groupishness" (p. 131)—and in that statement he is addressing both the impulse and the awareness as a potential cause for anxiety. And bringing this point back to the first theme of choice and freedom, both the existentialist and psychoanalyst agrees, that via interpretation:

Anxiety → Self-knowledge → The potential for new or different choices
(via a working F function ...)

An example: At the second to last session of a nine month long weekly learning group, a quiet and thoughtful member of the group did not look quite right at the start of the session. In short, group members noticed this and asked what was going on. The member replied that just prior to the group she received news that a friend of a friend, someone she knew, but was not directly close to had died earlier in the day in a car crash. She began to tear up. Members responded in a relatively conventional and sympathetic way. Then the member who received the news altered the conventional course of the group reaction. She explained that what was upsetting her was not just the news, but how the news represented the ending of the group. She was quick to add that she didn't mean to diminish the "actual" loss but rather to add to the meaningfulness that was in the room and to the end of the group that was coming. Several other members welled up with feeling after hearing that. Rather than treat one as "actual" and one as "symbolic," I made the following consultation. I said that in some ways a sudden, unexpected loss was easier to absorb. It was stunning, you reeled from it, the only choice was to react. But there was something exquisitely painful about a loss you anticipate, can see clearly coming, and have choice in how to deal with it. The consultation seemed to have connected at some level with the group as several members followed up by voicing they did have the wish to have the end of the group happen to them, as opposed to approaching the end in an active and engaged manner. The member with the news seemed to receive some relief and then, over the course of the hour the group said goodbye in an intentional and active manner.

## Death anxiety

In the freedom and choice section, it was noted that a disproportionate amount of the literature on groups is focused on the joining stage of group life. The same can be said about the ending of groups, generally called termination. In between the two, is life—the work and play done by the group. This may seem overly simplified, but it is worth noting that many theoreticians, from vastly different paradigms note that part of what makes groups so powerful, is that people quickly replicate life patterns upon entering a group. The group events become a microcosm of other important relationships for the members. Given that groups do this, and that at some existential level life is a series of joining others, connecting and creating relationships; contrasted by saying goodbye, disconnecting and ending relationships, this makes the life cycle of a group potentially powerful for the group members.

## Investing and withdrawing

Learning groups are usually time-bounded events—certainly for each session, but also regarding the total number of group meetings. Unlike therapy groups or support groups, they tend not to be open ended. Even more so, group relations conferences in the Tavistock tradition are typically defined as *temporary learning institutions*. The temporary and finite nature of these models and learning structures brings the issue of why someone would join such a group in the first place to the surface. The technical answer to this question is relatively simple: one joins to perform a task. But the task of learning does not "end"—so isn't it contrary to place an ongoing task in a finite space and time? The rational answer to that question is relatively straightforward too: all learning is not accomplished in the frame of the learning space, rather (it is hoped) that a piece of learning is accomplished.

But for readers who have ever participated in experiential learning, encounter groups, psychotherapy or the like, there is often the powerful sense that the group, the conference, the treatment is never long enough. There is always more to do. If only there was more time, another session, another meeting ... This tension, between the ongoing nature of learning and the closed nature of the learning frame becomes a dilemma, a struggle, even a conflict. The most manifest way this conflict is expressed by members and a group is how, when, and why they choose to invest in the process or withdraw from it. But before there is further discussion of investment and withdrawal, consider some of the key existential issues potentially joining a group can engender.

## Bion's point

Bion's notable quote that "The individual is a group animal at war, both with the group and with those aspects of his personality that constitute his 'groupishness'" (Bion, 1961, p. 131) is a significant one. First and foremost humans are relational entities, social creatures, and political animals. We are drawn to other people, groups, and communities to meet needs and wishes we cannot fulfill ourselves. Yet, we are at war with those needs and wishes. We deny them, distort them, and attack them. The vulnerability, potential rejections, and feared and real dangers make connection, even the wish for connection, a dangerous proposition.

### Yalom's point

Yalom identified four "core" existential concerns that undergird life. They are presented as on a continuum:

- Death → Life
- Captivity → Freedom
- Isolation → Connection
- Meaninglessness → Meaningfulness

All these "individual" concerns are easily identifiable (if not amplified) by genuine and authentic participation in a group.

### Heidegger's point

Heidegger said:

> As Being-with, man 'is' essentially for the sake of others ... Even if the particular factual human being does not turn to others, and supposes that he has no need of them or manages to get along without them, he is in the way of Being-with. (Heidegger, 2008, p. 160)

This quote resonates in some ways with Bion's comment about being at war with one's own groupishness. Direct participation in a learning group of a Tavistock variety calls attention to the existential dilemma of being alone in our subjective experience—no one is ever truly capable of being understood or connected with in a perfect way, yet the drive to connect, in order to understand the other better (and in turn ourselves) is ongoing, a timeless endeavor.

Participation in a group places people in an all too familiar paradox—one that is constantly in a process of investing in and then purposely withdrawing from others.

## Living and dying

Earlier it was explained that in an important sense, phantasies, the symbolic, or the metaphoric precedes the literal. We imagine and express impulses unconsciously and pre-consciously before we express or act on them literally. So it is true of existential conflicts and paradoxes group members find themselves in when participating in group life.

An example: At the last session of a nine month long weekly learning group, a group that had lost four members since it first started for various reasons, was meeting for the last time. The majority of the group members reported they had met up and gone out for dinner prior to the group session. The two members who did not go explained their reasons for not joining. One of the members who went to the dinner said that it was "no problem" and they could "always do it some other time."

Over the next ten minutes, another member began silently sobbing. It was as if no one could see it, and a fairly routine conversation started and then continued between two other members. A fourth member began taking copious notes. A fifth member said it was warm in the room, and despite a rainstorm raging outside, opened the door to fresh air and blowing rain. The conversation between the two continued. I felt like I was losing my mind. I was having a hard time believing what was going on around me. One member wrapped a scarf around her neck (despite the reported heat) and yanked it. The only thing I could think of was a noose. One of the consultants said that she felt like she was going crazy, it was as if she couldn't trust her eyes or ears. That consultation seemed to relieve the group for a few minutes, but then the "craziness" in the room began rising again. Still, no one commented on the silently sobbing member. I then made my consultation. I said that the group was suffering from a disorder, and that the disorder, specifically, was a delusional disorder. The group was under the false belief that it was not dying. That this was not the last meeting, that they could get together again at any time. I then said with an emphasis and intensity that surprised me. "Be clear. This is the end. After tonight, this group will never, ever be the same. Even if we all meet again, and have a group again, it will be different. At 9pm exactly, in thirty-four minutes this group ends." After a minute or so of silence, a member looked at the sobbing member and asked what was wrong. The sobbing member reminded the group that for her, major life changes coincided with the end of the group and that there was a frightened part of her that never wanted the group to end.

The Tavistock model of beginning and ending sessions exactly on time does enable the consultants and members to closely examine boundary dynamics. However, from an existential point of view it also marches groups toward death and death anxiety in a direct and some-times affrontive manner. As Ernest Becker asserts (1997), it is not death anxiety in itself that is problematic. It is rampant, unconscious death anxiety, the so-called "denial of death," and the personal and social defenses that are employed to keep that anxiety repressed, where prob-lems, distortions, and extreme reactions occur.

## *Authenticity*

As a general statement, existentialists posit that people should strive for authentic existence if they wish to achieve their potential and to feel "at home" in themselves and their lived experience. One defini-tion of authenticity is the degree to which one is true to one's own personality, spirit, or character, despite external pressures (Heidegger, 2008; Sartre, 1993). That said, most existentialists would also agree that the vast majority of people generally live inauthentically in the "public world," resulting in the denial to live in accordance with "one's freedom." This can take many forms, from pretending choices are meaningless or random, to convincing oneself that some form of determinism is true, to a sort of "mimicry" where one acts as "one should." This may sound familiar to psychoanalytic readers as being loosely parallel to Winnicott's (1965) concept of the "true self and false self."

As a general statement, Tavistock theory places a considerable amount of importance on the notion of authorization. In this context, authority is defined as: the right to perform work, utilize resources, and make decisions; the right to make decisions which are binding on others.

We differentiate between three types of authority: (1) authority from above, formal authority derived from a particular role in an external structure or system (e.g., an organizational hierarchy) and exercised on its behalf; (2) authority from below, informal or formal authority given by subordinates or colleagues; that is, one's authority is sanctioned or withheld from below; and (3) authority from within, one's individual capacity to take up one's own authority (formal, informal, and/or personal).

This definition and conceptualization adds another dimension to consider in the authentic/inauthentic continuum. In many humanistic models this congruence/incongruence is presented in some form of a venn diagram, Figure 7.

However, when one takes into account the Tavistock notion of other-authorization, people are only partially "free to be authentic to one's self, despite external pressures" (Bion, 1965, p. 50). A group must be "working" in the Bionic sense for a given member to have freedom from role-lock or repository functioning to express aspects of themselves or discover latent aspects.

Given this dimension, the visual model may look more like Figure 8.

An example: At a group relations conference, a group was meeting for the third time of seven meetings. The group had growing stretches of long silences. The group was devoid of play, spontaneity, and life. I and my fellow consultant had been working hard to interpret resistances, group defenses, and dangerous impulses that may have been preventing work in the group. The frustration by members and consultant alike was palpable. Tending to be overly technical, I tried to stop thinking about what was going on and tried to imagine a metaphor that might capture what it was like to be in the room at that time. After a few

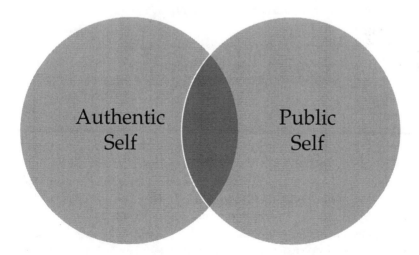

Figure 7. Authenticity congruence/incongruence model.

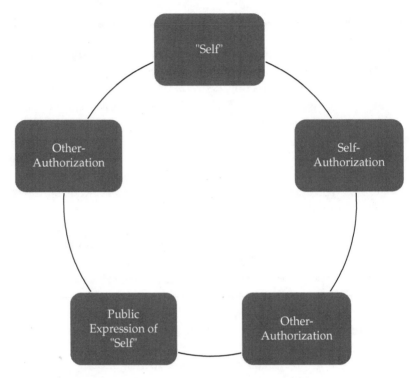

Figure 8. Authenticity as process of self and other-authorization.
*Note*: Note that this circuit does not suggest the quality, quantity, or direction of the variables interacting internally or externally. Note, it does not suggest whether the process is constrictive or expansive, promotional or deleterious to the sense of self. It does suggest that rather than viewing the "public expression of self" as a choice, behavior, or contrast, it imagines public expression as an event both preceding and following experiences of the self, and as such, a defining and interactive feature.

minutes one came to me. My consultation was, "If you have a baby that is born sickly and its prospects for life are uncertain, throwing it out into a snow drift may make sense. You save suffering for the baby and yourself. You can convince yourself that it was the humane thing to do. You can convince yourself that it is easier then loving and investing in something that may still go away in the end." That is what it felt like was going on in that room. The group's fragile life was uncertain; the members had unconsciously colluded to "pitch it in" before the life ever really had a chance. After a few minutes, a female member of the group, who was not showing, said she was pregnant after having problems conceiving. Another member said his six-year-old boy had died earlier that year of an undiagnosed congenital issue. Another member said he had considered suicide a few months ago. Over the next hour each member admitted in different ways that they were consciously aware of these matters upon registering for the conference. Even more telling was that each of the members had the conscious wish to explore, unpack or share these matters in the conference space. The "stuckness" of the group did not have to do with authenticity in the typical fashion—the members were aware and even eager to share their hesitancy to invest in the group process. What was missing up to the point of the consultation and cascade of disclosures was other-authorization from above and beside. True to form, this trigger event afforded the members to then invest in the here and now and "get into the room" and interact with each in a way that furthered the primary task of the conference.

## Connection and isolation

In general, traditional notions of existentialism focus considerably on the individual, individual responsibility, and individual choice. In contrast, Tavistock theory focuses on groups, social/systemic pressures, and deterministic dynamics. At one end of the continuum is the Tavistock model asserting the "myth of individuality"—the illusion of freedom from the social dynamics that appear universal; on the other end is existentialism's "existence precedes essence," which suggests that the most important consideration for the individual is the fact that he is an individual—rather than what labels, roles, stereotypes, definitions, or other preconceived categories the individual fits ("essence"). Whereas this philosophical contrast is beyond the scope of this essay, there is a window into these two dimensions of psychology that can further inform each.

Jean Paul Sartre in *Critique of Dialectical Reason* (2004) cites several types of groups. For the purpose of this chapter, three will be focused on. First is "The series." There is no common or collective purpose for the series. At one point, Sartre says a series is a "plurality of solitudes." To envision a series, think of the working class under capitalism—fighting each other for a piece of bread, people sharing a waiting room, people walking on the same block on a city street. The individuals in the series do not help one another realize their individual goals; the series is a loose collection of individuals who just happen to be engaged in the same activity. Next, Sartre posits "The group." A group, compared to a series, is based on cooperation. Groups are based on some common or collective purpose. The group is conscious, practices solidarity and leadership emerges. Examples include individuals under socialism, a lynch mob, or a reading club. Lastly, Sartre posits "The institution." An institution, unlike the former categories, involves an individual taking an "oath" of a particular sort to a pre-existing, and often bureaucratic entity. The oath and the structural nature of the institution involves formality and thus matters like codes of norms, rules of assembly, totems and taboos.

Although using a different verbiage and paradigm for study, presenting Sartre's ideas in this fashion clearly parallels important aspects of Tavistock theory. A Tavistock conference, for example, oftentimes starts with a "set of oaths"—from registration, to a letter of reference for participation, to the Director of the conference stating something to members in the opening event such as "… and your presence here authorizes me, and by extension the staff I have selected, to transact the learning agreement as outlined in the conference brochure …" In this sequence of formalities, the conference format overtly and consciously dis-abuses conference members from ignoring or suppressing the institutional nature of the social circumstance and contract they have entered. Indeed, Tavistock conferences are routinely referred to as "temporary learning institutions" by consultants and a significant part of the learning is the understanding of these institutional transferences, distortions, wishes and fears.

At Sartre's "group" level, the Tavistock model highlights how groups unconsciously cooperate, and in a sense distill and highlight that form of cooperation from the conscious intentions of the group. Regarding "The series," the Tavistock model makes perhaps its boldest claim, suggesting it only appears that a collection of individuals can be just that. As soon as a formal, or more insidiously yet an informal, task is introduced, the collection of people are launched into "The group" at an unconscious level, without members' consent or acknowledgment—thus spurring a host of dynamics, whilst maintaining the illusion of "The series." And as experienced members and consultants know well, arguments, protests, and resistances about this shift can consume much of the joining or initial stages in group development.

Which leads to the final suggestion of this section: As a parallel, it can be argued that the goal of a Lacanian analysis is to better appreciate, understand, and navigate the three fundamental spheres of one's psychological experience (the imaginary, the symbolic and the real). This does not come easy. Parts of our nature, development, and lived experience makes navigation from one sphere to the next difficult. Understanding our "group psychology" is similar:

The illusion of "The series," the unconscious cooperation of "The group" and totems and taboos of "The institution" are difficult to identify, harder to navigate and elusive in their ever changing machinations. Yet, it is the study of this that is at the core Tavistock work and which can propel further the existential understanding of wishes and fears to isolate and connect with others.

Rather then add a clinical example here, a brief synopsis of a typical group relations conference may better illustrate this point. Group relations conferences in the Tavistock tradition typically have small group events with a subgroup of conference members, large group events that include all members of the conference, and an institutional event

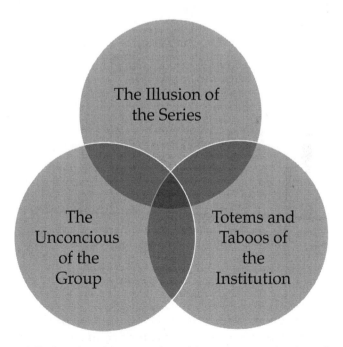

Figure 9.  A Tavistock re-interpretation of Sartre's categorization of groups.

of some sort that affords the members to determine and join groups of their own choosing.

Usually small study groups are the first here and now events of the conference. This group is oftentimes where the "myth of the series" is first encountered. Members discuss, test, and resist the concept, often assert ideas like:

- We are only a group after a while.
- We are only a group once we agree on a conscious task or group guidelines.
- Any individual can remain outside the group via declaring themselves not a member.
- We are only a group once everyone has begun participating.

These are all expressions of resistance and discomfort with the "Myth of the series" and are an endorsement of the "Myth of the individual." Confronting these myths, in short order, promotes the contemplation of "The unconscious of the group"—which is encountered in each of the events in the conference in different formats.

The "Totems and taboos of the institution" are also unfolding all conference long, from the opening plenary to the closing plenary. However it is the Institutional Event (I.E.) (or alternating conducted as an Institutional System Event (I.S.E.)) that this can be most clear. It is an operating premise that the groups, the themes of the groups, and membership of member groups created in the IE are projective in nature. They enact the "institutional model in the mind" in a psycho-dramatic and behavioral way. Meaning, the members construct the conference in the mind (including fears, wishes, conflicts, phantasies, and distortions) as represented by their choices, affiliations, and identities in the "free-er form" portion of the conference. The interactions amongst and between groups further illustrate this.

Two final points regarding these dynamics: The first is there is much difficulty for most conference members (and staff members) adjusting between events in a group relations conference. Whereas this can be viewed exclusively as role and task confusion or resistance in a B.A.R.T. (Boundaries, Authority, Role and Task) sense (Rice, 2013), the modified Sartrean existential components should not be ignored. The existential underpinnings, consequences, and significance of viewing, navigating, and working, groups and institutions this way takes considerable flexibility and can generate considerable anxiety. It disturbs personal, political, and social expectations and contracts. Whereas it can help members and groups become more realistic, rational, and educated in their efforts, it also generates existential concerns regarding identity, connection, and meaning making. This brings the last and probably most macro application of this chapter to the fore.

## The denial of death

Whereas there are differences, many profound, between psychoanalytic object relations theory and existentialism, the relationship between death anxiety, and more specifically the denial of death and psychotic anxieties in learning groups is quite complimentary.

As mentioned earlier, intrapsychic development from a Kleinian (1975) perspective unfolds in the following order:

The paranoid-schizoid position → The depressive position ≈ Capacity for K-links

These stages correspond with:

(Part-object functioning) → (Whole object functioning) → (Sophisticated functioning)

(Psychotic anxieties) → (Neurotic anxieties) → (Generative ideals and expectations)

And this parallels Bionic group development:

Basic assumption functioning → Rational group functioning → Sophisticated work group

In existentialism, meaning is often portrayed on a continuum:
Meaninglessness ⟺ Meaningfulness

However, this representation of meaning is extremely simplified. Meaning, unlike stage models of development, is a broad construct that can be part of other more specific models. To that end, a loose, qualitative correlation can be drawn between existential "meaningfulness" and Klein's concept of "depressive anxiety."

Depressive anxiety is characterized by a poignant quality, sometimes more angst-filled and agonizing, at other times more touching and moving in quality. Regardless of where on that continuum it falls, the experiences of the "depressive position" is like the concept of "meaningfulness" in existential theory, with "peak experiences" (Maslow, 2013) oftentimes characterized by mixed emotions, the experience of emptiness (Hazell, 2003) and sadness. So too are moments of "existential vacuums" (Hazell, 1984) and dread characterized by moments of "aha" insights and transformation. The classic example of this dynamic is the French word for orgasm, "petite mort" or "little death." It is with achieving an intense high that the end begins.

This said, the main thesis of this section has to do with psychotic anxieties. As mentioned above, in Kleinian theory, psychotic anxieties and part-object functioning is psychologically normative and developmentally necessary. However, like most psychological processes it can be retarded, regressed, or fixated and become pathological. Bion adds that groups have regressive properties and shift into paranoid-schizoid functioning naturally and without conscious effort. In the main, this is the primary explanation as to why Tavistock learning groups and conferences are psychologically anxiety provoking, sometimes distressing and oftentimes profound.

As with the other topics, existential theory can be applied to reveal another dimension of this process. In his book *The Denial of Death* (1997), Ernest Becker presented a bold series of premises and a powerful conclusion. Becker asserts all people are impacted psychologically by their personal awareness of death and the universal reality of death. People are impacted by this ultimate reality in such a fundamental manner that it is a key feature to psychological development. He suggests that at a personal level, people use defense mechanisms to combat death anxiety and the (relative) impending reality that all life ends. But, personal defense mechanisms fail. There are too many reality incursions on an everyday basis that puncture these mechanisms of denial, rationalization or avoidance. Thus, people gravitate toward and invest in ideologies that are "bigger" than themselves to give a social defense against death anxiety. For instance, reality principles suggest I do not matter in the grand scheme of things; my life (indeed all life) is fragile and finite; that wellness, happiness, and life can be ended at any moment. To deal with this painful and overwhelming awareness, people join ideologies and adopt a shared identity to compensate or neutralize these threats to self. For instance, being a devout Christian means an eternal spiritual life, being a patriotic U.S. citizen means being part of a strong and just country that protects its citizens and does good in the world, or that writing a book read by others means an author will always "live on" in some sense. Becker describes this sense of social safety as more rigorous and more effective then personal defense mechanisms. There are a number of problems that come with "denying death" in this manner—especially when ideologies and belief systems come into contact and conflict with each other—but for point being illustrated here, the focus will remain on the defensive quality of the paradigm. Becker suggests a core feature of affiliation is that the social defenses a group or collective can offer are more robust protection than any means an individual has at their disposal.

That brings us to the Tavistock learning group. As mentioned in the "Connection and isolation" section, participating in a learning group of this nature often has an unsettling quality to it. Many assumptions about individualness are questioned, the power of the collective is appreciated in a powerful and sometimes provocative manner, irrationality and emotionality are experienced in a personal and sometimes visceral way, paranoid-schizoid functioning is shared amongst members both overtly and covertly. Those reasons alone are enough to explain why the experience can be intense, anxiety-provoking, and powerful. Becker's paradigm offers one more reason. The Tavistock method is an excellent tool for unearthing hidden agendas and basic assumption functioning at work in systems. When this methodology explores, hypothesizes or identifies unconscious and defensive motives for group functioning, at the least, it results in a narcissistic injury for members (De Mare, 2011). By this, it is meant that the members assumed one thing about their experience but are offered data and rationale to the contrary—and that is psychologically "hurtful" in so far as it impacts ones' sense of confidence or world view (As an aside, many argue that all forms of interpretation results in small or symbolic narcissistic injuries, but that if tolerated, can lead to growth, development or transformation—as is true with a Tavistock learning group). Although it is not part of the theory or the practice of group relations work, the method cited above of exposing hidden agendas and basic assumption functioning in the psychoanalytic prism also open the proverbial door for the consideration of the existential prism. The Tavistock method identifies other reasons and mechanisms for group functioning, social defenses, and the role irrationally plays in system life, other than the conscious. With this possibility, the method implicitly fosters a questioning of the nature and possible defensive role group affiliations hold. This applies to the relational and psychological; it also applies to the existential. Learning that group affiliations and identities have irrational and defensive qualities ultimately lead people down a troubling path:

1. If there are ulterior psychological mechanisms for social, emotional, and work groups, there may be analogous mechanisms for ideological, spiritual, or political affiliations.
2. The possibility that ideological, spiritual, or political affiliations have a purpose beyond the conscious begins to increase anxiety as their defensive nature is contemplated.
3. As contemplation increases, the function of these affiliations as "death denying" illusions and their primary, but unspoken mechanism to reduce levels of death anxiety and accompanied dissonances deteriorate.
4. With the deterioration of these anxiety-reducing mechanisms there are increased opportunities for awareness and panic.

And whereas I would not assert most, if any people have ever left a Tavistock conference and said, "Gee, that group relations method is something, I may need to apply it to different aspects of my life, especially the existential. Whoa! I think I must be a devout [insert belief system here] because of the death denying comfort it affords me!" I do think many members leave with an increased sense of awareness and panic. The awareness has to do the potential utility of the model and the panic has to do with the types of rabbit holes the model may take one down. This certainly applies to the existential experience of people and all the intensity that brings.

# CHAPTER FIVE

# Lacanian discourses and the learning group

*Clive Hazell*

The purpose of this chapter is to demonstrate the applicability and utility of Lacan's scheme of discourses (2007) in group-as-a-whole work. First, I will outline Lacan's theory of the four discourses. Following this, I will address some applications of Lacan's ideas that have been dealt with by other writers and finally I will provide examples of discourse theory as it might be applied to group-as-a-whole work.

Lacan identifies four discourses and diagrams them as below.

Master    University

$$\frac{S1}{\$} \rightarrow \frac{S2}{a} \qquad \frac{S2}{S1} \rightarrow \frac{a}{\$}$$

Analyst    Hysteric

$$\frac{a}{S2} \rightarrow \frac{\$}{S1} \qquad \frac{\$}{a} \rightarrow \frac{S1}{S2}$$

KEY
S1:   The master signifier
$:   The divided subject

S2:    The signifying chain
→:    The direction of production
a:    l'objet petit a, jouissance
—:    The bar

In addition, each of the corners of the quadrant has a fixed definition as diagrammed below.

$$\frac{\text{Agent}}{\text{Truth}} \rightarrow \frac{\text{Object}}{\text{Product}}$$

Thus we can see that each of the four symbols (S1, S2, a, $) rotate, one quadrant at a time, over the four positions of Agent, Object, Product, and Truth. This rotation creates each of the qualities and attributes of each of the four discourses. Thus, in the discourse of the Master we have the agent as the master signifier (S1) who produces desire (*objet a, Jouissance*, surplus production) in those who are the targets of the action. Such desire is barred from complete awareness by a signifying chain (S2). The truth of the matter is that the master signifier is him or herself, a divided subject ($). An example of this might be the cult leader who speaks with absolute certainty and mastery as if has a hold on the ultimate truth, as if he has "the word" (S1). This "truth" is manifested in signifying chains (sermons, dictates, proclamations). The followers are a flock who follow and worship the master, creating for him a surplus value that the master enjoys but of which they are largely unaware (a). The master, guru or cult leader is unaware, as is everyone else, of their "feet of clay" of their secret divisions and uncertainties, symptoms, fetishisms, and neurotic conflicts ($).

A further example would be the old fashioned aristocrat who lords it over the serfs. They pontificate and moralize while the serfs labor and produce a surplus. This master–slave relationship is cloaked in a discourse of fealty and obedience while the aristocrat harbors secret neuroses. We can see here the derivation of Lacan's scheme, for this last example is the first "move" in Hegel's discourse of master and slave (1977). Hegel points out that this discourse is an inherently unstable one and goes on to outline a theory of history founded upon this instability. This is later elaborated upon by Kojeve (1980) and Fukuyama (2006). Lacan takes a different tack. As we can see he posits these four discourses and, rather than posit an inevitable historical evolution from one discourse to another, seems to argue that each of the discourses necessitates the other and that we will observe a fluctuation from one discourse to another as we observe human interactions at all levels.

When we turn to the discourse of the university we see that the agent produces a chain of signifiers which creates a divided other. The object becomes overtly filled with desire. The secret truth is that while the agent in this discourse appears to be holding forth free of a master signifier, in fact the entire discourse rests upon an unacknowledged master signifier, a basic unquestioned assumption, without which, the entire discourse crumbles into meaninglessness.

As an example of this discourse we may turn to a university lecture hall. The professor holds forth upon a topic creating a signifying chain (S2). This produces hidden conflicts in the students as they learn new perspectives and are called upon to alter their world views. They feel mixed feelings about this ($). Ideally, the students are filled with desire to learn and an interest in the subject at hand. They are hungry for the words of the teacher (a). The professor may claim that she is unbiased, that what is being presented is "science" and they are pursuing an open-minded inquiry. The truth of the matter is, however, that all the signifying chain is based upon, and must be based upon, a master signifier, an assumption that is "taken as read" that cannot be proven by the signifying chain that it has enabled, but is assumed as a starting point, as a *"point du capiton,"* a quilting point. Godel's incompleteness theorem (Franzen, 2005) demonstrates that the basic assumptions of a theorem cannot be proven by the logical consequences of that selfsame assumption. This leaves the basic assumption, as it were, "hanging in space." Such arbitrary beginnings to our discourse are rapidly forgotten and the ensuing discourse is assumed to be independent of such leaps of faith. This we find in the conception of the master signifier.

In the discourse of the analyst the symbols have taken another quarter turn and we have the opposite of the discourse of the master. The agent is "a," that is the agent is set up as the overflowing point of desire. This agent produces discourse that acts as a master signifier and it is addressed to the divided subject, the subject that is at odds with itself, in conflict. The barred truth of the discourse, that is the lower left quadrant, is that the analyst speaks from a chain of discourse. The comments (let us call them "interpretations") may seem "crazy" and saturated with desire, but they actually follow a logic, a theory, an organized praxis, as in a craft. A common situation in psychotherapy can illustrate this discourse. The patient forgets to bring a check to pay for the session the week after there has been a break in sessions because the therapist was away on vacation. The therapist may offer an interpretation that this is the form of a retaliation for the pain caused by the therapist and his absence. In this the therapist seems to be placing themselves as an object of desire in the patient's world by implying to the patient, "You love me and you missed me. You are angry and hurt." The therapist is also producing a superfluity of meaning, of excess, a surplus, as it were. "It is not just forgetfulness; it is love and hate." The patient, seeing the analyst as the *sujet supposé savoir* hears the interpretation as having the stamp of authority (S1). Although the statements of the analyst may appear "crazy talk" to the naïve observer, they are, in fact founded upon one or several organized and serviceable theories (S2). These theories are not explicitly addressed. They are "barred." If they were addressed, the discourse would probably become educational, that is, the symbols would rotate back a quarter turn and it would become the discourse of the university.

In the discourse of the hysteric, another quarter turn of the symbols takes place and the subject that speaks is divided ($). The subject is in conflict with itself. This captures the essence of the neurosis, "Should I or shouldn't I? Did I or didn't I? Do I or don't I?" and so on. The hysteric produces a chain of discourse, linked symbols (S2) that are directed at the master signifier (S1). In a way, we might say that the hysteric is fascinated and mystified by the master signifier. The secret truth is that the hysteric is the object of desire, a source of surplus, of *jouissance.*

The discourse of the hysteric is perhaps best understood by starting with the symptom. For example, a daughter, filled with both love and hate ($) for her angry, obsessive, and frightening father, faints when he walks into her room unexpectedly, as if god has just been sighted (S1). The secret is the barred awareness of the desire inherent in the situation—the desire for and of the love of the father. It was in such passionate domains that Freud got his start, and the analyst is ideally suited to speak to the hysteric. Note that in the discourse of the analyst, the agent (a) speaks directly to the divided subject ($). The daughter in the above example might well benefit from a discursive relationship of the analytic kind.

Figure 10 is meant to demonstrate that in any social situation there is likely to be an oscillation between the four discourses, often with the preponderance of one type of discourse over the others, and that this preponderance is what will define the nature of the discourse. The discourses are both synchronic and diachronic. In many fundamentalist cults, there will be a preponderance of the discourse of the master,

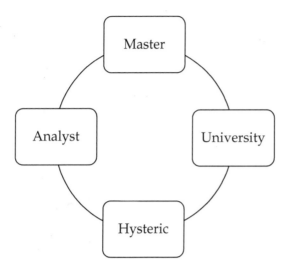

Figure 10.    Relations between the discourses.

although close observation will usually show instances of other forms. Similarly, in a classroom, there will be a predominance, usually, of the discourse of the university, while in the analyst's office or in a group relations event, one would likely see more of the analyst's discourse. In groups and individuals who are conflicted, who state they want to do one thing while they busily set about doing the opposite in some way, we would find the discourse of the hysteric.

While we may have a preference for one type of discourse over another, the discourses flow into one another and rely on one another for their very functioning. Each discourse also serves different functions and is arguably related to different individual and group tasks. For example the discourse of the master can be seen as linked to Bion's basic assumption dependency. Bion has shown how this assumption can be yoked to group functions we find in religion or human needs for stability and permanence. The discourse of the university is clearly linked to individuals and groups involved in tasks having to do with the transmission of knowledge. In groups and individuals coping with ambivalence and conflict and the intrusion of anti-task behavior, the discourse of the analyst would seem to be useful and perhaps the discourse of the hysteric is a group's or individual's way of bringing into the discussion that which cannot be uttered; the inchoate, the conflicted, the unbearable. This leads us to a formulation of the task of the group consultant in terms of discourse theory. The task of the consultant can be seen in part as involving the identification of the discourses operating in the group in the here and now and to explore their relationship to the task at hand.

## Žižek: Authenticity and consistency in the discourses

Žižek (1993) provides a different avenue for understanding and utilizing Lacan's scheme. His fourfold categorization is amplified and applied to legal theories by Lorraine Schroeder (2008). Figure 11 illustrates his ideas.

We thus see, following Žižek, that the analyst's discourse is consistent, that it is internally logical and forms part of an integrated coherent and cohesive system of thought and language. It is also authentic. Sidestepping, for the moment, the many problems surfaced by this troublous term, we may state that the discourse of the analyst is open to an encounter with the truths of the self, the truths of desire, and mastery.

The discourse of hysteric is authentic, the symptoms speak to the truths of a divided subject, but it is also inconsistent. Now one thing is asserted, next another; now one thing is done, then it is undone. Ambivalence and ambitendency prevail throughout the discourse.

The discourse of the university is consistent; there is a logical flow to the presentation; there is a syllabus and a set of guidelines, but the discourse is inauthentic. Desire is held by the other and the truth of the existence and dominance of the master signifier is kept under wraps.

The discourse of the master is both inconsistent and inauthentic. The master does not have to "make sense" and doesn't. The discourse can be full of rampant unacknowledged contradictions. In addition the truth of the "feet of clay" of the master is a closely guarded secret and

|  | Consistent | Inconsistent |
|---|---|---|
| Authentic | ANALYST | HYSTERIC |
| Inauthentic | UNIVERSITY | MASTER |

Figure 11. Authenticity and consistency of the four discourses.

desire is kept in the other, not acknowledged as present in the subject. The Wizard of Oz provides an example of this phenomenon as depicted in popular culture.

This fourfold table helps again visualize the opposition of the discourse of the master and the discourse of the analyst. The discourse of the master is the "other side of psychoanalysis." Interestingly, by extension, we see that the discourse of the university is the opposite of the discourse of the hysteric.

Struggle occurs within the discourse, for example between master and slave in the discourse of the master and slave as described by Hegel (1977) and struggle or conflict also occurs between discourses as we see in conflicts arising between the master and the university. An example of this might be the conflict arising between fundamentalist religion and scientists forwarding the theory of evolution. An example of the struggle between the discourse of the university and the analyst might be exemplified by the history of Lacan's conflicted relationships with actual universities and schools of psychoanalysis. Such ideas are connected, perhaps to Bion's notions of "container and contained" (Bion, 1977). Many narratives are founded upon just such combinations and permutations of "collisions of narratives." The movie *Analyze That* (Ramis, 2002) or the therapist/patient relationship in *The Sopranos* (Chase, 1997) dramatize the tensions between the discourse of the analyst and that of the master (mobster). Similarly the romantic comedy (or tragedy) where the college professor (standing for the discourse of the university) falls for the coquettish student (standing for the discourse of the hysteric) still seems to fill theater seats.

A group consultant can thus not only identify what discourses seem to be operating in the group in the here and now and to consult to the inherent tensions in such discourse, they can also observe in groups the types of tensions that seem to arise from the co-existence in the group of different types of discourse and the tensions that emanate from this. Often, there is a competition in the group so that one discourse might be established to the exclusion of the others. At other times, it is as if certain types of discourse will only be tolerated in a highly managed form. The group consultant can also analyze their own contributions. Ideally, these should be in the discourse of the analyst, but often counter-transferential, institutional, managerial, and other issues (symbolic, real, and imaginary) will cause the consultant to shift discourses, so that instead of analyzing, they educate (discourse of the university), pontificate (discourse of the master), or seduce (discourse of the hysteric). Sometimes the roles in these discourses will be reversed and it is the consultant who is scolded, educated or quasi-seduced. These deviations are in themselves analyzable, and probably they should be analyzed. Following Langs (1979) we think that deviations from the task and role of the consultant should be at least implicitly acknowledged in an interpretation.

If the consultant is reasonably consistent in their maintenance of role and they do, in fact, deliver the discourse of the analyst, then this usually, especially in the early stages of group formation, will stand in contrast to the other prevailing discourses in the group. This again provides much fodder for observation and interpretation in the group insofar as the consultant may observe what happens to his discourse and what seem to be the preferred discourses in the group.

The following are examples from groups to illustrate the four discourses in action.

## The discourse of the master

This pattern is quite common in groups. It can be seen when the group insistently asks what the consultant wants them to do, what the "right" way of behaving in a group is. The group is on a quest for the holy grail of correctness-the master signifier. Perhaps a member will read from the syllabus or the conference brochure and quote in a forceful way the manner in which members are supposed to behave and what the true task of the group is. At other times the consultant will be criticized for having deviated from the groups inchoate, yet firmly held notion of what a leader should be and how they should behave. The consultant to the group will often be referred to as the leader even though the role has always been carefully described in the group literature and preparations as "consultant." There is frequently the feeling in the group as if there is a strict paternal function in the room, a strong, brittle, unforgiving "superego" that will weed out deviants and enforce the rule of law. However, in a Tavistock or a leaderless group, the exact nature of that law remains unclear. Referring back to origins, namely Hegel's discourse of master and slave, it will often seem that the group is a want-to-be slave searching for an absent or ill-defined master. This desire for a master is frustrated because the consultant stays in the role of consultant, abjuring the role of dictator and remorselessly offering up only the utterances of the analyst. Thus the discourse in a Tavistock group often plays out as frustrated desires for domination and submission. In several ways this discourse is a manifestation of Bion's basic assumption dependency (Ba/D) and it is also reminiscent of Reich's "emotional plague" (1980a).

### The discourse of the university

As the name for this discourse implies, this discourse will be seen to be present whenever something ostensibly "educational" occurs in the group. Perhaps the consultant starts to offer consultations that get quite lengthy and have a didactic and explanatory tone to them. It might even start to feel like a traditional seminar in the room, with students manifesting a desire to know, curiously asking the consultant for clarifications and explanations, acting like good students, hungry for learning. Of course the consultant can be pulled into this "feeding" role if she feels rewarded by such interest. If the consultant herself is unwilling to take up the role of professor, then perhaps a group member will oblige, especially if they have more experience in group work or a predisposition to be the instructor. They may bring in some printed material or share their wisdom with the group and start to educate. Because this mimics so many other classroom situations, the group, and sometimes the consultant will feel that "work" is going on. Of course, if the stated purpose of the group is examination of the group's dynamics in the here and now, it is not. This is a flight from the task.

Lacan informs us that this discourse of the university which seems so free from the dynamics of the master–slave discourse, has in actuality, a hidden truth, namely, that the discourse emanating from the "professor" which seems so free and "liberal" (S2) is in actuality founded in secret upon the assumption of a master signifier which serves to anchor the meanings of the symbolic chain (S1)—the master signifier. The secret of this discourse is that it too is founded upon basic assumption dependency (Ba/D). The dependency however is not as rank as that in the master–slave discourse. It is mediated by a signifying chain, a set of linguistic or logical rules that can at least be played with to some extent. If one pushes for the ultimate basis of these rules, however, one finds that it is an arbitrary starting point that must stand as a master if the system of rules is to stand. If the beginning assumption is challenged the entire system falls. Further, following Godel (Franzen,

2005) we cannot prove the validity of the beginning set of assumptions with the rules that emanate from it. It remains radically arbitrary and unfounded, yet if we are to communicate and think we must act as if this is not so while at the same time acknowledging it. Of course, such ambiguity is not appreciated by the group when it is in full flight of enjoying the discourse of the master or the university. Such ambiguities belong consciously only to the discourse of the analyst. Such ambiguities, as we shall see are acted out in the discourse of the hysteric.

## The discourse of the hysteric

The discourse of the hysteric can be seen to be operating in a group when there is a symptom—a symptom understood in the "old fashioned" sense of a divided subject. A group member would like to run away and not run away; to kick someone, but not kick someone; to spread their legs but not spread their legs; to stand on their own two feet, but not have a leg to stand on. They are a tangle of conflicts. How are these conflicts spoken? In a symptom. The group member inexplicably gets her legs all caught up in the chair such that she cannot budge. In the language of Lacan's discourses, the subject is divided, in conflict, desiring and also not wanting to do something. These wishes are directed towards the "master signifier," usually personified by an authority figure, real or imagined, often the consultant or what the consultant is seen to stand for. The discourse of the hysteric produces speech, a signifying chain (S2) but it is riddled with conflict and the secret is the secret unfulfilled desire of *l'objet petit a* that is barred from recognition in this discourse.

Much "small-talk" in the group can be understood as the discourse of the hysteric. Examples are legion. A common theme in groups of students is the topic of "other professors, other classes." Here, the group will discuss the pros and cons of other professors—who is nice, who is not; who is hot, who is not; who is easy, who is hard; who is cool, who is stodgy. The divisions of approach and avoidance, love and hate, fear and trust are captured in the topic itself (the divided subject). Behind the division and ambivalence lies the secret of desire (*l'objet petit a*). The discourse that is created is, on a manifest level, quite sensible and sequential (S2) and the entire discussion can be seen as a derivative, in the sense used by Langs (1979), which is all about the group's attitudes towards and feelings about the consultant, who is seen as the master signifier (S1). To anticipate the discourse of the analyst we would say, in the role of consultant to the group, that the group is discussing, in disguised form, its mixed feelings about the consultant.

## The discourse of the analyst

The discourse of the analyst can be seen in the group when individuals in the group speak to the divided subject, producing a "master signifier" (S1). The one in the role of analyst positions themselves as the object of desire (a). The secret truth is that the analyst "sits on" a body of schematized knowledge and ideas that guide his understanding of the discussion, even though this comprehension might appear to be free-floating (S2).

The discourse of the analyst can be seen when a consultant makes an interpretation regarding group behavior. Such interpretations have been hinted at in the previous examples. Another example: a group composed mostly of young adults pressured the singleton, old white male to be more forthcoming and generous in his contributions to the group. They were irritated that he had not shared much of himself emotionally, and that when pressed all he seemed to do was offer thoughts. He did not spend enough time with them or seem warm enough. Although this feedback had some merit, to the consultant the pressure did seem somewhat disproportionate. The man had been making an effort and other members had been far less forthcoming. The consultant then offered the hypothesis that the group was displacing its anger at the consultant (an old, white man), whom they experienced as overly distant onto the person that most resembled him, namely the singleton white male in the group. In thus doing, the consultant had initiated (or attempted to initiate) the discourse of the analyst in the flow of the discourse of the hysteric. The consultant had placed himself as the object of desire (a). In making the interpretation, he was saying to the group, "You think you want him, but you actually desire me." He was addressing the divided subject in the group in saying, "You want me but you also do not want me and that is why you displace this desire on to someone else. You are a divided subject." The consultant delivers the hypothesis out of the authoritative role of "consultant," thus imbuing it with the power of a master signifier (S1). The secret truth is that the consultant is practicing a craft, a craft based on a theoretical framework (a signifying chain) (S2).

Often a group will respond to consultations such as these with comments like, "Why does the consultant have to always make everything in the group about them? Can't we just be mad at someone or do something and it is not about how we feel or what we want to do with them?" In this, we see a recognition of the discourse of the analyst, where the subject places themselves as the object of desire, and in this is the key to the transferential interpretation.

## Summary

There is a seemingly inevitable tendency towards the apodictic, towards the normative—an urge to ask, "Which one of these is best and how do we encourage its further use?" Lacan is quick to stall such attempts. As we saw at the outset of this chapter, the four discourses are not hierarchically organized, no matter how much we may prefer one over another. They are arranged in a circuit, as in Figure 10 (Relations among the discourses). As in the Borromean knot, where we have an inevitable intertwining of symbolic, imaginary and real, so we have a dialectic interdependence among the four discourses. A metaphor I find helpful is that of Tesla's rotating magnetic field in his induction motor. Motive force is created as the core "chases" the rotating magnetic field in a never-ending charged circle of coils. Similarly, the energy of a group endlessly "chases" and is engaged by these four discourses. Just as if one of the coils should fail in an induction motor and the energy stalls, so, if one of the discourses is absent or weak, the energy in the group falters. There is a parallel to Lacan's Borromean knot here. If any of the symbolic, the imaginary or the real is not adequately heeded, we end up with "problems." Lacan always seems reluctant to adopt any pragmatic stance (such talk is markedly Anglo-Saxon). But the things seem to go much better when all four discourses and all three registers are pulsating, alive, and well.

The following table gives a further illustration of the application of some of Lacan's ideas to groups. This was a very brief demonstration group given as part of a class in a graduate school of psychology. There were six members, three male, three female and the instructor a female, was joined on this occasion by a guest lecturer, an old white male who co-consulted.

## Illustrative example: a short student group

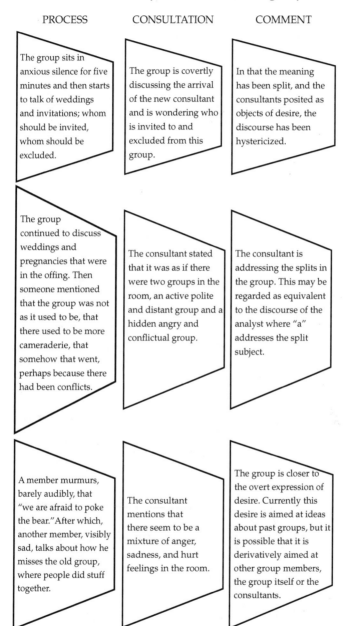

Figure 12.  Lacanian discourses and the learning group.

### The discourses as a way of conceptualizing
### the concept of capture

The concept of "capture" is one of the first concepts I learned when working on the staff of a Tavistock conference. I did not know much, but I quickly gained the impression that it was bad and to be avoided. There was a distinct psycho-galvanic judder in the room whenever the possibility that some staff member had been "captured" was forwarded. It was quite frightening. In technical terms, a harsh, rigid, and punitive superego was activated around this concept and I at times felt quite paralyzed in terror.

The basis of the concept of capture, despite these powerful emotional responses I had, is really quite rational and even prosaic. When one is a consultant, one's job, one's role, is to consult to the group as a whole. If one strays from this task and gives advice, offers encouragement or sympathy, shares one's personal history, or has an argument or personal interaction with a group member where your desires and wishes might be manifested, then you have strayed from your role as a consultant. Linked to this is the idea that this straying from one's role was motivated, at least in part, by your own wishes and the wishes of the group to whom you ought to be consulting. You have been "captured." The undertow of the group has pulled you out of role. Perhaps you were complicit in this capture. Perhaps even the staff with whom you are working and its dynamics contributed to your capture. Perhaps you were offered up by them to the membership. If the group is capable of getting beyond the paralysis induced by a harsh superego and the terror of having "done something wrong" and being seen to have done so by the group such thoughts as these can lead to some very interesting, illuminating, and useful re-conceptualizations of the group and its matrix. In this sub-section, I will demonstrate how the Lacanian discourses provide another useful and interesting way of attending to and thinking about the phenomena associated with "capture."

A Tavistock style consultant has signed on for the job of providing group-as-a-whole consultations that relate to ideas about the unconscious dynamics of the group at hand. This clearly locates the consultant's task in the realm of the discourse of the analyst. When the group, on day one, launches into a discussion of safe and dangerous neighborhoods in the city and techniques for identifying and avoiding them, the consultant in this role might consider sharing with the group the idea that members are afraid of the group, concerned about their safety and would like to develop ways of ensuring same. The consultant might also consider adding (on a more transferential note) that the group is wondering if he (the consultant) is a safe or dangerous neighborhood. The consultant as "agent" is offering themselves up as an *objet petit a*, insofar as there is a playing with language, there is a willful stepping into a potential, transitional space—Langs' area of illusion (1979). Interestingly, this speech is intensely in the mode of assimilation (Piaget & Inhelder, 1969) in that it plays "fast and loose" with the rules of language. In everyday terms, it is like "crazytalk"—lallations. In addition, these comments are aimed at an object that is treated as if it was split ($). The group thought it was talking about safe and dangerous neighborhoods. After this consultation, it is as if they are in two minds—one talking about the city, the other talking about the current group dynamics.

The product of this consultation (that which occupies the lower right quadrant of the discourse diagram) is usually a dreadful feeling that some master has spoken, and has uttered terrible, dreadful words. Often this will manifest in the group joking about the "oracle" or the "mad scientist" who is conducting an experiment for his amusement. Paranoia and death anxiety mount in the presence of such a one. Sometimes a brave soul will attempt a rebellion of sorts.

Finally, the lower left quadrant, the truth. In the discourse of the analyst, the letter that occupies this quadrant is S2, the signifying chain. Although the consultant appears to be speaking "crazytalk," or seems to be trying to drive people crazy by splitting them in two, or seems to be making pronouncements from on high, or all of the above, the truth of the matter is that there is an organized chain of signifiers that bring a rational order to his consultations—theories, supervision, reading, training, ordered studies, observations, thinking, and research. This is the truth of what the consultant is "sitting on" when he speaks in the discourse of the analyst.

Having grasped this mapping of group consultation onto the discourse of the analyst, we can, with relative ease, proceed and see how when a consultant drifts into any of the other discourses, it is indeed a "capture." Such a reconceptualization is useful in at least two ways. First, it provides a finer grained categorization of the type of capture. For example, was the consultant captured into the discourse of the master, the hysteric or the university? (I will leave aside my proposition that there is at least one more discourse, that is, the discourse of the clown). Once this determination has been made, one may ask why this particular form of capture was chosen and this will lead to some interesting hypotheses regarding the dynamics of the group. Second, when the question as to the form and function of capture is posed in this way, there is a considerable relief of the aforementioned paralyzing superego pressure and the way is more open to migrating the discourse back to that of the analyst in a way that is not driven by numbing senses of shame and guilt. The pathway is better lit by curiosity.

## Capture by the university

Here the consultant becomes the professor. She offers educational consultations to an avid audience that is split in its love and hate for the professor who, while looking like an open-minded, even handed type is sitting on an unacknowledged throne of a "master signifier." Many anxieties can drive the group and consultant into this form of capture. First, it often has an "obsessive-compulsive" quality to it and indeed it will serve as a good defense against affect and any ideas of chaos or lack of control and order that might be present in the group or its context. Second, it is often too hard to differentiate from analytic work, especially if one only hears about it from reports—"the group addressed oedipal issues in a particularly interesting way." This type of discourse in a group maps neatly into the "speculative" row of Hill's scheme (1965). It often has the feel of "this is what psychotherapy looks like" and is found often in groups composed of psychotherapists in training. This discourse also has a feeling of usefulness that derives from its attempts at orderliness and functionality. It can thus serve as a defense against feelings of uselessness, powerlessness, and void. Sometimes consultants will feel impelled to "educate" when groups start voicing their dissatisfactions and saying things like "We aren't learning anything! I wish I was in that (other) group where things are actually making progress!" It is difficult indeed to follow Bion's edict of being without "desire, memory or understanding." In the discourse of the University there is plenty of each—desire that there be learning, memory for what has been learned and understanding of what is being learned. Recall, this is not a panning of educational discourses or psycho-educational groups. They are extremely useful. However, even in psycho-educational groups, there is "discourse migration," from the supposedly predominant discourse of the university into and around the other discourses. An aspect of being a competent teacher is knowing how to "manage" such situations—the emotional outburst in the classroom, the wild comment from left field, remarks on the here and now situation in the room ... The assessment of the discourse and its utility is best related to the task of the group.

## Capture by the master

When the consultant is "captured in the discourse of the master," he will be seen laying down the law, admonishing, praising, castigating, blaming, exhorting, and using the techniques and wiles of the master. Sometimes this master will be the frightening heroic brute of Hegel (1977) sometimes the philosopher-king of ancient Greece, sometimes a good shepherd, sometimes the Prince of Machiavelli, sometimes a mad scientist, sometimes a King Hal, "... we precious few ... filling the breach with the English dead!", as in Shakespeare's *Henry V*, sometimes "Big Brother" and sometimes combinations of the above or any of the other many forms of mastery over others.

Consultants might be captured by this discourse when anxiety of certain forms runs high in the group. Sometimes an element in the consultant's superego is stepped upon and a flare up of "conscience" results in an attempt by the consultant to master the situation. As suggested above, this mastery may take "old fashioned" forms, as in Kingship or manifestations of force. In the postmodern era, however we are more likely to see "soft mastery", it is a "soft machine" that stealthily emerges and exerts control in order to create an absence of dialectic, a "one dimensional" man, woman, group or institution (Foucault, 1980; Marcuse, 1991). Consultants can subtly communicate to groups that the rules of discourse to be followed emanate from the consultant and that the group serves at the pleasure of the consultant. Groups also, which are frequently operating under the aegis of a dependency assumption will readily encourage the consultant to become their leader and tell them what and what not to do. And although the consultant's perceived position as master is often bridled against, this master/servant situation, for all of its unsatisfactoriness, still meets deep dependency needs.

Consultants may also be suctioned into the discourse of the master when boundary issues arise, especially if these are unexpected. For example, members who are dedicated anti-work leaders, members who consistently act out by, for example, missing sessions and showing up late, interruptions of the work from persons "outside" the group (administrators, cleaners, security personnel) can all serve to render a consultant unsure of his footing and legitimacy and might cause them to swerve their discourse to that of the mastery in an anxious attempt to re-establish their role as a consultant. In their attempt, of course, they paradoxically further undermine their role as a consultant.

In addition, it may be that the consultant has their legitimacy or authority under question in the institutional surround of the group itself. This may cause them to compensate in the group by adopting a more "masterful" stance. Further, it might be that issues operating in the wider society touch on hot spots for the consultant. These topics might be broached in the group and the consultant finds themselves "holding forth" from some "bully pulpit' or another, telling the group, "how it is!" For example, perhaps the issue of race and leadership, or abortion or sexism is powerfully charged in the wider society. The consultant is galvanized by this issue. The group starts a discussion on it in a rather tendentious (perhaps even provocative) way and the consultant rises to the bait and stops analyzing and starts laying down the law. Once this is done, then the discourse becomes quite complex, because the group will perhaps pick up that there has been a deviation in the frame." After all, aren't consultants only supposed to consult?" And then the group, in turn, starts to make derivative comments (Langs, 1979) aimed at commenting upon the deviation in the frame that has just occurred. All this is intermingled with the previous substantive discussion which had its own latent and manifest meanings so the discourse is now quite chaotic and will remain so unless it is consulted to. I believe, along with Langs (1979), that perhaps the best consultation should include an admission on the part of the consultant that they have made an error. It might be helpful (and not too defensive) to offer a hypothesis as to why this error had been made accompanied by a curiosity as to why it was made. This would constitute something of a return to the discourse of the analyst.

## Capture by the hysteric

If we recall the structure of the discourse of the hysteric, we see that it involves a split subject, directing discourse at the master signifier, producing a chain of signifiers while holding *l'objet petit a*, desire. When the consultant has been captured by this discourse it manifests in the panoply of ways traditionally seen as "hysterical" as well as other, perhaps more disguised forms. The consultant may, for example, develop symptoms in and around the group but, importantly will not utilize these symptoms in the formation of analytic comments. She may fall asleep, forget the beginning and ending times of the group, get names wrong, leave buttons or zippers undone, get their feet caught up in the chair, develop a physical symptom, or any of the many symptoms often associated with "hysteria" in its multiple forms. Perhaps the consultant will engage in an oedipally tinged competition with a group member for victory or affection. This competition may be waged with intellect or charm, humor or even references to physical strength or sexual prowess. It might also show up in seductiveness, preening, endorsements of certain member's comments, cuteness or sexiness in clothing or demeanor, in the frequency of eye contact or even in smiles at certain select members and veiled criticisms of others.

Sometimes groups will symbolically offer one of its members as a "gift" to the consultant, a bride, wife, companion or partner. Sometimes this is sexualized, sometimes it might be less so. Sometimes groups will offer a young bride or lover to the consultant, perhaps with the aim of placating them or numbing them or getting them to stop the uncomfortable work of consulting to the group. If the discourse of the hysteric is holding sway, these offerings might be successful or might cause group dynamics that occupy much of the group's time without ever being analyzed.

At other times the discourse of the hysteric can show up in the context of the group and this might to a greater or lesser extent bleed into the group. For example, the consultant might be engrossed in oedipally charged conflicts with their fellow staff members and those who are in charge of the conference, department or institution. "Games", such as "who is daddy's or mommy's favorite?", "who owns the phallus?", "where is the phallus?" or "who has the biggest phallus?" might be played out, sometimes in "hissy fits," sometimes in highly disguised and often intellectualized and rationalized form. Frequent disguises involve struggles over authority, connections, linkages, and access to power, leadership, and influence, ownership of the most important ideas or the most powerful techniques and so on. While these scripts are being enacted in the context of the study group, or therapy group, they can easily walk into the room with the consultant and affect the dynamics of the group because the "consultations" have now become affected unconsciously by these hysterical dynamics operating in the organizational context of the group.

A key issue is that these dynamics are not examined. They can be examined. In fact, it is often the discourse of the hysteric that is most easily rendered examinable through the interposition of the discourse of the analyst. Lacan points out that these discourses are quite dynamic and that a transition from one discourse to another is usually (always) accomplished by a recourse to the discourse of the analyst, through an analytic interpretation which interrupts the hypnotic thrall of the other discourses. Or, as Bion, might put it, the analytic discourse interferes with "the numbing sense of reality."

We argue that it is this very interruption of the numbing sense of reality that is a major contributor to mental health. It offers "binocular vision," being able to look at things from a different perspective or vertex and opening one's mind to new horizons. In Piaget's terms, this might be framed as reintroducing a functional balance between assimilation and accommodation.

*Illustrative vignette*

The following vignette will perhaps help demonstrate the utility of this Lacanian framework in thinking through group phenomena, especially those involving capture. This example also helps show how the discourses are not only diachronic, that is occurring in a switching sequence, one after the other, but are also synchronic, that is, they are all going on to some extent together, simultaneously in any given discourse.

It is the penultimate small group of a sequence of eighteen one and a half hour sessions. The first fourteen were conducted at a school of professional psychology and the last four at a weekend retreat in a rural setting some 100 miles away from the school, which is located in a large city. This group is the last here and now group and its stated purpose is to examine group dynamics. The group is composed of eight persons, seven white, one African American female, seven female and one male. There is a consulting team comprised of one senior faculty member (myself) and two white graduate students in their twenties, one male, one female. There is one heterosexual married couple in the group, and they tend to sit together. Briefly, the history of the group has been quite calm, the major dramatic event being the expulsion of one member by the faculty member for non-attendance. This was a white male member who missed four sessions when it had been clearly stated in the beginning syllabus (the group is also a credit class at the school) that only two absences were permitted. The group did not do much work on this event.

About half way through this session the singleton white male initiates a discussion on race, affirming that he is blind to color and that this is the way it should be, that he is saddened by the extent to which the city he has moved to for this schooling is so segregated and obsessed with issues of race. He does not understand why this should be the case. Why can't people just get over it? His peroration seems to go uncontested. He seems to get some support from his wife. A mild challenge is made by the black woman who is in her early twenties, but he continues in his statements of frustration and bewilderment over why race is such a big deal.

As an aside, the consultant becomes aware that the rural retreat at which the group is being held is in an area that is perceived by persons of color to be very, very "white" and that whites rarely experience this whiteness since it is continuous with their own identity. Frequently, persons of color, especially African-Americans, in the past have evinced great anxiety at coming to the retreat. Interestingly enough, this is rarely stated in explicitly racial terms at the outset. It is usually "disguised" as an anxiety about getting lost, bugs, insects, cleanliness of the housing, and concern over the nature of the tasks of the retreat. Usually further examination reveals the underlying concern of racism in rural areas and the danger that blacks are exposed to in the "collar counties" around the metropolis.

The conversation continues in the same vein and the lead faculty consultant, a white male, becomes filled with powerful feelings of rage and sadness. He finds himself associating to his stepson, who is in his early twenties and is brown, since his parents are Mexican and Puerto Rican. He recalls the way in which his stepson is routinely stopped for no apparent reason while driving, frisked and searched and sometimes detained. His driving documents have to be in squeaky-clean condition if he is to be able to move on. He has been called down from the steps of the back porch where he lives by the police to be searched and to have his car searched. When he was a child he was picked on by other kids for being of color. Racist teachers would scapegoat him. He was threatened violently and abusively by gang members routinely. At work, whites would torment and exclude and test him and make life very difficult for him. It was a continuous uphill battle. The consultant overflows with these feelings and breaks role. He becomes captured and breaks into the discourse of the group by sharing these experiences, arguing, as it were, for the silenced opposition that one cannot ignore racism in the face of such virulent, violent daily evidence of it.

At this the young black woman bursts into tears of mixed pain and gratitude and the awareness and thinking of the group seems shifted. There is also the tacit awareness, unspoken, in the group, that *this is different*. The consultants have never spoken this way. They have never shared so much of their personal lives nor have they evinced such strong feelings. The group seems to end on a reparative note. The white protagonist male seems to act in a chastened, if not chastised manner and others seem to feel a mixture of sadness, guilt, and concern. The group ends.

Afterwards, the consultant trio get together to discuss the group, only briefly since there is much else on the agenda of the group. The lead consultant is concerned to a moderate extent about the "capture," as is the female consultant. Both seem willing to examine it but also to not worry overmuch. The younger male consultant on the other hand is very upset about this capture, sensing it as a violation, a betrayal of some sort. This is especially the case because the apprentice consultant had previously looked up to the lead consultant as an exemplar of good group work and yet here he has clearly broken the rules.

Clearly this vignette is pregnant with interpretive possibilities. What we seek to do in the following is to suggest some ideas that follow the outline of the four Lacanian discourses just described. In so doing, we hope to demonstrate the utility of this way of thinking. We also hope to demonstrate that the discourses are (like the Kleinian positions) both diachronic (occurring sequentially) and synchronic (occurring at the same time). We also will see how the discourses in a group setting are dizzyingly polycentric. At one moment one member is in the position of master, and the next they are in the position of the hysteric, and so on.

We find the discourse of the master at several locations in this vignette. The disappointed student, co-leader who asserts that the lead consultant abandoned their position and did not play by the rules speaks with the voice of the master. The lead consultant, insofar as he feels abashed and chastened, while aware that he should have done something different is the split subject of the hysterical position, perhaps addressing the master (student). This can be seen as a role switch of a radical kind since usually it is the professor who will take up the role of master (S1) or teacher (S2).

When the lead consultant sits with his ambivalent feelings as the peroration on racism is proceeding in the group, he is experiencing the split subjectivity of the hysteric, on the one hand aware of the role of being expected to speak as an analyst and yet filled with feelings and fantasies that contradict this position. When he finally "lets go" and is captured, he abandons the discourse of analyst and seems to occupy several discourses all at once. First, he has insofar as he has become captured, become "a symptom" and is speaking the discourse of the hysteric, addressing the "master racist" in the (imaginary) group. He is also delivering a counter argument, an educational diatribe and is thus taking up the role found in the discourse of the university. And finally, he is attempting to wrest control from the hegemony of the culture of "racial blindness" in the group. In this, he is adopting the discourse of the master.

The consequences of this capture are equally interpretable along these lines. Of particular interest are the feelings that suddenly pour out of the African American female who was previously in a rather subjugated, silenced position in the group, her captivity is ended by the successful capture of the lead consultant.

In addition we see a contrariwise movement in the two other white men. One, the group member, is challenged by the old white consultant and "backed off"; the other (the co-leader) suffers a loss of idealization as he mirrors the loss in status of the white male in the group.

## Summary

We hope that we have shown that the application of the four Lacanian discourses to the understanding of the "social bonds" that occur in groups can be of use in various ways—perhaps of as much use as the "basic assumptions" of Bion (1961) and other assumptions forwarded by other authors, for example, the assumptions of "massification" and "aggregation" posited by Hopper (2003). Thus, just as the consultant's experience of being seen as a "guiding shepherd" can be the source of "basic assumption dependency" interpretations, so may the four

Lacanian discourses be used as templates for generating potentially useful interpretations.

For example, when group members ask the consultant for his expert guidance and leadership out of an eagerness to be obedient or when they are concerned about whether or not they are doing the right things in the group, this can be understood as evidence for the discourse of the master. When the consultant finds they are being pressured into and perhaps complying with the act of teaching, of delivering "educational" consultations or when the group members take notes and refer to theories of group development and papers they must write, then the group can be seen as participating in the discourse of the university. When something that feels very much like a "symptom" emerges in the group, often an event that seems to challenge the very nature of the group and its *raison d'etre* as for example when someone has a pizza delivered or members decide to give each other backrubs or move the group to another space, these can be seen as manifestations of the discourse of the hysteric. Finally when we see in the group the deployment of concepts such as displacement, condensation, double entendres, transference, splitting, denial—any of the vast armamentarium of psychodynamic theory that addresses latent content as well as manifest content, then we have the discourse of the analyst.

We trust that the preceding has shown that this is not an empty classificatory exercise but one that lends further insight into group dynamics or, as Lacan would have it, into "social bonds." Once we arrive at a tentative classification of the discourse we have at hand a number of logical consequences and explanatory themes that can offer further insight into the unconscious dynamics of the group. We believe that this system can be of general use and is of especial use when attempting to understand the highly charged phenomenon of "capture of the consultant by the group."

The strength and utility of this fourfold Lacanian template lies not only in its interpretive fecundity but also in the reflective distance it can provide in such highly charged group situations. The fluidity of these social situations is more fully recognized as one sees the discourse slip, slide, and rotate around the quaternity and especially as one sees that in any social situation all four are operating at the same time. It is just that some are more apparent than others.

# CHAPTER SIX

# I'll disappear: data and the absence of data in the learning group

*Clive Hazell and Mark Kiel*

The use of the term "data" tends to conjure up dry rows of numbers rather than the close contact with emotions, fantasies, and impulses that is often part and parcel of Tavistock group work. This section aims to examine the types of data that the Tavistock consultant may use, examining situations that may lead to overwhelming floods of data and deserts of absence of data. Finally, ways of coping with data floods and droughts will be suggested. A thread running through this will be the openness to data that comes from ideas beyond the traditional frame.

When training to become a consultant in Tavistock learning groups, I was frequently asked, upon describing a consultation I had delivered, "What is your data?" Often, when consulting to a group, members would respond to consultations as if they came out of the blue and would ask, in one way or in another, "From where did you get such an outlandish idea?" I soon developed a habit of attempting always to have fairly reliable answers to such interrogations. I even developed a "rule of three," that is, that before I would deliver a consultation to the covert processes operating in a group, I would have at least three data points to substantiate my offering. Thus, for example, a consultation having to do with the group's boundaries might be backed up by my observation that the door had been left open, that someone had mentioned that they had found something in their purse that was not theirs and yet another had wondered if the group had the same start and end times every time.

## Types of data in groups

Freud reminds us that we do not have to look far for the unconscious. It is there, right in front of us, in us, surrounding us. It is mostly elusive because of our own unwillingness to encounter it and its contents. We are unwilling to hear what it has to tell us. The same might be said of groups and their covert processes. As we sit in a group, ready to consult, we are immersed in data—data that floods in along multiple channels.

First, there is sensory data, light, color, heat, smells, tactile data. There is proprioceptive data, how we feel in our bodies. Often these data are elaborated upon with imagination which, while it itself is data will transform the sensory data. Thus a brightly colored shirt might jar us or cheer us up. The sniffling and coughing of a member might cause us to recall comforting times in bed with a cold or might annoy us. Sensory data is colored by associations and fantasy. These fantasies can migrate into symbols, such that the stuffiness of the room comes to symbolize an uncaring administration of the facility, the "Black Hole of Calcutta" and the lack of power of the group members. We see how sensory data does not stay simply sensory for very long, it is almost instantaneously colored by imagination and symbolism. There might happen to be a television screen in the room. Fairly quickly the group is talking about being monitored by "Big Brother." Lacan's Borromean knot (2007), with its overlapping venn circles of the symbolic, the imaginary and the real helps chart our way through these waters. The cup of coffee that is spilled at the beginning of the group for the third time in a row occurs in the real as a sensory event, but it is also capable of being elaborated upon in the imaginary realm (Are we wetting the bed? Are we overflowing with passions? Does our cup run over?) and can be rendered in the symbolic realm, where it might become an interpretation, a means of exploring the shared meanings of this performance. Perhaps we could call these data streams I data, R data, and S data respectively, corresponding to the imaginary, real, and symbolic of Lacan's scheme.

Heidegger (1988) too, reminds us that Hegel cautions us that the immediacy of sense-data is illusory. Sense data is mediated. When we see an object, we tend to see it as an example of a category and thus miss its essence. Sensory data, however, seems to provide a sense of certainty. Heidegger calls this "sense certainty." However, Heidegger argues, along with Hegel, that "what is known by the senses is altogether a one-sided knowing" (Heidegger, 1988, p. 57) and "Sense-certainty is as little interested in itself as it is the *this-as-object*" (1988, p. 56). Thus, "what is known by the senses is altogether a one-sided knowing" (1988, p. 57) A group consultant, therefore, following these ideas would, janus-like, look, or rather, sense both ways, both upon the object, that is, the group and also upon the subject, that is themselves. Thus the observation, the sensing of the consultant is a different type of "looking on."

> This looking on is not an indeterminate, arbitrary, unprepared staring, guided by whims, but is a looking on within the attitude of undergoing an experience, the way this experience sees. This looking on is a looking with the eyes of absolute knowledge. (Heidegger, 1988, p. 53)

One could say that a dialectic is set free to play between the group and the consultant.

With regard to S data, symbolic data, there has been considerable emphasis on words. This is quite reasonable since this language is very powerful. However, there are multiple languages, multiple coding systems and each one can provide consultants or whomsoever with valuable data streams.

Musical data abounds in interpersonal settings. It is useful every now and then to turn off the content of *what* is being said and simply listen to the music of *how* it is being said. The consultant may fruitfully ask, "If this was a piece of music playing in this group, what would it be? A dirge? A military march? A pastoral? Who is performing? What instruments are being played and to what effect?" Thus for example, one might hear several of the group members playing a funeral march in low tones with sad sounds while the youngest member has been elected to chime in every now and then on the piccolo, as if to cheer everyone up. Meanwhile there is a tension in the room as if we all know that soon, unexpectedly, the braying horn section will interrupt. Perhaps this group orchestral piece reminds the consultant of "Three Places in New England," by Charles Ives. This association itself renders forth a welter of ideas about social processes. After this, the consultant tunes back into the manifest content of the group only to find they are talking about beaches in Mexico and how they long for a vacation. The consultant becomes aware of a divergence between the "music" of the group and the manifest content of the groups discourse and this itself is saturated with interpretive possibilities. The ground is set for some consultations.

Manfred Clynes in his book, *Sentics* (1989) offers a theory that the emotions are coded into "sentic shapes" of great precision and that the human brain recognizes these shapes across all sensory modalities. Thus, anger is characterized with a shape that involves a rapid expression of energy, followed by a very rapid decay. Sonically, musically, this would be expressed as a staccato effect; visually as a sharp edge or a point; gesturally, as a rapid jab, as in a karate chop. The emotions of grief, love, reverence, joy, hate and so on each have their own distinctive shape. Each shape can be recognized across modalities, rather akin to synaesthesia. This capacity is reminiscent of Stern's (2000) notion that the infant has the capacity for translation of sensory inputs and outputs across modalities. In addition, these shapes or codes are very precise, down to milliseconds. If they are altered by a few milliseconds this way or that, so that they last a tiny fraction of a second longer or if the rate of acceleration or deceleration is altered by a tiny amount so as to alter the contour of the shape, then the emotion that is experienced is changed or nuanced or, if the change is too great, the emotion is felt to be false, or fake. We think that the processor for these shapes, for this language is found in the mammalian brain. Fluency in this language can be trained, as we see in musicians who can take the same set of notes on a stave but give different readings of the feelings in the composition. If group consultants (or anybody who has to work with people) train themselves in this language they can become more effective by opening themselves to a flood of data in the situation. Hazell and Perez (2011) show how such processing might be of use to bodyworkers, chiropractors, naprapaths, massage therapists and so on.

The body, in its movement, structure, gestures, and positioning offers a form of language, another code, as it were, and thus, another data stream for the consultant to consider. There is a decent sized literature on these topics and a growing interest in incorporating bodily expression into therapeutic work, especially in dealing with trauma. Much of this work hails back to Janet (1889), Ellenberger (1981), and Reich (1980a, 1980b). More recently we see contributions by Lowen (1972,

2003, 2005, 2012), Levine (video, 2010), van der Kolk (2015) and Fisher (2008). The field is rich and varied. A summary far exceeds our space here but an illustrative example might demonstrate the integration of these bodily modalities in Tavistock work.

A group has, as its focus of attention a member, J, who is complaining about his depression, and loneliness. The other members have either "checked out" or are involved in an attempt to either "cure" J or at least get him to cheer up. They suggest exercise, hobbies; ask about his parents and so on, but to no avail. They are starting to get frustrated and J is starting to look like a "help rejecting complainer." It also looks somewhat like one of Berne's "games people play" (1996) "Why don't you? Yes, but." If we were to place this group interaction on Hill's chart (1965) it would occupy the intersection of "group/speculative" where a sort of pseudo-psychotherapy occurs. All of this would perhaps be enough data to give the consultant something to offer in the way of an interpretation, perhaps something like, "The group seems to have elected someone to play the role of patient and others to be therapists. Yet others seem to have checked out."

However, perhaps the consultant looks at the bodies in the room. They are slumped and the breathing seems to be shallow. Even the consultant is slumped and is suspending their breathing. The consultant checks in with what this feels like and then shakes this off by sitting up, lengthening his spine, and taking a few deep breaths. He then notices that J, the central person of the moment has a strangled, whiney voice and it looks like his body has been immobilized. He fits the description of the "masochistic" body structure as described by Reich (1980a, 1980b) and Lowen (2012). This is an unfortunately pejorative term but Reich and Lowen are not just putting labels on people, calling them names. They also inquire as to the underlying dynamics of this bodily structure. They argue that this bodily structure is found in individuals whose will and initiative have been thwarted. They have a lot of energy, but this energy is bound in by tight constricting belts of muscle. They fear they might burst if they let their repressed feelings, often of rage and sexuality out. Thus much energy is spent on containing these feelings. Now all this may or may not be true. However it does provide an interesting template that might be connected with some of the group dynamics. If all these formulations do hold for J and if he has been selected as some repository for the group perhaps the fact that he contains these dynamics of helpless, immobilized, pent up rage gives us a clue as to what might be another useful interpretation. Now we may offer a more elaborate hypothesis about what is going on in the group:

> The group seems to have elected someone to play the role of patient and others to be therapists. Yet others seem to have checked out. All of this might be connected to the group feeling tied up with feelings of helplessness and rage.

Thus a glance around the room at body structures and dynamics might give ideas as to individuals' predispositions to perform certain repository functions. These awarenesses might enable more deeply empathic consultations. It also might enable members to become aware of roles they recurrently play in groups as others pick up on the language of the body and the readiness to play certain roles that this language communicates.

Sometimes consultants might experience what might be called "intuitive" data, data that seems to come out of nowhere, often in a vivid and compelling way. Sometimes a word, sentence or phrase will pop up into the consciousness of the consultant (much like an instant message pops up on a computer screen). A phrase such as, "You never took enough care of me!" or "Why won't you listen?" might suddenly enter the stream of consciousness. At times this is reminiscent of the movie character in *What Women Want*, (2000) who suddenly finds himself blessed (or cursed) with the capacity to hear what women are thinking. As he walks down the street past women he hears such words and phrases being uttered or blurted out by the female passersby. This phenomenon is somewhat akin to patients who hear voices and in fact we have worked in groups where just such phenomena have occurred (Semmelhack, Ende, & Hazell, 2013; Semmelhack, Emde, Hazell, & Freeman, 2015) and they were treated as if they provided intuitive or eidetic data on the here and now of the group. This seemed to be effective for these members and for these groups. Sometimes the intuitive or eidetic data may be verbal, but it can also occur in other sensory modalities. A tune may keep playing in the head of the consultant, with or without words. This tune may be profoundly connected to latent dynamics in the group. Is the song a song of longing, sadness, anger, desolation? How does the timbre and meaning of this melody relate to the current process of the group?

Sometimes a vivid visual image may occur in the mind of the consultant or member. At a particularly intense moment in the life of a conference a staff member reported just having had a "vision" of a baby left to die in the snow. This image captured the profound feelings of isolation, disconnectedness, vulnerability, and danger of the group.

At other times the intuition is directly emotional. As an Englishman and an Irishman were talking in a somewhat heated fashion about what was happening in the group, the person sitting between them became overwhelmed with a deep and mysterious sadness and sorrow and dissolved in tears, tears that seemed in part connected to the current dynamics of the group, in part to his own history and in part to the history of the English and the Irish. In large part, the origin of the tears remained mysterious and profound.

Intuitive data such as these are different from "free association" since free association can be somewhat directed by one's will. One can ask oneself, "What does that remind you of?" or "What is that connected too?" These eidetic data arise with absolute spontaneity, rather like the "wild thoughts" of Bion (1997) and related to the prized "spontaneity" of Winnicott (1965).

Turning to linguistic data we find Freud's work is filled with ideas as to how these may be utilized in uncovering that which is unconscious. In *Interpretation of Dreams* (Freud, 1900), we find extended sections where a word from a dream (Boltraffio) is stated and disassembled again and again, each time revealing a new layer or perspective on unconscious meaning and intent. In his study of Schreber, (Freud, 1911) we find that meanings are revealed when we reverse the overt, immediate meaning of a statement. Thus, "I love him," and "He loves me," can become, "I hate him."

Freud demonstrates the use of the rebus, where "eye" can become "I" (Freud, 1905). Many parapraxes are linguistic, as in the well-known, "slip of the tongue" (Freud, 1901). The mechanisms of condensation, where one word assumes multiple meanings at the same time and displacement where a word may be used to symbolize something not consciously intended (Freud, 1900) are linguistic turns.

In addition, the very concepts of transference and derivatives (Langs, 1971) manifest as linguistic data when it takes the form of the common consultation,

> The group seems to be talking about a mad professor who teaches such and such, but there is a very good chance that this discussion refers to the consultant in this room as he or she is being experienced in there here and now.

Thus, for Langs, the speech in the group which appears to refer to a there and then set of phenomena can be taken as a here and now comment on the current "adaptive context" or situation in the group. Again, sometimes these derivatives can be painful for the consultant to countenance. For example the group may be discussing a series of bosses, teachers, colleagues, and acquaintances who just do not "get it," who just do not understand them. Taken as a derivative, this could be taken to mean that the group is experiencing the consultant as absent and unempathic. If there is supporting data, this somewhat unflattering perception should be built in to a consultation, especially if the consultant thinks it is true.

Many of the jokes Freud discusses and analyzes, (Freud, 1905) involve *double entendres*, plays on words, rebuses or linguistic set-ups that cause the listener to abruptly change frame of reference, resulting in anxiety, mastery, and laughter.

Thus, if we are faithful to Freud, we should have no shortage of data when listening to a group. These interpretive riches are such that even if the group is quiet (perhaps in attempt to starve out the consultant) a short statement here and there will be enough grist for the interpretive mill. A little can go a long way when we have the armamentarium bequeathed us by Freud.

Viewed in this way, we can perhaps understand why Lacan goes to such lengths to show that it profits us well to reread Freud from a distinctly linguistic framework.

But we may derive benefit from pushing this linguistic analysis a step further. We may, for example, treat the discourse of the group as a text and listen to it with the ear of a literary critic. Once we venture into this realm, we find a flood of ideas.

Bahktin (1982), for example, posits the differences between the epic and the novel, arguing that the epic speaks in one voice of a time long past while the novel is multi-voiced and radically engaged with the present. The epic aims at maintaining the status quo and is distinctly propagandistic in its motives, while the novel with its polyvocity involves a tremendous, highly energized flux, very close to the "dialogue" described by De Mare in the median group (2011). One might be able to listen to the "text" of the group with the question as to whether it is epic or novelistic in its nature and intent. Further, one might ask why such a form has been adopted.

Empson (1966) in *Seven Types of Ambiguity* presents many more than seven types for each page seems to have several types of ambiguity or slippages in linguistic meaning. The close reading Empson exemplifies uncovers many nuances and shadings of meaning. Such methods can be profitably applied to the discourse of the group so as to reveal subtexts, hidden possibilities in the stream of language. These interpretations themselves may stimulate further notions, further curiosities in members and consultants alike.

To illustrate how Empson's ideas on ambiguity can be applied to group consultation, we may use, as an example, an ongoing large group occurring on a monthly basis in a nursing home. The group averaged twenty-two members, usually about fifteen female and seven male and was conducted along Tavistock lines with three consultants, two male and one female. This is the same group referred to in Czochara, Semmelhack, and Hazell (2016).

First let us briefly describe Empson's categories of ambiguity:

- The first type is the metaphor, where something is described by comparing it to something else.
- The second type is where two metaphors operate at the same time, thus delivering at least two possible meanings.
- The third type is where two ideas are contained in a single word. The word may be read in at least two ways.
- The fourth type is where a statement contains two different meanings and this is intended to communicate the complex state of mind of the author.
- The fifth type is like the fourth type except that the author discovers an alternate meaning in the very process of writing or communicating.
- The sixth type occurs when the statement means nothing and the reader creates the meaning. Usually this meaning is at odds with the original intent of the author.
- The seventh type involves a statement where two words carrying the opposite meaning are used in close proximity with the intention of communicating a division in the mind of the author.

## The first type

The fourth group started off with a disparate discussion of hobbies, horse riding, quitting smoking, problem drinking, and a variety of other topics. A member blurted out, "Don't believe a word they say!" and this was hard to make sense of. Then, after a pause a lady asked the group if anyone had a crochet hook, she needed one. At this, the consultant felt that they had been offered a metaphor and was able to offer the following consultation. "The group feels like it is drifting. It cannot find anything to hook onto, not a book nor words that will help." The metaphor of the crochet hook also has allusions to thread, to losing the thread, to threading the needle, to stitches, fabric and so on. The consultant went on to hypothesize that this loss of the thread was perhaps related to some significant changes in personnel that had recently taken place in the home.

## The second type

In group twelve two visitors from France, sisters of one of the members, were present. Shortly after the beginning of the group, one of the members spilled her coffee on the floor. Several members helped clean up the mess. This was consulted to as being a possible metaphoric performance—and a metaphor that had several possible meanings. Could it be that the group was filled to overflowing? Was it overflowing with feelings? Was this a reference to the over-full room with two members from France? Could it be a statement that our cup "overfloweth"? Could it be all of these and more? The fact that there had been a spilling of water in the previous group, group eleven, suggested that whatever it was, if it was anything, it was an ongoing theme. We see in this example a metaphor which has at least two meanings and remains indeterminate until the group has worked with it to some extent.

## The third type

This type, where two ideas are contained in one word can be found in session seven where members shared their experiences of homelessness in their lives. Many had been foster children and many had lost their homes. Later, there was a discussion of the possible closing of the nursing home in which they resided. The word "homelessness" now becomes loaded with two contextual applications. On the one hand, the possible homelessness they face should the nursing home be closed and second the homelessness of their earlier lives. This double barreled meaning of the word "homeless" and the way in which it becomes "overloaded" with meaning and affect was addressed in a fairly straightforward consultation.

## The fourth type

This type of ambiguity where a statement communicates two different meanings, communicating the complex state of mind of the author is to be found in group seventeen which occurred after a three month hiatus owing to scheduling difficulties in the consulting team. Seemingly in response to this adaptive context the group spoke about the importance of persistence in gaining skills. This was consulted to as being perhaps related to the consultants' lack of persistence and being absent for three months. At this a member turned to the older male consultant and said forcefully, "Yes. Where were you Dr. H? ... Oh, don't worry, I know people need a little break now and then." This was followed by a discussion among the members speaking to the deep sense of gratitude they had for the group. This in turn was consulted to by pointing out that the rupture in the group seemed to have been smoothed over. At this the same member said, "Oh don't worry Dr. H. We have ways of getting rid of bad people." This was followed by an extended discussion how they had driven away unpleasant staff members in the past. This sequence, we think, nicely illustrates the complex state of mind existing in the group as it struggled with love, gratitude, hate, longing, and revenge.

## The fifth type

This type of ambiguity is found when the author, or speaker or group discovers what they mean to say as they say it. It is not an uncommon phenomenon for someone to realize, in the middle of a speech, for example, what was on their mind. Much of group work in the Tavistock tradition is of this nature.

In the fifth group, for example, the group started off by talking about Halloween, which had just past. This led, naturally enough to a discussion of death and sadness over loved relatives who had died. At this a consultant mentioned that in addition a group member had died in the previous week. Then the lady who had been the room-mate of the dead member opened up and shared her grief at the loss of her friend. It was as if this was the topic that really needed to be discussed but had only been alluded to in the previous flow of discourse.

## The sixth type

In this type the statement, or more broadly the discourse or the performance, means nothing at face value and it is up to the reader or audience to decide on its meaning and, according to Empson, to usually get it wrong.

An example of this type of ambiguity is fairly easy to find in a group comprised of individuals who are prone to loose associations, hearing voices, and with other ailments that might cause thoughts and language to become disordered.

One example occurred in group seventeen where a member asked if he might share techniques of Tibetan chanting with the group. He did so and the group joined in. Since there was no introductory explanation people were not quite sure what to make of it. After it was over the group sat in some anxiety and one member opined it felt like a cult. Another said he was afraid of the KKK. Another said it felt calming. Overall, there was a paranoid atmosphere in the room. Perhaps this is a frequent reaction to type six ambiguity. The consultant opined that something new had been brought into the group and that the group was not quite sure what to make of it. This prosaic consultation seemed to help the group think through the experience.

## The seventh type

The seventh type where two words of opposite meaning occur in the same statement, communicating a division in the author's mind is found very prominently in the writing of Blanchot (1988). In groups it will be found we believe, when the group is under stress. For example, in group one we find such opposites in abundance as the group has dual reactions to the prospect of joining a large group. There was a dread of loneliness and a dread of emotional contact and where it might lead. There was a strong wish for rules that would prevent a free-for-all and yet a strong wish for freedom from the restricting roles they had experienced in other groups. We are reminded here of Bion's observation that humans are group animals at war with their groupishness. When this conflict surfaces we seem to encounter Empson's seventh type of ambiguity.

Eagleton (2008) offers clear "snapshots" of the different frameworks of analysis that might be used in literary criticism—Marxism,

Postmodernism, Psychoanalytic, Deconstructionism, for example. Each one gives a different reading of the text at hand, in a fashion that is reminiscent of the different crystals that are revealed in a slice of a rock sample as light with different polarizations is shone upon it. In this, we are perhaps close to Bion's notion of "vertices" of science, art, and religion each of which has its own truth.

Blanchot (1988, 1998) leads us into a space where conventional notions of subjectivity, alterity, time, space, life, death, and being are transmogrified so as to take us beyond that which can be captured precisely in language. Such states are fairly frequent in groups and are resonant with the writing we find in *Finnegan's Wake* (Joyce, 1999), *The Waves* (Woolf, 1978), Kafka (1926a, 1926b), and is also found in the writing style of Lacan (1981), Freud (1928), and Winnicott (1965). This type of literature perhaps delves into the nature of the transitional space prior to the formation of an identifiable transitional object, prior, thus to the formation of culture, to follow Winnicott's argument (1965). This space is also the equivalent of the "différance" of Derrida (1982).

The most telling moment in Beckett's *Waiting for Godot* (1982) is Lucky's speech and it can be regarded as a group phenomenon. Present are Lucky, Pozzo (Lucky's owner), Estragon, and Vladimir. Lucky holds forth in an incomprehensible, yet authoritative presentation at the behest of Pozzo, his master, while the other two gaze on. One wonders how a Tavistock consultant would have interpreted this moving event. There is certainly a terrific amount of data in Lucky's outburst. However, when he is done, they carry on as if nothing of import had happened. Which interpretive frame to use? Could one even turn to critical theory? To Adorno (2001, 1983)? To Marcuse (1991)? To Dr. Seuss, who in *Horton Hears a Hoo* (1954) provides a telling metaphor for the unheard elements of a group and the pressures activated to ensure that these inconvenient truths are not exposed to the light of day, do not become part of the dialogue of the group, do not become part of its "novel."

Kohut reminds us that psychoanalytic work involves both empathy and introspection (1971, 1977). Thus while the consultant is attuned to the external world of the group and its context, she is also attuned to her inner world. Part of this involves perception of one's internal bodily states, imaginings, and cognitions as they occur as direct unmediated reactions to the group. Another part involves the self-aware reflection on these impressions and the chain of associations stimulated by them, free association. Great care is needed when using this type of data, because one's associations are conditioned by one's predispositions emanating from multiple sources—personal history, cultural background, and training, for example. However, sometimes one's free associations are linked in meaningful and useful ways to the dynamics operating in the group. If one bases consultations on one's free associations without filtering them for personal bias, one is imposing these idiosyncrasies on the group willy-nilly. How can one draw the boundary between what might be useful and what is more or less purely personal? One recourse is to the rule of three data sources as the foundation for a consultation. A free association can be one of the data points. Perhaps the other two can come from other sources—the discourse of the group, an action in the group, a rearrangement of the physical setting of the group, the emotions being expressed in the group and so on.

Often, when scanning and integrating these multiple data sources one arrives at a consultation that can be troubling in a number of ways. Perhaps the image or idea is very impassioned or involves violence or sexuality to a frightening degree. At others the images are at odds with material reality. Such formulations run counter to materialistic models of reality, to thought processes dominated by "concrete operations" (Piaget, 1969) or to cultural norms of what should be thought or uttered, especially in public. At such points we recall that Freud's theory is a "metapsychology." This means in part that it deals with the non-material, with the mind. In a parallel fashion, Hegel's philosophy of the "spirit" is metaphysical, that is, in examining consciousness, it is examining that which is beyond physical manifestations. A helpful image is that of the popular cartoon. These movies, usually humorous, depict a reality that is not dominated by conventional notions of physical reality—time, space, motion, physicality all operate in what we might call a "cartoon space." Creatures fall off cliffs, are flattened, die, spring back to life again, break into thousands of pieces and reassemble and morph into different forms. We watch and are amused. Perhaps part of the wonder for us is that these cartoons, which are so much, "child's play," so accurately portray the cartoon space of our minds, especially our unconscious minds, where mommy and daddy combine into one being only to separate and become grandmother and a cat. All of this is done seamlessly and without contradiction in the cartoon and in the mind. This possibility can perhaps enable the consultant to entertain a wider array of data and consequent hypotheses without too quickly discarding them as "too far out," or "impossible."

It seems that there are so many sources of data, how could there possibly be an absence of data?

Freud reminds us (1916–1917) that even though the unconscious is "unconscious", its manifestations are all around for us to see. It is our repression that makes it invisible. When we meet a client or sit in a group, it has already spoken volumes in the first minute or two. Our defensive maneuvers and our collusion with the other or others, however, ensures that we do not "read" these volumes. When the defenses are high in intensity, then there will be a subjective sense of a paucity of data. Bion refers to this as the "numbing sense of reality," where the group and the consultants become locked into a transcription of the experience that is "taken as read." "A spade is just a spade," and this very comment, under the spell of the numbing sense of reality will not be open to multiple meanings—a winning card, a black card, a digging tool—perhaps for a grave or perhaps for a garden. The experience has become frozen solid and there is little or no flow. Any attempts to create flow are nullified through various means—ridicule, subject changing or perhaps an attack. The frozenness manifests itself in a lack of dialogue in the sense used by De Mare (2011) or, to use ideas from literary criticism, one feels as though one is participating in the recitation of a stable "epic" rather than a lively exchange such as one would find in a novel. The numbing sense of reality is maintained in what seems to be a hypnotic state and it can be powerful enough to hypnotize and capture the consultant and they are pulled out of their role as commentator on the process into a participant in the "real discussion." At times this hypnotic thrall can be so powerful as to actually put the consultant to sleep. Sometimes the consultant picking up on that which the group is defending through this flattening and freezing will fall asleep either physically or metaphorically as a way of protecting themselves from the psychic pain that lies beneath the surface. If the consultant becomes aware of this, then this dynamic in and of itself becomes valid material for a consultation such as, "The group seems to be harboring some extremely painful and frightening thoughts, feelings, and fantasies. Numbing everybody in the room might be one way of seeming to deal with this."

At times the group might seem as if it is in a shock state, like the proverbial deer in the headlights. Sometimes this can seem to come out of nowhere and some work has to be done to find the event or idea that initiated the stupefaction. Bion's *Taming Wild Thoughts*, (1997) can offer a few ideas here for sometimes it seems as though a wild thought has just entered the group mentality and has terrified everyone. Bion offers pertinent ideas on how one might work with others towards the "taming" of the wild thought. One of the first steps is that the wild thought must be entertained by the consultant, metabolized without retaliation and then offered back up to the group in the form of a useful consultation.

As an example, we may go back to the previously cited group where a newly admitted member shared some chanting techniques and encouraged them to join with him since he found them very calming. The group obligingly chanted for a minute or two and then paused. Then someone said, "This is like a cult." And another member said, "It's like the KKK!" At this point a dread seemed to overtake the group. Even the members who could usually be relied upon to break the ice with a sermonette or a lecture were silenced. The not-infrequent feeling that there was something very bad hovering over the group, waiting for a victim emerged and everyone was still. The fantasy that someone would soon be attacked and maybe killed flashed through the consultant's mind.

Eventually the consultant offered up the following, "Something and someone new has been introduced to the group, and this seems to stir up some anxiety. It is as if the group is frozen." This seemed to help and the flat, frozen quality of the group seemed to melt. This example is telling in a number of ways, because it not only illustrates how a group might seem to give itself and the consultant a dose of curare, or play possum in the face of the new and anxiety provoking, it also demonstrates the impact of bodily processes on group dynamics. For a minute or two, while chanting, the group was breathing a bit more deeply and thus increasing the flow of energy in the system. This, predictably, lead to more feelings coming to the surface challenging the coping mechanisms of all the participants. The example also illustrates the role of a consultant in a Kleinian modality insofar as they may act as a sort of psychological dialysis machine—taking in highly charged emotions and fantasies from the group (in this case seeming to have to do with terror) metabolizing them and handing them back to the group in a form that can be managed by the group as a whole and its members. In addition, if the "reading" of the group is accurate, then the members move from a state of contactlessness (to use Reich's felicitous term (1980a)) to a state of being very afraid but in emotional contact with others while in this state. One is reminded of how important this is by Bion (1961) in his recollections of having been in groups of soldiers who were in panic along with his astute observation that the leader is the one who stays in emotional contact with the group even though everything points towards just taking care of oneself.

In conclusion, it seems that absence of data is more likely to be the result of a "data overwhelm" and the consequent defensive maneuvers to rid oneself and the group of any vestiges or evidence of this disquieting data, than it is to be the result of an "actual" absence of data. The term "data overwhelm" is used here to deliberately invoke the useful "models of the mind" of Gedo and Goldberg (1976) insofar as it provides a useful map to the consultant (or anyone for that matter) as to the nature of the overwhelm and its attendant conflicts and anxieties.

Having charted out the sources of data in the group and the possible causes of its fluctuations, we may now proceed and generate some ideas on how to cope with these vicissitudes.

Among these is the virtue of patience or, stated in a different way, what Bion, (1978) calls, following Keats (1899) "negative capability" which is the capacity of the individual to sustain a frame of mind of "not knowing" for a while, to endure the anxiety of confusion or of ambiguity without getting rid of this irritation by doing something or hastily, too hastily, creating an idea, a theory or an intervention that "makes sense." This premature making of sense can foreclose possibilities and conceal valuable truths, truths that are perhaps harder to bear (this difficulty being witnessed by the slowness with which they are coming to consciousness) but which, nevertheless are far more useful in grasping the here and now dynamics of the group. Stated in a slightly different way, we may invoke Lacan's notion of the *point du capiton* (2007a), or the "catching point", the morsel of data—perhaps a word, or an association, a grimace, an intuition or a gesture that is usually affectively charged that serves to offer some organization to the welter of data that has beset the consultant for some time. This catching point is functionally identical to Bion's "selected fact" (1978). This waiting for the selected fact is additionally useful insofar as the selected fact (or catching point) yields an organizing framework in the nature of a theory, an assemblage of interlinked hypotheses. This is very different from the situation where there is no waiting for the selected fact, where the negative capability is relatively absent, when the consultations are not so organized and one is reminded of Reich's notion of the "chaotic situation." True, Reich applied this concept to disorganized individual psychotherapy, (that is a psychotherapy not based upon a hierarchically constellated layering of character defenses) but it may be equally applied to group consultation.

Are there techniques for enabling the appearance of the selected fact? Yes, but they are subtle and delicate. We get one clue from Heidegger as he explains Hegel (1977, p. 51). Quoting Hegel, he states, "Our approach to the object must also be immediate or receptive; we must alter nothing in the object as it presents itself. In apprehending it, we must refrain from trying to comprehend it." We are surprisingly close to Bion's idea of approaching the patient without "desire, memory or understanding" (1978). This is one of the senses of the term in the title of this section, "I'll disappear." One can make oneself receptive to the selected fact by suspending oneself temporarily, perhaps allowing a wild thought to be entertained in one's mind for a while.

Enabling the emergence of a new perspective or "wild thought" on the group might be understood through the application of Bion's theory of thinking. Thinking involves the surpassing of the "numbing sense of reality" (Bion, 1978) and approaching the object of examination "without desire, memory or understanding."

### Group consulting without desire, memory, or understanding

This advice from Bion (1978) not only sounds absurd, it also has a Zen-like paradoxical quality. First, isn't a consultant supposed to offer a perspective, information and even, perhaps, advice? Second, if we strive for absence of desire, isn't that also desire, desire of desirelessness? It is reminiscent of the "paradoxical communications" of Watzlawick, Bavelas, & Jackson (1967) that are argued to be a part of the "schizophrenogenic family." It is a command that is impossible to fulfill, like, "Be spontaneous!" or "Ignore this sign!", if you obey these injunctions, you disobey them.

So what is Bion attempting to convey here? A short cut can be found. One could simply say that he is simply repeating Freud's advice to utilize "free-floating attention" over the data one experiences as a group consultant. Let your mind wander freely, without impediment and take close and careful note of where it goes for this will inform you as to the latent processes operating in the interaction.

But Bion's admonition has three parts to it. It is more detailed. It seems to give some deeper guidance on how to have free-floating attention and seems to offer some ideas on what might impede such freedom of thought and feeling.

Another quick response might be simply to avoid coming across as a fount of knowledge, filled with memories, understandings, and goals for the group because this will feed right into the usual dependency assumption that we find in groups. Such an approach will end your role as group consultant and initiate your role as group leader with followers who are dependent upon you. The goal of the group, which is to study itself and its dynamics has been subverted by the new goal which is to follow (or not) the consultant-leader.

Again, Bion mentions several times in his writings his admiration for Keats' notion of "negative capability," the ability of a person to live with uncertainty and not "irritably" jump to an explanation, a conclusion, a theory or "the answer." In more conventional terms, it might be called tolerance of ambiguity. Ambiguity is usually uncomfortable. It comes in different forms. Empson (1966) identifies seven types. Perhaps Bion is advising us to live with the discomfort of not knowing for a while, of just letting the confusion ride in our minds for a bit before we tidy it up in a neat package. There is also the good possibility that this ambiguity matches the experience, the phenomenology of the group-as-a-whole so that in these moments the consultant is more in touch with the group process.

Bion gives us another clue to help explain this advice. Desire emanates from the pleasure principle. Following Freud, we may argue that the pleasure principle is opposed to the reality principle. Our goal in conducting Tavistock style groups is pitched towards our constructions of the *reality* of group life. This learning, since it is done through experience, is difficult, uncomfortable, and anxiety-provoking. The parts of people that dislike or even hate reality will turn away from this task towards more pleasurable pursuits even if they subvert the stated task of learning. Such desire is perhaps inextinguishable, except maybe upon death. However, if desire holds sway over the group dynamics, little learning will take place. The reality principle will get short shrift. Desire follows the pleasure principle. The pleasure principle leads us away from reality.

Lacan tells us, "Desire is the desire of the other" (Lacan, 1991, pp. 223–224). This statement itself has several possible meanings. One that is fairly commonly cited is that at root, humans desire to be desired by the other. This reading of the statement harks back to the Hegelian idea that humans' deepest yearning is for "recognition," a desire that is played with fatal consequences in the discourse of the master and the slave (Hegel, 1977). Perhaps Bion's dictum can be understood as counsel to the would-be consultant that he should avoid confusion in the domain of desire. If desire is the desire of the other then perhaps one's consultations will be automatically biased towards those that cause the group to desire the consultant. This of course constitutes a drifting away from the stated purpose of the group which is that of understanding. The consultations may be pitched in such a way that the consultant's desire to be recognized is the primary aim, instead of uncovering hidden group dynamics or enabling curiosity about group dynamics. If the consultant is not aware of the primordial wish to be recognized there could develop a subtle and insidious collusion between the group and the consultant involving a non-analytic discourse: that is of the hysteric, the university or of the master. Perhaps the desire cannot be eradicated but consultants can perhaps be, to a greater or lesser extent, aware of this desire for recognition and, observing its vicissitudes, render more helpful, on-task consultations. For example, in one group we have consulted to, in a nursing home, the group members developed a very strong idealizing transference on to the consultant, offering a very strong "recognition" of him that was very gratifying to many parts of his personality. This desire to be idealized and the desire in the group for an idealizable object when lived out mindlessly is off the task of the group, which is self-study and in many ways it curtails certain types of thoughts, feelings, and fantasies in the group, especially if they are more aggressive. However, we wonder if it is possible or desirable to "analyze away" these impulses, these desires for recognition. Perhaps they can be yoked to the task, much in the way Bion argues that the basic assumptions can be yoked to the various tasks of groups—fight flight assumption, for example can be yoked to the learning task where the enemy to be destroyed is ignorance. In this case, perhaps the obvious libido involved in the dynamic can perhaps be yoked to the task of learning by bolstering cohesiveness, morale, and encouragement. But again, we are working in an unstable area here. We are sounding similar to Kohut (1971) when he argued for the utility of the idealizing transference and was criticized for using patients for his own narcissistic ends. We do not accept these critiques and think that there is a boundary here that can be fruitfully worked (perhaps suggested in the title of Žižek's text, *Enjoy your Symptom!* (2012) where desire is acknowledged, even enjoyed, but one has the desire, it does not have you and it is utilized in the realization of the task. This is probably more functional than to pretend the desire is not there and to erect defenses, usually in the form of reaction formations, against it.

So what is left if we subtract memory, desire, and understanding? Perhaps a form of being, a form of being that is not sustained by any of these three. Tome after tome has been written on the topic of being. Perhaps part of the irresolution is that there has been confusion resulting from the fact that what is taken as "being" occurs in multiple forms. It is an umbrella concept. There are several different forms of "being."

First, being occurs at the level of what might be called facticity. Something simply "is." It attains being simply by existing or as being seen to exist.

Second, there seems to be what might be called phenomenological being which arises from the subjective sense that sentient beings might have that they, themselves exist. This itself can be experienced on a gradient. Sometimes the individual is barely aware of their existence, at other times, perhaps when facing an existential crisis, they might be very sharply aware of their being. Allport writes of this in his *Becoming* (1955) and Tillich in *The Courage to Be* (1952). This type of "being" is often experienced as one's "core" being, as related to enduring and valued elements of the self. This type of being is closely related to what Stern (2000) calls the "core self."

Third, is what might be called "narrative" being. This is the type of being that rests upon the story of one's life, one's history. It includes key events, turning points, explanations, and even anticipations. The element of time and memory is clearly important in the determination of this sense of being. For these reasons, it seems to be close to the being to which Heidegger refers (1994). Since memory is mutable, this sense of being is also subject to modifications, as evidenced by the theories and practice of narrative therapies (Madigan, 2010).

A fourth type of "being" is captured by Stern's (2000) "Emergent Self." This involves the being as it is experienced in a state of becoming. This type of being like "isness," but unlike narrative being is predominantly nonverbal. Some poetry and other art will capture the ineffable of the being coming into being. It is the mysterious process of the being in the process of coming into being. It is at the root of deep psychological change. It is very closely tied to Winnicott's idea of the true self, that self which emerges free from impingements from the other. Its emergence rests upon relaxed states of "unitegration" or what Khan calls "lying fallow" (1996) where a true impulse or perception can emerge and being may take on a new form.

A fifth form of being is found in the experience of being we have in relation to others—call it interpersonal being or intersubjective being. This sense of being is a complex amalgam of thoughts, emotions, fantasies, and bodily states that are experienced when we are in relation to others. Perhaps we feel a relaxed sense of "being in the presence of the mother" (Winnicott, 1965). Perhaps we feel battered and pushed upon. Perhaps we feel like we have to step on eggshells and so on. All these interpersonal experiences are sometimes taken as the experience of being. Again, this is close to Stern's idea (2000) of the intersubjective self.

The sixth form of being is that of one's role identity. This is to borrow from Erikson (1993). One might say one is a plumber, or a policeman and experience that as one's being, "It's who I am." The role identity, as Erikson amply demonstrates, is a complex amalgam of multiple forces, developmental, cultural, social, economic, technological, and historical. It is a far cry from some of the other forms of being just described, but it is inextricably bound up with them.

One is here reminded of Jung's discovery, described in *Mysterium Coniunctionis* (1977) that the alchemists of the Middle Ages believed that

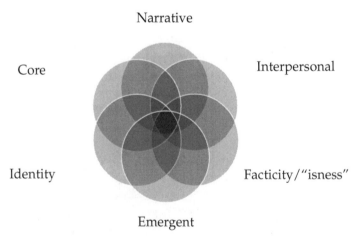

Figure 13. Different forms of "being".

their success or failure in their efforts depended crucially on their state of mind as they performed the experiment. While much of the conventional attitudes in modern science would scoff at such an idea, those scientists who would attempt to explore the structure of the atom would revisit it with some respect. The famous example of "Schrodinger's cat" which is in a box and only becomes alive or dead upon the opening of the box and being observed is a modern, less "magical," more "epistemological" way of reformulating the alchemists' belief. Schrodinger's problem, to oversimplify a great deal, was, "Is light waves or particles?" The answer seems to be, it all depends on the cognitive frame of the observer.

Here we are very close to Bion's grid. This theory of thinking offers another way of conceptualizing the consultant's approach to the group

| Bion's Grid | | | | | | | | |
|---|---|---|---|---|---|---|---|---|
| | | Defin atory Hypo theses | Psi | Nota tion | Atten tion | Inquiry | Action | ...n, |
| A | beta elements | A1 | A2 | | | | A6 | |
| B | alpha elements | B1 | B2 | B3 | B4 | B5 | B6 | ...Bn |
| C | Dream Thoughts | C1 | C2 | C3 | C4 | C5 | C6 | ...Cn |
| D | Pre-conception | D1 | D2 | D3 | D4 | D5 | D6 | ...Dn |
| E | Conception | E1 | E2 | E3 | E4 | E5 | E6 | ...En |
| F | Concept | F1 | F2 | F3 | F4 | F5 | F6 | ...Fn |
| G | Scientific Deductive System | | G2 | | | | | |
| H | Algebraic Calculus | | | | | | | |

Figure 14.  Bion's grid: a theory of thinking.

in a suitably fertile state of mind. The term, "fertile" is used deliberately to imply related concepts of meeting, mating, and giving birth, for these ideas are central to Bion's theory of thinking.

The grid above is an attempt by Bion to communicate his theory of thinking. The vertical column expresses the step-by-step assemblage of particles of sense-impressions (beta bits) into small linked pieces through the alpha function—a linking function and on into dreams and myths. Crucial in the evolution of thought is the "preconception–conception–concept" sequence. "Preconception," in this context implies not the usual notion of a stereotyped idea, but the thought just before it becomes a thought, that is, a preconception, something prior to a thought. This preconception meets up with, "marries", or becomes contained in a mind and then issues a concept. This concept can then be assembled with other concepts to form theories and might even become mathematized in the form of equations. We can see that in this process of the sequential linking of bits, impressions, pre-concepts, concepts, hypotheses into explanatory templates, the process of linking is essential. Bion understands this linking to be fraught with all the risks of linking addressed in several psychodynamic theories. Klein's theory and Freud's theory both describe the pleasures and pains, the excitements and risks of linking things together. Bion's paper, "Attacks on Linking" (1959), describes some of the forms in which this linking process, so essential to thinking, can be disrupted by unconscious processes. In this, we believe, he is close to describing some of the mechanisms outlined by Fairbairn (1952) and the activities of the "internal saboteur."

The horizontal arm of Bion's grid describes the hierarchical arrangement of activities related to thinking, from the forming of hypotheses, to paying attention, to taking action. By cross-hatching the two axes, he arrives at a typology of activities and the underlying thinking. For example, cell A6, where action is taken upon beta bits, in the absence of piecing together thoughts, we would have something akin to "acting out." Cell F5, where a hypothesis is shared as a result of a conception would be close to a consultation being delivered to a Tavistock group.

We may fruitfully use both Hill's matrix as delineated in Chapter Two where cell IIE is a confrontation of the group as a whole and Bion's matrix to discern the nature of the confrontation in Bion's typology. It is as if Hill's matrix will tell us what city we are in and Bion's matrix will tell us what neighborhood of that city we are in.

We are now in a position, using Bion's grid, to restate the issue of consulting without desire, memory or understanding. To be without desire, memory or understanding is to be in such a frame of mind as to allow the emergence of beta bits, to allow for the alpha function and the stepwise mating of ideas, the coming together of inner objects, such that a "wild thought" can enter the consultant's mind (Bion, 1997) be tamed by mating with the elements in the consultant's mind, usually with some emotional strain on the part of the consultant. Bion wrote that if one did not experience fear in a session, then probably not much was happening in that session (1978). The resulting thoughts are then shared in a digestible, that is, relatively comprehensible or bearable, form with the group.

A technique that might stimulate a new perspective or "binocular vision" (Bion, 1978) is that of looking in the background of the phenomena as they are presented. This idea occurs in an array of contexts. It is used in deconstructionist literary criticism, for example where pertinent details may be sought in the marginalia of a text. Fritz Perls (1965, 1973) in his technique of dream analysis would routinely direct the dreamer's attention to something that was in the background in the dream and seemingly of no importance to the central narrative or message. Thus, one might report that one was dreaming of being in a room with several significant people in the room and one would be asked to speak as if one was the couch or the wallpaper in the room. This idea is consistent with the notion that the censoring of the dream may well have located some important ideas in the background of the narrative as means of repressing undesirable thoughts, feelings, and fantasies. Once again, we may invoke *Horton Hears a Hoo* (Seuss, 1954). The consultant, Horton-like, listens for the denizens of Hooville in the room, gives them voice and initiates a dialogue.

As an example, a group member shared a dream with the group that was very colorful and dramatic. There were wild animals, diseases, parents, and many dramatic and sudden shifts in location. Throughout, the issue was not, "What does this mean?" the issue was more, "Which of the umpteen meanings available in this dream should be selected for interpretation?" Instead the consultant selected a fact that was in the background of the narrative. The last scene happened to take place in front of Mount Rushmore. All the action was in front of the mountain. But the consultation was framed around the silent watchers, the observing father figures in the background. The consultation brought these into the foreground.

It was as if the narrative had been turned inside out, reminiscent of Lacan's *"échelle renversée"* (reverséd ladder), a Klein jar (a three dimensional object where the inside and outside are one continuous surface) or a Moebius strip (where two sides become one side and then again two). These experiences are characteristic of the arrival of a selected fact— truth, unity, ambiguity, and paradox collide in a fruitful way.

Returning to Kohut (1971, 1977), we are reminded of his admonition that the keys to analysis are empathy and introspection. In empathy, the consultant seeks data (although of course the dry word data does not capture the richness and power of this experience) from the group. In introspection, the consultant would look inside herself, scanning her emotions, thoughts, fantasies, wishes, and bodily experiences for data that might inform them of the processes operating in the here and now. There are many barriers to the free ranging of introspection. One that is key and acts as a powerful barrier to the flow of data is the experience of shame. Shame is a powerful and very "primitive" emotion and it can have a paralyzing effect on a consultant. In a mild form, a consultant might experience shame when he becomes aware that for the past ten minutes or so, they have been psychologically absent from the group, thinking about other things—what they have to do next, a fight they had with their spouse or bills they have to pay. Suddenly, they realize they have been "off task" and they feel a stab of shame for they know they are supposed to be finely tuned to both the group and their own inner task. They have been "asleep at the wheel." The consultant at this juncture, faces some choices. They can castigate themselves for being inattentive, feel some shame and proceed with the intention of paying more attention in future. Or, they can "lean into" the painful affect of shame and approach it more with the attitude of a curious anthropologist and less with the attitude of a moralistic missionary. Asking a few questions might unleash some useful trains of thought. What in the group led to the absenting of the consultant's attention? Was it something that stimulated anxiety? Was it boredom? Was the boredom perhaps a cover for something that was anxiety or depression-inducing? Was the very sense of shame resonant with some shame in the group that was projectively identified into the consultant for them to metabolize? Such a series of curious interrogations might pry open the group and its workings in a useful and interesting way.

Of course, not all the experiences of shame are this benign and easily coped with. Fantasies involving sex, helplessness, and violence could be much more troublesome. With powerful experiences of shame, much more is demanded of the consultant's internal world and support from colleagues so as to enable the working through and redelivery of painful and potentially disruptive thoughts, feelings, impulses, and fantasies by the group. Shame is much more effectively coped with in an environment that is psychologically safe. Once a Tavistock group has reached the stage of development where it is a working group (or what Bion (1961) would call a "sophisticated group") such safety can be found for in such a group there is a reasonably ready comprehension of the dynamics of projective identification and of the "group mentality" (Bion, 1961). In this situation the painful and frightening experience of shame can be worked through in the group-as-a-whole.

Techniques such as those we find in *Synectics* (Gordon, 1969) where two seemingly unrelated phenomena are brought together so as to provide a creative solution to or perspective on a problem. Thus, one might conjure up a metaphor that characterizes the group and then pursue the metaphor in more detail to see if light may be thrown on the group's process by aspects of the metaphor that might at first seem irrelevant. Thus, if a group seems "constipated," the metaphor of an alimentary canal might fit the group. One could then "push" on this metaphor by asking what other attributes of an alimentary canal might possibly illuminate the situation— the gut operates via peristalsis, it is in a constant state of sub-clinical inflammation, in its upper reaches it floods with water, in its lower reaches it extrudes this water back into the body, it has its own nervous system (the enteric nervous system), utilizes serotonin and is very susceptible to stress. In some ways it is like a worm. Each of these features might in turn lead to further insights on the group. For example: Are there signs of inflammation in the group? What stressors have caused the peristalsis to slow down or cease? What is it in the group that is so hard to digest? Such a creative technique may unlock some ideas that can assist the group in the examination of its own process. The process of synectics is similar to the process of "bisociation" described by Koestler (1967) in *The Act of Creation* where it is argued that the bringing together of two matrices of knowledge is at the heart of creativity and humor. The latter of these two brings us back to Freud (1905) who argues that jokes are a road to the unconscious.

The use of such techniques, however, is not always smooth sailing, for not only may they unearth unconscious processes that stimulate the experience of shame, they may also induce states of terror in the group. The uncovering of unconscious material can be likened to a re-traumatization, a recovering of that which has been disavowed by the conscious mind. At times this recovery might evoke anxiety or shame, but at others, the reaction can come close to an abject terror. This terror or the anticipation of it may paralyze the group-as-a-whole, including the consultant. This paralysis may result in the experience of an absence of data and a terror-stricken frozenness that wards off the acquisition of any more data. This may manifest in numbness, vacancy, emptiness, flattening of affect or in the exact opposite, panicked, manic flight—a superfluity of pseudo-data. If the consultant attempts to follow this they are led on a merry chase "around Robin's red barn," issuing a sequence of consultations that have little or no sequence or meaning. Sometimes this will pass unnoticed. At other times the group may comment on it in derivative fashion. For example they will talk about "wild goose chases" or Hansel and Gretel forgetting to leave breadcrumbs and getting lost as a way of derivatively, unconsciously remarking upon the "adaptive context" (Langs, 1971) of the consultant who has been led astray.

Finally, while all these techniques have utility in the task of generating, sorting through, and interpreting data; they can only take us so far. Polanyi (1974) describes the process of learning how to read an X-ray as an illustration of what he means by "tacit knowledge," that is, the kind of knowledge one has but finds difficult to verbalize or elucidate. It is, as the title suggests, "personal," that is, not easily transmitted. When Polanyi first looked at X-rays all he saw was a mess of smudges and bright spots, perhaps with a few landmarks. After years of struggling, he arrived at the point where he could quickly look at an X-ray and come to valid and reliable conclusions quickly. However, when challenged to describe exactly how he does it, he is stumped. In a similar way one is stumped when trying to describe the process of riding a bicycle. One might know the physics of it and be able to describe it but the actual process is the domain of "personal" or "tacit" knowledge. This kind of knowledge is gained through experience. It results in knowing something rather than knowing about something. Bion (1978) reminds us how difficult it can be to learn from experience. Thus in the process of learning "about" groups, especially consulting to groups, language, such as that in this book, can only provide a few pointers. The last steps which involve personal, tacit knowledge are gained through the challenging process of learning from experience (Bion, 1978).

# CHAPTER SEVEN

# Anti-work and the capacity for abstraction

*Mark Kiel*

G iven that a primary lens of Tavistock learning groups is a focus on the irrational, unconscious, and covert barriers to group functioning, it is no surprise that there is extensive literature on the phenomena of "anti-work" leaders, subgroups and group cultures (Bion, 1959, 1961; Edelson, 1970; Ganzerain, 1989; Gould, 2006; Hazell, 2005; Hopper, 2003; Hill, 1965; LeBon, 2002; Lipgar & Pines, 2002; Obholzer & Roberts, 1994; Yalom, 2005). As a common working definition, anti-work is a broader term, more expansive then simply the opposite of "group work." Anti-work can apply to any group activity that is not in the service of furthering the primary task of the group or system. Thus, a range of neutral actions or inactions, novel or banal contributions, convergent or divergent experiments or endeavors may qualify as anti-work. Indeed, the differentiation of such phenomena as work or anti-work is at the center of much of Tavistock theory and practice.

There are a few conventional notions of anti-work that will be discussed here to serve as a brief reference, and to further the main thesis of this chapter. Aspects of anti-work include being off task, out of role, being under or over-authorizing, or the blurring of or inattention to boundaries. Many consultants identify anti-work as a stage of group development, a form of resistance, or a set of defenses attempting to ward off anxieties. Pragmatically, this anti-work is oftentimes overcome by a critical mass of the group members partnering with the consultants, the group task, or each other in a way that serves to further the primary task and which is rational, self-reflective and productive. Once this "critical mass" is reached, it becomes much like a tipping point that shifts the group into a new and more effective work mode. In general, the "lead member(s)" who works toward the primary task in a genuine, self-reflective, interactive, and interpretively curious manner is known as the "work leader(s)," and member(s) who do much of the opposite are "anti-work leader(s)." As one would expect given the nature of the Tavistock model, both are considered repositories. Like any repository function, in order to become a "working group," a group needs to identify the roles and split off parts they have given these leaders, garner a deep understanding as to why the repository function happened in a group/context specific way, reclaim the projections and projective identifications, and adjust and change group norms, work style, roles, etc. accordingly. However, these generalities do not capture the range of anti-work. Consider the following brief examples:

- A member of a group almost always agrees with the consultant's interpretations and usually spends a good amount of the group time trying to "sell" the group on the value and applicability of the consultations.
- A group member tends to monopolize most sessions. When confronted on this he says he is being as authentic as he can be, and given that he is in a process-based group, what other option is there but to keep processing and sharing?
- A group member cannot accept the rationale for the consultants' interpersonally "unengaged, flat demeanor" and will not participate in the group until the consultants start to participate more like the members.
- A group member arrives halfway through a conference and immediately changes the topic and tenor of the group by making disclosures about group members in an attempt to "be transparent" about covert dynamics.
- The only person of color in a group refuses to participate fully as group tends to scapegoat singletons and he does not want to be a casualty of the group process.

No doubt, some of these circumstances may sound familiar. The purpose of mentioning them is to begin to further bridge the discussion on anti-work. First, the Freudian notion of resistance is applicable here. Resistance is a sign something important is being approached. Thus, resistance is not something simply to be overcome. The very process of exploring resistance is important. This leads to the second concept, which is that anti-work leaders and work leaders are two sides of the same dynamic. Without the so-called "anti-work" member or members, there is no symptom, no expression of what is a point of disruption or distress to the group (See Chapter Five for further discussion of the so-called hysterical discourse). The "anti-work" member is a key voice for what is reluctant, stuck, or dysfunctional for the group. However, due to a vast number of reasons, certain "anti-work" members seem fundamentally un-workable in this sense. In clinical terms this may be a member with a personality disorder, in systems terms they may have an "identified patient" status that both the group and or the individual needs to keep a homeostasis in order, in Tavistock terms it may be a persistent and resistant "role lock" that is actively (in the intrapsychic sense) invested in preventing change or understanding. Consider:

• The member who does not attend regularly.
• The member who shouts and emotes in a way that other members find threatening.
• The member who does not appear to have the capacity to distinguish phantasy from reality.
• The member whose reason for joining the group was to "experiment" by breaking, not agreeing or otherwise manipulating group norms and group material to see what sort of impact it has on themselves and others.

There are two typical responses to such examples (or perhaps more frequently, some combination of the two):

1. The managerial: this includes actions like better pre-group screening, member selection methods, and psycho-education for prospective members. Administrative actions like the removal of a member from a group or conference fall into this category. As does the clarification of contracts or agreements made in exchange for group membership in conscious, direct or pragmatic manner.

2. The interpretive: the frame of the Tavistock theory—group dynamics, repository functioning, unconscious dynamics, and a failure to have adequate insight into dynamics is the cause of all dysfunction—the motto here is don't just "trust the process," invest in it and stick to it even more when anti-work expressions are rampant.

## Metaphors

When it comes to the "interpretive" response mentioned above, perhaps it is easier and more educative to think about dimensions of so-called anti-work metaphorically rather than explaining specific aspects of theory or techniques.

Consider, for many psychoanalytic and systems-oriented group practitioners, terminology and conceptualization of the technical variety are imperative tools and scaffolding for understanding, deconstructing and intervening with groups. Homeostasis, heterostasis, repository functions, role valencies, the mechanics of projections and concurrent or concordant identifications of those projections, open-system *vs.* closed system capacities, the list goes on and on ...

Each, of course, is important and even essential for a sophisticated understanding of a group, system or organizational life. Yet, so is the symbolic. The right-brained. The metaphoric.

The following metaphors are anchors, lens, or alternative ways of knowing when studying and participating in Tavistock learning groups.

### The ocean

Imagine you are on a beach, looking out at the ocean. You see the waves progressing to the beach, the water white-capping, a boat off-shore, debris or seaweed may float on or near the surface, swimmers may splash and paddle in a given direction. Are those things just listed really there? Without getting into a discussion of "reality", yes, they are there. So when a group member says something about their favorite book—*The Lord of the Flies*, or a member shows up ten minutes late to a group because they had to use the bathroom, or a member takes the group leader's usual chair, are they talking about a book, a necessary function, what's most comfortable? Yes they are. But as you look out at the ocean, would you not see another scene if you put your head under the water line and opened your eyes? And would not the things you saw have direct and not-so-direct relationships to that which you saw when you were above water? Rip-tides, under-tows, and cross currents as well as another entire world—both beautiful and terrible—co-exists, or perhaps intersects with that which is above. And if you could understand some of the most important goings-on under the water, might you not have a better idea of the phenomena (wave patterns, the direction of floating debris, possible danger areas for swimmers) that you witnessed above the waterline?

Psychologists and clinicians argue whether the idea of the unconscious is necessary, helpful or even possible to work with as a concept when understanding an individual. However, groups and systems evidence, time and again, that covert processes exert considerable influence on the functioning and capacities of group life. Conformity and obedience, spontaneous psychodrama, riot theory, the bystander effect, scapegoating, risky shift decision-making, groupthink, system push-back, the list again, goes on and on. Social inertias are clear and demonstrable and often start, gain momentum, and occur before those in the group can even identify them, mainly in the large part, because people are not on the lookout for them. Those things happen in "other groups."

Learning from and navigating in groups begin with attention to what is above and below theses waves.

## The storm

The simplest explanation for a weather storm is that two fronts of different temperature collide. The result of the collision is a storm, replete with rain, lighting, and thunder if the fronts are significantly different from each other in their temperature.

Storms happen in groups for the same reason. Subgroups, sometimes as small as two members, sometimes encompassing every member, collide, their tonal, relational or thematic differences produce what appears to be unpleasant-ness: conflict, disagreement or disengagement. Simply weathering a storm in a group is a missed opportunity. Unlike the weather metaphor, people in groups are often in a group to work on tonal, relational or thematic differences. To work up to the point where these matters intersect and simply wait for it to blow over is both exhausting and frustrating. Exhausting in that members have often committed a lot of themselves to form and move fronts and frustrating because this work is then for nothing. If too many storms occur without working through the why and how they occur, the storms tend to escalate into the truly damaging or dissipate never to see possibility of understanding again.

When you see heat lightening in the distance, the barometer drops in the room, or you feel the first drops of precipitation, do not run to batten down the hatches. Look, listen, and feel. Identify the fronts, think about precipitants and feel the accompanying pressures. These fronts are different in important ways. Understand these and you are well on your way to understanding a key part to group life. Moreover, don't be frozen in place by the flashing lighting or loud thunder. This is a time to be a storm chaser.

### The knot

Knots are like the flip side of the storm metaphor. Whereas storms crash, produce flashes, and you can feel the by-products of the fronts colliding, knots are just stuck. In fact, the more you pull, the more stuck they get.

If you spend enough time in groups, you will find yourself stuck, tangled or gridlocked. At these times, a loud and flashy storm may seem like a joy too much to hope for because of the mind-numbing death of paralysis.

Like the storm metaphor, this is an opportunity as well. Tangles, like storms, happen for a reason. Learning that reason can be very important, but can take a decidedly different course of action to identify. Yanking a knot rarely unravels it. Sure, every once in a while, but more likely, it simply makes the process of untangling that much more arduous. And as groups trend toward homeostasis, they will likely try what they are comfortable with (whatever tangled the knot in the first place) rather than trying something new. Thus, they yank away.

Whatever the cause—a storm dynamic that becomes entrenched, misunderstandings that can never seem to be worked through, even a failure to seemingly join in the first place—knots in groups happen for lawful reasons, and at least a bit of data is present with all knots—the threads lead back to where they started.

Pause. Follow the strands of the knot back to the representatives of the group associated with the tangle, then work your way back to the knot. See what symbolic issue—for the group—the knot has centered on. The knot is part of the specific members who were active in the entanglement, but not theirs alone. For a real knot to happen, the other group members are complicit in some way with the dynamic that has frozen the group. When you look at a particularly wild knot, it looks like there must be three or four cords tangled up in the mass, not one or two. In a group there are actually more than the one or two threads leading back. Notice how members "not involved" have gotten stuck in there too, notice how the group leaders have been snared, notice how the "issue" is both those that are literally involved in the tangle, as well as the group-as-a-whole's issue. Like the storm metaphor, the "cutting out" the knot is the in the long term the worst option as the opportunity to learn, work, and develop from these very real entanglements is eradicated or denied. And usually, to cut knots out of a group process means denying or disavowing aspects of self and group, leaving them more incomplete then when they started.

## The horde

There is a saying that you never have to put a lid on a bucket full of lobsters. And why is that? Because if one lobster starts crawling its way out, the others will pull it back down. Again and again.

For many who have had powerful, positive experiences in groups, some of these metaphors may seem awfully ominous. But as mentioned above, groups go "wrong"—they are unable to accomplish their tasks, injure members, or arrive at erroneous decisions—as often as they go "right." An important part of this dynamic is the horde nature of a group.

Many models of group dynamics focus on leadership, but group relations or the Tavistock tradition, looks at authority—as a concept separate but related to leadership and power. Freud spoke about this dynamic eloquently in his psycho-anthropological work *Totem and Taboo* (1912–1913). A horde is a group that is an undifferentiated mass that can engulf its members at times. Not only do members of a horde lose degrees of identity as a cost of membership, but members are extremely ambivalent about other members of the horde who take up authority and lead. The term "alpha"—as in "alpha male," was first identified in pack-like, or horde-like animal groups. Alphas are something needed by the group, are feared and challenged by the group, and often—particularly during times of weakness or particular vulnerability—are disposed of by the group. So too is the dynamics of leading and claiming authority.

The ambivalence has to do with wishes and fears around strength and weakness. To be a member of a faceless or undifferentiated member of horde has a certain amount of safety and anonymity. Deferring to a powerful alpha means having someone else sit with the burden of leadership (like making wrong decisions or inspiring wrath in the horde). But to see another take up their potency—to work, to make decisions, to risk-take—is painful too. It inspires envy. So then, when the alpha is weak, vulnerable or otherwise compromised, the horde may take the one who has jutted out ahead back, just like those lobsters. And often, a group will go through many machinations to cleanse its collective hands of tearing down the alpha that may well have helped the group to survive or thrive at certain points (see the Totem part of *Totem and Taboo* …). This is a form of undoing in the Freudian sense, a spoiling attack in the Kleinian sense, and enactment in the psycho-dramatic sense.

Regardless of what maybe going on at a process and content level in a group, remember the anthropological, social, and psychological roots of groups. Part of us still has one foot back in the horde, regardless of the sophistication we may present. In fact, the more clever the group, the more subtle the rise and fall, the envy and the spoiling, the authority and the attacks on that authority.

## The hourglass

Learning groups, unlike the often open-ended nature of individual work, are usually time-bounded. Logistics alone suggest that it a more complicated task to manage getting eight people together, rather than two. Couple those logistic realities with the tendencies for groups to be run in immersion formats, to meet at the same time each week, to be time-limited or to have trappings like "checking in" or "checking out" rituals, and time takes on considerable meaning. For the purpose of this metaphor, consider an hourglass filled with sand. Turn it over and watch the sand run into the newly made space.

At first, it seems like the top bulb isn't changing in volume at all, even though the sand continues to run. And at the end, the sand races, at a seemingly disproportionate rate. Why is that, psychologically speaking? Because endings are catalysts. They are boundaries that can bring matters into focus. When there is an ending, there is an exquisite knowing that it is now or never. And groups, like people, do a lot of important things when that realization sets in.

A number of things that is true for individuals are true for groups when it comes to matters of time. For instance, some comments or disclosure may be made right at a time boundary—testing the time boundary to see if it is firm or flexible—or perhaps the comment is said so it can be made but not processed at that exact moment.

A particularly salient feature for groups is trust. Yalom (2005) states groups only have one issue: trust. It is simply revisited time and again, at deeper levels—like a spiral staircase winding downward. Tuckman (1965), when studying the developmental tendencies of groups, observed that the joining process, the stage where group members decide to commit to a group has immense ramifications for later stages where actual "group work" occurs. These two ideas are related. A group needs trust to join, and joining begets trust. A third variable in the mix is time. What happens to joining and trusting at deeper levels when you know that the process is coming to a stop? A usually sudden stop in the Tavistock model.

As the group notices the top bulb is more empty than full, and the sand runs quicker and quicker, what is to be done? Do you continue to join, risk-take, and trust, or does the group stop, terminate early, or rush forward denying the death or ending staring it in the face. That said, the key to this metaphor is to remember the illusionary effect of the hourglass. Remember, at the beginning, the group does not have all the time in the world. Each group meeting is important and part of the finite amount of time the group has to live, develop, and work. And at the end, when it is clear the stopping point is drawing near (either in a specific session or in the overall life of the group) there is still time to work and learn. Premature endings, just like the denial of endings, are to be acknowledged and balanced. Time crawls and time races. It is a hallmark of a working group to understand that psychological experience and to work in a more conscious and rationale manner with the experience.

There are more metaphors and traditional concepts of anti-work to be sure, but, in keeping with the book-wide concepts of symbols, abstraction, and surplus, let us take a step back and examine "anti-work" from traditionally non-Tavistock contexts.

## Abstraction and shared symbol systems

In the review of the traditional forms and mechanisms of anti-work mentioned at the start of this chapter, concepts not listed included the terms "symbol system," "linguistics" or "abstraction." However, in the literature on psychoanalysis, the ability and importance of language, linguistics, symbols, and abstract thinking are numerous (Bahktin, 1982; Berman, 1988; Berne, 1996; Bion, 1959, 1978, 1997; Birdwhistell, 1970; Empson, 1966; Freud, 1911, 1916–1917, 1921; Gordon, 1969; Heidegger, 2008; Lacan, 1981, 1997, 2007a, 2007b; Langs, 1979; Madigan, 2010; Parsons, 1971; Stern, 2000; Watazlawick, Bavelas, & Jackson, 1967). So let us, in the Tavistock vein, apply some of these notions to the entity of the group.

Groups can function at different levels of development, employ various degrees of ability to use language, to understand abstract phenomena, and to perceive events or behaviors from various points of view. It is the main thesis of this chapter that this is not "just" one of many "developmental lines" (A. Freud, 1965), but a key developmental nexus that is directly correlated with the capacity to do group work and understand (or at least contemplate) complexity.

A visual may be helpful here:

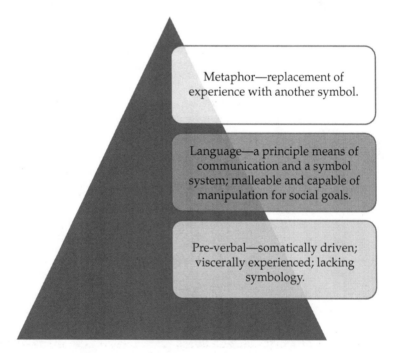

Figure 15. Hierarchy of abstraction.

Before a fuller explanation of this model proceeds, please note three caveats: (1) Somewhat like Maslow's "hierarchy of needs" (2013), people and groups do not "achieve" a level of abstraction and then statically remain until further development occurs. Rather, depending on the circumstances outlined below, there can be fluid progressions and regressions up and down the abstraction hierarchy. (2) Whereas higher order developments afford the capacity for sophisticated work, they do not necessarily invalidate the lower order conceptualizations. Rather, a higher order capacity expands on the lower order expression adding to it, rather than negating it—hopefully the explanations and examples will help illustrate this. (3) The stages of the hierarchy presented in relationship to Tavistock group dynamics are both descriptive and derivative—descriptive in so far as they define the capacity for abstraction, but is also derivative as those definitions have analogous correlates to work and anti-work functions.

The model that follows offers both an inclusion of additional terminology and a change of emphasis to traditional Tavistock group development. The alteration has to do with the inclusion of more lingual terminology associated with overt language-based abstraction. The change in emphasis has to do with a focus on transitioning from a working group to a sophisticated group (rather than the more prevalent focus from a basic assumption group to a working group) and identifying elements of anti-work in seemingly functional working groups.

| Stage: | Capacity: | Hallmarks: | Anti-work expressions: |
|---|---|---|---|
| I. Metaphoric | Somatic | Projective identification | Extreme BA: Me-ness or One-ness, Part-object relatedness |
| II. Lingual | Language | Rhetoric | Bionic basic assumptions Illocutionary confusion |
| III. Pre-Verbal | Abstraction | Irony | Pseudo-work Metonymy & Synecdoche |

## The Pre-verbal

On one hand, this first constellation of phenomena is in many ways well worn. It is the fundamental concepts of Freud (1921, 1916–1917),

Klein (1975), Bion (1961), and Winnicott (1965). Yet, if indulged, it paves the way for the reconsideration of the two next stages.

"The Pre-verbal" unit may be considered developmentally "primitive" compared to the type of functioning many think of when they consider the dynamics of a learning group. Yet as will be demonstrated, that may be a misperception on at least two counts.

Long before language, early attempts at communication, even before the experience of empathic attunement, (Kohut, 1971) is the bodily experience. As Freud stated so eloquently, "The ego is first and foremost a bodily ego" (Freud, 1921, p. 20). We "know" our experience via what we viscerally experience. Initially in development, this experience is without words—something that becomes harder to remember or contemplate the longer one has had access to language. Due to the psychological profile of this stage of development, it was initially believed that the methods of psychoanalysis were not applicable to people or groups functioning from this level of ability. Yet, as my co-author writes about in Chapter Eight regarding trauma and later in Chapter Nine regarding the body, this is an experience that is key to understanding both the so-called "high functioning" neurotic groups as well as the "low functioning," fragmented or regressed group. Here, we are not simply talking about a "silent group" or one that is at a loss for words (although, dynamics like that may be aided by a conceptualization of this nature). In a developmental sense, this is more akin to Mahler's concept of "normal autism" (1975) in so far as there is only the ability to have access to the bodily or sensory sensations. What does this look like when a group of "adults" are functioning from this stage? A psychiatric ward of catatonics. The traumatized that have sought relief by radical dissociation. The sounds of shrieks, sobs, or cooing; the movements of rocking to and fro, hitting, or molding the body into comfort. In clinical and applied circumstances, it is more likely that this stage is regressed to from a previous higher order stage, oftentimes due to trauma. This stage becomes more salient for Tavistock learning groups when considered in a constellation of frequently related phenomena:

### Projective identification and object relations

As Klein (1975) explains, projective identification is both a defense (ridding oneself of an ego-dystonic experience) and a form of communication. Before words, the transferential mechanism it is a powerful primary

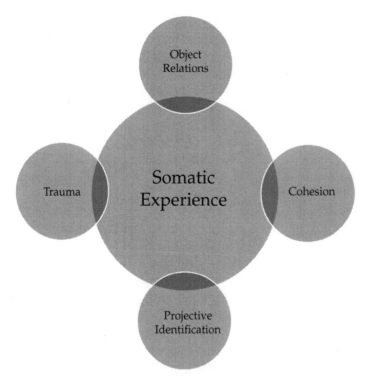

Figure 16. Somatic abstraction capacities.

manner of communicating one's experience to another. It is evidenced from the earliest moments of life and the mechanism remains available throughout the life cycle, becoming reactivated especially during times of distress, regression, abandonment, and of course, in groups.

The study and application of this concept is a core feature in the theory and practice of Tavistock learning groups. In this presentation, note its placement opposite object relations.

As Bion (1959), Fairbairn (1952), and Klein (1975) explain, object relations follow processes of introjection (internalization of experiences, affects, and relationships) and projection (externalization of experiences, affects, and relationships) in the presence of relationships (both real and in phantasy). Object relations also developmentally evolve from fragmented part-objects perspectives to whole-object integration and even complex object synthesis. As volumes have been written on these matters, a recitation will not be offered here. However, as it will become important later, brief definitions of the latter terms will be offered here:

*Part objects* are a function of splitting, which takes place in phantasy. At an early developmental stage, experience can only be perceived as all good or all bad.

*Whole objects* replace the splitting and part object relations by the capacity to perceive that the other who frustrates is also the one who gratifies. Schizoid defenses are still evident, but feelings of guilt, grief, and the desire for reparation afford the capacity for integration.

*Complex objects* expand on the depressive position's anxieties, affects, and capacities and afford the ability to comprehend uniqueness, foster benevolent curiosities, and synthesize self and other's projections and introjections.

## Cohesion and trauma

When groups are under stress or distress, they tend toward one end of the cohesion-incohesion continuum as defensive compensation (Hazell, 2005; Hopper, 2003). When groups are traumatized, they tend to radicalize toward one end of the continuum to an even greater degree. Radical or irrational cohesion is one defining feature of the neo-Bionic basic assumption: One-ness (BA: O)—where there is an undifferentiation of group membership to the extent of perceived merger. At the other end, there is radical or irrational incohesion, one defining feature of the neo-Bionic basic assumption: Me-ness (BA: M)—where there is differentiation to the extent of denial of group or systemic existence or influence (Hopper, 2003).

Both BA postures are social defenses, distortions, and provide some fantasy of safety from threats real or imagined. The relationship between trauma and group or system cohesion is important in several ways. For the purpose of this topic, it should be noted that BA: One-ness/Me-ness functioning is a developmentally early manner of functioning, or a regressive one if the group has evidenced previous "higher order" functioning. Second, fusion or detachment in group development has parallels to child development dynamics, replete with accompanied defenses, pathology, and wellness. Finally, trauma oftentimes activates defenses and regression in the unsupported/under-resourced group. In regression, the group over-utilizes projective identifications at the expense of mature symbol systems and more flexible and adaptive capacities. This, in turn, fosters anti-work as the task of the group pitches toward distortion generation, avoidance, and expulsion of projective identifications and defensive or retaliatory acts.

## The anti-work profile

A Tavistock learning group functioning from a regressed, pre-verbal level of development, oftentimes due to trauma, has several features familiar to traditional group-as-a-whole theory and some novel: rampant projective identifications left unclaimed and ignored, repository functioning bordering on burnout or casualty, and irrational cohesion or incohesion as social defenses. The non-traditional description of these phenomena include: loss of previously acquired rhetorical capacity, over-use of emotional pleas and enactments, the inability to differentiate between literal, implied, and metaphoric communications and symbols.

## An example

At a group relations conference, during a large study group, a member discloses an experience of abuse by an authority figure in the military as a child. As this member's emotion grows in intensity, sectors of the group—those especially near to him become silent, a tense waiting quality to see what happens next. The few sectors that are not quiet attempt to sooth the member and each other with rationalizations and attempts at empathy, "This is transference," "This must be painful for you," "It's hard to trust authority." The member with the abuse history turns his focus on one particular consultant in a still growing intensity, voice raised, saying things like "you need to know" and "it's not ok." Although it is in the conference materials and various members are aware that the consultant receiving the attention of the member has a duel professional identity as a mental health professional and former military member, it remains uncommented on by consultants or members. "This is cathartic for him," "we are his witnesses," "should he be a member in a conference like this?" are comments lobbed in the direction of the member and consultants. A consultant comments that this is displaced rage at the director for his abandonment of the group; perhaps for not being part of the large group consulting team. The member with the abuse history has moved toward the "military consultant" and is now addressing the consultant in the first person "you did it," "fuck you." Several other members leave their chairs and get out of the established seating arrangement—either distancing themselves from the now shouting member, or to make an attempt to calm or intersect the distraught member. Members and consultants—with the exception of the distressed member who is now reduced to wailing and a somewhat flailing physical posture and the military-consultant, who consults that this is the group's rage and disappointment with the failure and harm caused by authority—are almost universally silent. A member on the outer ring of the seating gets up to leave, she is ashen, "I'm going to puke," and leaves for the washroom. This is done at the time boundary of the event and the consultants stand up, and as the events unfold, appear to be led out of the room by the "puker." Sounds of retching can be heard from the adjacent bathroom seconds later. Members break into three major groups, those that flee the room immediately, a small group that try to console the still crying member, and a larger group that want to generate an intervention of some sort—to have the member removed from the conference, to leave the conference themselves, or to make a direct appeal to the director for some sort of action.

## Summary

The example above will be familiar to Tavistock-versed folks as it is replete with several phenomena traditional theory does an exceptional job explaining. Rather than a drawn out analysis of dynamics, contrast the example with the capacities and dimensions of the second stage (with particular focus on the over use of pathos, loss of language, and increase in communication via enactment). Regarding the somatic stage, note the impact on object relations and the sub-grouping/splintering of BA: Me-ness and One-ness.

### Lingual Stage

The capacity for language and the utilization of shared symbol systems is also a familiar stage to those with experience in Tavistock learning groups. Here, Klein's and Bion's theory, practice, and research on traditional basic assumption functioning are in practice with accompanied trappings of interpersonal, unconscious, and systemic engagements. As volumes are written on these concepts and models, they will not be repeated here. For reference please see (Bion, 1959, 1961;

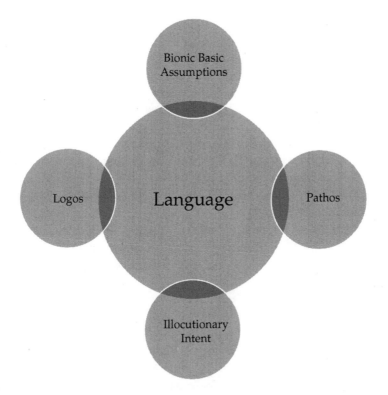

Figure 17. Lingual abstraction capacities.

Edelson, 1970; Ganzerain, 1989; Gould, 2006; Hazell, 2005; Hopper, 2003; Hill, 1965; Klein, 1975, Lipgar & Pines, 2002; Obholzer & Roberts, 1994). However, a few comments on the utilization of language as an expression of anti-work are appropriate before this constellation of concepts are offered.

First, with the use of shared symbol systems comes two tendencies: to over use them and/or to forget language is a place holder for other, more literal experiences. Regarding the over-use of language, we are reminded again that language does not outright replace experience. As Lacan states, "I always speak the truth. Not the whole truth, because there's no way, to say it all. Saying it all is literally impossible: words fail" (Lacan, 1990, p. 3). Of the multiple dimensions to this comment, one salient aspect for this section is that language systems are incomplete. Yet, words and clarity of meaning have a privileged place in this model:

- The psychoanalytic discourse of interpretation is at the center of the Tavistock model.
- Consulting, commenting, and verbally expressing matters is preferred to behaviors, actions or enactments.
- The visceral, bodily or somatic experience is oftentimes left as a trapping of earlier stages until it is unavoidable.

There is no arguing that this "privilege" is not merited and necessary. However, it is equally problematic to view language and shared symbol systems as an end in its own right. As Lacan goes on to comment, "… Yet it's through this very impossibility that the truth holds onto the real" (Lacan, 1990, p. 3).

In this model, the lingual stage is positioned between the somatic stage and the metaphoric stage. An over-reliance on a single symbol system or the view of language as the experience itself, can cut the group and its members off from the visceral experience (a common mechanism resulting in neurotic processes amongst other things) and prevent the development of sophisticated work processes (fueled by metaphor, irony, and play). Not only is this one of the distinctions that separates the Tavistock methodology from other group modalities such as the interpersonal processing technique, but it serves as an important premise for the dialectic tension between rationality and irrationality.

## Logos and pathos

Tavistock theory prefers the terms "rationality" and "irrationality." At a simplistic level, rationality is equated with employment of the scientific method, working or sophisticated groups and emphasizes realistic, goal-directed functions in line with a primary task and role flexibility in the membership. In contrast, irrationality is equated with basic assumption functioning, groups that are off task or otherwise invested in defensive activities than the primary task, and that foster repository functioning and/or role lock.

As mentioned at the start of this chapter, work leaders and anti-work leaders were presented as two expressions of a shared dynamic. So too is irrationality and rationality. To that end, in a stage hallmarked by the capacity for language the terms logos and pathos are used slightly redefined terms. Logos is traditionally considered a form of persuasion through the use of reasoning. In this context, it is a form of rhetoric used when presenting consultations, hypotheses or social scientific claims as they are often data-driven, include shared observations, and follows rules of a given logic (such as the "lawfulness" of psychosocial behaviors). Pathos is traditionally a form of persuasion through the use of emotion. In this context, it is a form of rhetoric used whilst participating in "here and now events," using the experience of affect as a form of data, or can be an attempt to translate the personal/visceral experience from the somatic level of experience. Pathos includes emotional appeals and expressions, vivid language, or sensory details and are often affect-driven, including phantasies and impulses, and can be an appeal to the group's sympathies, empathies or imagination.

Individuals familiar with this model will no doubt be able to recall experiences of phantasies being quite accurate ("I have a hunch Sharon won't be present in the large group today"—and she is indeed nowhere to be found) and expressions of logic failing to alter events in the least ("The director shared that information with the membership and gave them a copy of his speech in their folders"—yet there they wander, looking for the room they have been assigned). Whereas these are simple examples, they illustrate the time honored tenets that the unconscious, irrational, and emotive are an engine as much as a barrier to deep learning and understanding of complex social systems, and that the conscious, rational, and cognitive are a barrier to understanding the multi-dimensional nature of psychosocial complexity.

Thus, the pivot to logos and pathos. Here the terms are slightly different than their denotative definitions and are used as constructs representing the cognitive-emotional continuum. Failure to identify the "pleas" or argument made in these forms and to privilege one over the other is a potential trap. They are represented in the model as opposite ends—as tensions rather than dichotomies—representing two aspects of "rhetoric." Two dimensions to the psychological whole.

## Bionic basic assumption and illocutionary intent

Whereas in the first stage object relations (the structure) was paired with projective identification (the communication mechanism), here BA functioning (the social defense structure) is paired with illocutionary intent (the communication dynamic).

The Bionic basic assumptions of BA: Dependence, BA: Fight/Flight, and BA: Pairing (Bion, 1961) will not be commented on with the exception of a reminder regarding language. Whereas it may be elementary, dependence, fight/flight, and pairing are all literal impulses and behaviors until language and maturation make them also symbolic, defensive or transferential expressions. This is noted as they are literally present in the somatic stage, and are literally and symbolically present in the language stage.

Illocutionary intent, is in contrast, absent from Tavistock theory. It is "of or having to do with that aspect of an utterance which relates to the speaker's intention as distinct from what is actually said or the effect on an auditor" (Webster's Dictionary.com, 2016).

The ability to comprehend complex and unsaid meaning, as opposed to what is literally said, is a key part of development (both linguistic and psychological). This is known as illocutionary intent. As children begin to grow into their schooling years, they develop skills to manage more and more complex conversations. The term illocution was introduced by the philosopher John L. Austin (1953) in his investigation of the various aspects of speech acts. For example, in uttering the locution "Is there any salt?" at the dinner table, one may thereby perform the illocutionary intent of requesting salt. A definition, even simpler yet, is knowing what was meant, even though it was not directly said.

This concept is related to projective identification to the extent that something "unarticulated" (or under-articulated) is transacted between the sender and the receiver of a communication. While trappings of illocutionary intent have linguistic, communicative, and cultural dimensions to them that are oftentimes more conscious and identifiable than projective identifications, they too remain rife for enactments and distortions. The capacity to understand or contemplate illocutionary intentions and acts has roots that go back to very early parent–child interactions, communications, and expectations and have derivative extrapolations for group-as-a-whole functioning, or given the topic of this chapter, dysfunction or anti-work.

## The anti-work profile

A Tavistock learning group functioning from a language-based level of abstraction has several features familiar to traditional group-as-a-whole theory and some novel. The traditional: Bionic basic assumptions of dependency, fight/flight, and pairing, the developmental anxieties and defenses of the borderline stage—vacillating between the paranoid-schizoid position (and accompanying dynamics), and the depressive position (with accompanied dynamics). The non-traditional: distortions, subjective definitions, and diffuse terminology in the use of shared symbol systems. Anti-work, confusion, and resistance is oftentimes anchored in a form of hermeneutic or expressive absolutism—where only one meaning or interpretation can be tolerated or contemplated.

An example: As part of a group relations conference, an administrative team (admin) is formed several months before the conference to work with the conferences directorate to plan and prepare for the conference. The admin team is primarily a work group performing tasks but regularly holds "processing sessions" led by the Assistant Director for Administration (ADA) to explore repository functions of the team for the conference, experiences elicited by having contact with the conference membership, and to explore and hopefully prevent repository functioning or role lock. In one of the early "processing sessions" an admin team member intimates her contributions are not being heard or valued to the same degree as others in the group. She attributes this at first as having less conference experience than her teammates. As the work continues, she requests more processing time to explore this dynamic and time is made available for this. At an interpersonal level the team is polite with each other, offer empathy readily, and actively explore what this undervalued/under-authorized member is holding for the admin team as well as perhaps for the conference membership. Between sessions, the member in question writes an email saying that her teammates are not responding to her in a timely fashion and this is impairing her ability to accomplish tasks. She then outlines the tasks she is willing to do for the week—all of which do not require collaboration, partnership or much other-authorization.

The next weekly meeting is designated as a time to process this event and to understand the perceived difficulty in collaborating and communicating. The frustrated member does not show, texting the morning of the meeting saying she is "fighting a cold." The admin team is conflicted, on one hand there is a growing need to address the dynamics of the team, on the other, there is hesitancy to process without the full team for fear this would further out-group the absent member. Ultimately, the ADA asks the admin team members present to consider what split off parts of the team they have located in the frustrated and absent team member. This is a somewhat superficial conversation only speaking in generalities to anxieties and fears of the pending conference, but without much emotional content. After a short discussion, the team agrees to make it a "work event" and get caught up on tasks and they will process when all members are present. Before that can take place, a regularly scheduled meeting with the Associate Director (AD) of the conference is held to update her about the admin team's work, membership registration, and some tentative plans for room assignments, SSG membership assignments, and some protocol for receiving the members on the first day of the conference. The absent member is back for this meeting and several of the admin team's proposals are a surprise to her as the admin team had made those decisions when she was not present the previous week. In the meeting, the frustrated member critiques and disagrees with some of the proposals. The ADA says her comments will be taken into consideration, but that would have been more helpful earlier. Quickly a blame dynamic emerges. She can't complain when she doesn't come to the meetings. He, as team leader, should have informed her of the decisions made while she was absent. She was the one who had asked to be left alone to do work. He should be trying to bring the team together. She sabotages team trust by "throwing their work under the bus" when they met with the AD ... Ultimately it comes down to a fight pairing. The female team member feels persecuted for "being genuine," for "using the process time to really process" and for "honestly pointing out problems as she sees them." The ADA feels like the two of them are "fighting for the team, or maybe the staff," dynamics of her authorization are under-explored, and she is not taking responsibility for the "surplus meaning" behind his actions. The AD assigns the admin team a consultant from the staff for their next processing meeting. The consultant makes three main points over the course of the meeting: (1) the gender dynamics in the admin team appears like an exaggerated parallel of early staff dynamics. (2) The experience of the frustrated admin team member appears as a parallel to early communications conference members have made about a lack of confirmations to submitted applications. And (3) The "critique" made by the frustrated member of the admin's team work to the AD echoed a "stab in the back" image one of the consultants had made during the consultants pre-conference processing meeting that including a lengthy discussion on competition.

The consultations did not appear to have any effect, and for the last two weeks before the conference the ADA allowed the frustrated member to pick tasks she could do on her own, that she did not need collaboration to accomplish. As the conference loomed, work was accomplished but a building sense of dread gathered in the admin team as they considered their sub-system's process on the conference as a whole.

During the staff "check in" on the eve of the conference, the formerly frustrated admin team member, now self-identifying as the "ignored one," spoke at some length about what it was like to be an outsider in conference designed to make sense of scapegoating, out grouping, and repository functions. Although the word hypocritical was not said, it was implied. Staff took up the themes of her comments and further considerations, interpretations, and hypotheses offered to the member, the admin team, and to other consultants.

The first day of the three-day conference was a whirlwind of activity, reports, and team meetings. All said, conference logistics worked fine, the conference operations ran smoothly and members were responded to by staff in an orderly and efficient manner. At the checkout at the end of the day, a consultant noted a parallel in the small study group he was consulting to and to a particular member who like the admin team member was expressing a continued sense of disappointment with the conference process and his group. The consultant started to hypothesize about system level contributions to this circumstance when the admin team member interrupted and began recounting what a miserable day it had been for her being "so alone" with her experience. At that point another consultant asked everyone, including the admin team member to wait, so the first consultant could finish his comment on the system level contributions to the dynamic. At this point the admin team member said, "Unbelievable!" and left the staffroom much like an angry and misunderstood adolescent.

## Summary

Again, the example above will be familiar to Tavistock-versed folks as it is replete with several phenomena traditional theory does an exceptional explaining. Rather than a drawn out analysis of dynamics, contrast the example with the capacities and dimensions of language stage and contrast it to the following metaphor stage.

The admin staff member who appears as a repository for fear, me-ness, resistance or anti-work is also a clear expression of pathos— making an emotional appeal much like a group member or group navigating through the "Borderline" functioning between part object and whole object relations. The other staff who consult to the dynamic mostly employ logos to interpret the dynamic. For all her frustrations, the repository does "quit," leave or disengage fully until a boundary is put down by the consultant who asks (requires) the admin team member to put her process on hold.

While there does not appear to be the one and only way to interpret this dynamic, one main consideration from this stage and one main consideration from the next stage may help widen the traditional group-as-a-whole conceptualization. One avenue to access the pathos being communicated to is consider the derivative communication of the repository with an ear toward illocutionary intent. When the staff member claims she is "not being heard or valued to the same degree" as others at the start of the example, she may be twisting language to a more ego acceptable statement rather than a more vulnerable request to be in some way acknowledged for what she is capable of or has contributed. The consultations based in logos "miss" in a sense, and do not release the role-lock for the repository or the larger staff group. Good minds may disagree as to whether this sort of illocutionary interpretation and response is appropriate in a group relations conference context. That said, however, it is hard to consider the comments, the actions, and the outcome as complete and fully considered given the dysfunctional nature of the dynamic. A second point for consideration comes from the next stage and involves the concept of synecdoche. (Although it will be expanded on down below, the repository and the group appear to have very different definitions of what it means to "process" in the context of a conference staff task and this prevents a truly shared symbol exchange as would be expected).

*Metaphoric Stage*

Departing the most from traditional Tavistock terminology is the metaphoric stage. The reason for this is threefold:

1. Sophisticated work groups demonstrate a type of interpretative flexibility that is not as readily or linearly plotted by object relational theory.
2. These "higher order" functions appear to parallel a capacity for abstraction represented well by literary theory.
3. The anti-work manifestations in working groups parallel phenomena from early stages, but with a form cloaked by language and intellectualism.

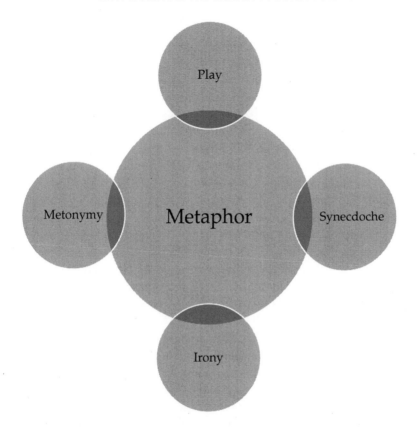

Figure 18. Metaphoric abstraction capacities.

This stage is presented with two underlying premises: one, even in sophisticated groups, anti-work elements are present; and two, pseudo-work, much like anti-work is a combination of authorization, resistance, and hermeneutic dynamics. As will be demonstrated, authorization dynamics tend to involve over-authorization at this stage, resistances tend to involve castration and superego anxieties, and hermeneutic dynamics tend to be of the post-modern variety. This tends to be in contrast with the under-authorization, annihilation and loss of object anxieties, and literalism of earlier stages.

## Metonymy and synecdoche

Metonymy is a figure of speech in which a thing or concept is called not by its own name but rather by the name of something associated in meaning with that thing or concept. For instance, "Wall Street" is often used metonymously to describe the U.S. financial and corporate sector, while "Hollywood" is used as a metonym for the U.S. film industry because of the fame and cultural identity of Hollywood, a district of the city of Los Angeles, California. Similarly, "The White House" may be used as a metonym for the Executive branch of the U.S. government.

In contrast, synecdoche, meaning "simultaneous understanding," is a figure of speech in which a term for a part of something refers to the whole of something, or vice versa, often by means of either mentioning a part for the whole, or conversely the whole for one of its parts. Examples from everyday English-language idiomatic expressions include "bread and butter" for "livelihood," "suits" for "businessmen," or "boots" for "soldiers."

Object relationalists may already see where this is going. With the capacity for abstraction and metaphor, object-relational limitations and distortions can take new forms. Like the part-object relations of earlier development, metaphoric object relations pay a price for collapsing constructs. Instead of overtly shearing away aspects of the object via splitting and denial, here dimensions of the object are assumed to be nebulously present (metonymy), or distorted around one overarching and defining feature (synecdoche).

In many ways, the attributes of these expressions of categorization are more difficult to discern as the use of metaphor can disguise nuance in a manner good/bad splits make obvious. Is referring to the director as "The Man" a 1970's anti-establishment sentiment? A commentary on gender dynamics? A reference to the localization of authority a single person? Or a compliment of a somewhat anachronistic variety? Similarly is referring to the membership as "a sea faces" a commentary on anonymity or uniqueness? An indirect reference to affect via expression? A defense of depersonalization? Or perhaps a wish or fear to disconnect identity from the body?

Use of metaphor is a "higher order" capacity in this model. It is oftentimes associated with complexity and even as a conscious means of relating to unconscious or multiply determined phenomena. Unlike seemingly set vocabulary or terminology, metaphors can be joined with in a variety of mutually inclusive ways. Metaphor can simultaneously hold several dimensions or properties (consider groups in an institutional event picking names or identities like the "Riot Police," "Hard Candy" or "Pawns").

Yet, these constructs have defensive and limiting dimensions to them as well. American literary theorist Kenneth Burke described four "master tropes" in *A Grammar of Motives* (1945):

Metaphor—a substitute for perspective;
Metonymy—a substitute for reduction;
Synecdoche—a substitute for representation;
(... and to preview the next section ...)
Irony—a substitute for dialectic.

These literary tropes have correlates to psychological defenses and displacements as well as the capacities this stage can achieve.

## Irony and play

Play: According to Winnicott, play offers the experience of a "non-purposive state." It opens up a space of trust and relaxation in which the need to "make sense"—operationally defined as the need to defend oneself—is absent, so that genuinely free association can happen. It is out of this state alone, that "a creative reaching-out can take place" (Winnicott, 1965, pp. 55–56). Therefore, although creative adults are cultivating their world in very sophisticated ways compared to an infant, it is just as applicable that adults need to rediscover or re-engage in this "formlessness" in order to further creative engagements.

Whereas Winnicott began with the mother–infant pair, groups of different varieties become the social platforms where the transitional space that is needed for play can happen. Learning groups in a Tavistock tradition are ideal for such "formlessness," transition and play.

Play is an engine for exploration, search for the self in the "reflecting back" or "summation" of others, and for creativity. In a working group, defensive and compensatory stances are less necessary, less intrusive, affording members the forum to play more. This, in turn, allows groups to be platforms for learning and engagement with whole objects and even complex objects. Relating to whole and complex objects both requires and advances the consideration of multiple meanings, Lacan's double entendre, and general interpretive flexibility and scope.

Irony: Henry Watson Fowler, in *The King's English* (1908), says

> any definition of irony—though hundreds might be given, and very few of them would be accepted—must include this, that the surface meaning and the underlying meaning of what is said are not the same. (Fowler, 1908, pp. 434–435)

The use of irony may require the concept of a *double audience* as well. Fowler's *A Dictionary of Modern English Usage* (1926) says:

> Irony is a form of utterance that postulates a double audience, consisting of one party that hearing shall hear and shall not understand, and another party that, when more is meant than meets the ear, is aware both of that more and of the outsiders' incomprehension. (Fowler, 1926)

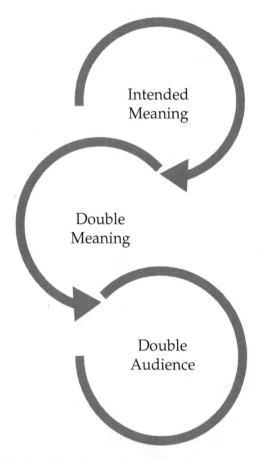

Figure 19. Flow from intention to irony.
*Note*: Hopefully, the connection between play and irony comes into relief here. As play increases, the opportunities to witness or experience irony increases; as members witness or experience irony, more transitional spaces are created, thus giving more opportunities to play.

Lastly, The *American Heritage Dictionary*'s (2015) secondary meaning for irony: "incongruity between what might be expected and what actually occurs" needs inclusion here. These various definitions speak to aspects of irony that apply to a particular hermeneutic capacity. The ability to reflect on, contemplate or otherwise integrate the unintended or incongruous meanings of expression is very similar to catching glimpses of the unconscious in parapraxes, irrationally in a defense or derivatives in a commentary. However as the second Fowler definition suggests, another dimension to irony is not only the awareness of the double meaning but also the double audience. In this ironic layering, one audience is aware of the other audience's incomprehension of the double meaning.

## The anti-work profile

A Tavistock learning group functioning from a metaphoric level of development will tend to exaggerate otherwise functional operations, defenses or impulses just like any other problematic or dysfunctional dynamic. Common features include a "surrender-like" approach to irony, the unconscious, or synchronicity—when confronted with covert processes members will by word or action act as if it were fated, lacking curiosity or motive to incorporate, understand or apply the phenomena. Pseudo-play will hold hidden agenda compromising formlessness. Metonymy will serve to keep constructs vague and undifferentiated. Synecdoche will be employed to keep objects over-determined or over-defined. A caricatured version of post-modernism, where anything can mean anything, will be offered or accepted without utilizing the tapestry of resources available in the group for comparison or investigation.

## An example

A group relations conference was planned at a university setting with a double task—the traditional goal of putting on a dynamic and rich conference experience for members and staff, but secondly to prepare staff for mounting multiple conferences in the same year due to student demand. In a sense, it was a training conference in the way a teaching hospital may work, by provided service whilst preparing physicians for more independent practice.

The first meaningful "conference event" for the full staff was a notification that the conference had been over-enrolled. The intended cap had been sixty-five, but the focus on future demand seemed to result in an under-estimation of the current demand and seventy-two members were given formal acceptance to the conference before the importation boundary was closed and a waiting list created.

In a sense, this paralleled staff dynamics as the full staff included twenty-eight people as pairs and observers were deployed to all teams to further learning and experience.

Dynamics of "size" manifested quickly on the staff's preparation day before the start of the weekend conference as phantasies and considerations of literal and figurative room capacities were considered (it was unclear if the large study group room could hold the 100 people for the plenaries due to the "Fire Code"). Staff joining was short and fairly mechanistic as only an hour was available for the twenty-eight staff members to share what outside life events or matters were being imported into the conference. One or two staff perpetually sat outside the staff table as there did not appear to be enough room around the table, even though there were enough chairs (and this was sometimes further obfuscated by admin team members who were absent at times dealing with matters outside the room).

During the first day and a half of staff preparation the following dynamics were identified:

• A younger (twenty-something) admin team member who had used social media outlets and point and click email links to recruit was identified as a main source of the robust recruiting efforts.
• Wishes and fears regarding shifting from a one conference a year model to a multiple conference per year model were expressed. The two main reactions were "more was better" (more staff positions, more room to move up in conference responsibility and or authority), and fears of "watering down" what was considered a strong staff, model and conference.
• Subgroups formed between "older" staff and "younger" staff, "guest staff" who had been invited in from other systems or organizations and "long timers" who worked the conference multiple times over the years, and staff formally affiliated with the university and those who were not.

Overall it was a very rich, complicated, and multi-faceted conference, an analysis of which could fill a book in its own right. Having set the scene, four particular events are identified for description and analysis:

## The director's first reaction

The director was also the head of the Large Study Group Team (LSGT). After the first LSGT preparation meeting, he reported to the full staff that he had never felt as unsafe and fragmented in a team meeting as he had earlier in the day and he was very concerned for the efficacy of the LSGT. After the LSG on Friday, he reported his fears were confirmed to an extent as the LSGT struggled to work together or with the membership in their consulting task. This report left the conference staff on an ominous note as the LSG was the last event and last report on Friday night before staff went home.

## The ISE convener's dream

I was assigned the convener of the consulting team for the Institutional System Event (ISE) (DeLoach, 2009), a model where management (the directorate and admin team) are separated from the consultants in the ISE to better explore the members' relation to management. Although I had performed the role multiple times before, there was a great deal of trepidation I associated with the large membership, being responsible for a large portion of the staff for the ISE event (eighteen of the twenty-eight staff), and the disconcerting message from the director/LSGT head.

That Friday night I had a dream that was based in reality: a dream recollection of a trip I made alone to identify a dead loved one's remains at a morgue after a car accident. The affect in the dream was of dread and an unnerving sense of loneliness persisted upon my waking.

## Disclosures

Although not identified until later in the day, during midday on Saturday, both the director and I made personal disclosures to our teams, in what seemed in the service of the task. The director spoke personally about why diversity (a formal task on the conference brochure and certainly a matter that was omnipresent in the backgrounds and identities of the membership and staff) was so intimately important to him. This included intergenerational trauma and oppression. I had been struggling with how and in what form to deploy the consultants in the ISE and I shared my dream as data as to why the consultants should work in pairs during the event, regardless of experience or expertise—I thought the dream may be a "conference dream" warning of working alone while others were available. Later in the day, a staff member who was part of both teams identified the parallel disclosures, and then several staff shared how the disclosures allowed them to differently authorize the director and me in our roles (and therefore themselves)—for the better.

## Hybrid vigor

During the ISE, well after the events above took place, a consultant returned from sector and began reporting on what was taking place with the sub-system where she was consulting. She was reporting that the sub-system was considering merging with another sub-system and used the term "hybrid vigor" to describe the fantasy the sub-system had regarding how the merger would strengthen them as a collective. Another consultant interrupted at that point with a bit of confusion and surprise on her face and said, "Did you just say 'hybrid nigger'?" The reporting consultant (who was multi-racial) seemed to take the question as some version of a parapraxis and humorously, and a bit warmly, thanked the questioning consultant (a white woman) for the question. The reporting stopped and several of the consultants asked in various ways, what had just happened and why. After the phrase was used a couple of times, an exacerbated consultant in training (a Latino woman) said, "Stop saying that word!"

What followed was a fragmented process where different consultants had different ideas on how to proceed with "unpacking" the misspoke/mis-heard phrase. One consultant (a black man) was hesitant to start a discussion unless all agreed to give it the time and gravity the issue merited (fairly unlikely given the work task that was going on for the consultants at the time). For another consultant (a gay, white woman) it triggered memories where slurs were used and she was not accepted based on her sexuality. For another consultant (a white male) it echoed a staff competition parallel between he and his black colleague where each thought the other had a privilege of sorts. However, these many directions led to gridlock in so far as they appeared opposing or in conflict with each other. Ultimately the boundaries and tasks of the event brought the subject to a close as reports were prepared for the management group, consultants left to consult in sector, and the time boundary of the session ended.

Not surprisingly, the issue did not remain confined to the ISE. ISE consultants were reconfigured to their SSGTs and LSGT roles and the matter resulted in gridlock, to different degrees, in those sectors as well. In the SSGT, the matter was difficult to discuss and the associate director/SSGT head had to finally ask what was actually said, as she remained unclear as the topic and related topics were raised, and as she had not actually heard what was said that triggered the various reactions. For the remainder of the day the dynamic served as a group paralytic where it was raised.

## Summary

While an encapsulation of a whole conference in under five pages cuts many corners, I hope the brief outline of particular events demonstrates several key points. For one, the conference staff was certainly a working group—accomplishing task after complex task—creating and maintaining a learning space for members as well as managing unexpected circumstances. Members of the staff were able to wed personal life experiences with the life of the conference to forge meaning and direction. The entire staff managed a double, perhaps triple, task of participating in the conference life, consulting and managing the conference boundaries and tasks, and performing training tasks to prepare additional staff for multiple conferences.

On the other hand, several circumstances have dimensions to them that traditional Tavistock theory would identify as dysfunctional, irrational or as basic assumption functioning. These include the (under) management of the importation boundary, the subgrouping amongst staff, and the real and imagined anxieties regarding "Fire Codes." These matters have problematic dimensions to them, but were dealt with readily enough to the point they become inert dynamics with a commensurate amount of attention and processing.

However, the extended anti-work bouts experienced by this largely "working" staff group center on the "disclosures" and the "hybrid vigor." The two dynamics juxtapose each other in certain ways. The self-disclosures by the director and convener that served to "jump-start" joining and work also had an anti-work undertow to them. The director and I are both white men with enormous amounts of privilege in various domains of our identity. Despite the majority of the directorate being woman, the majority of staff being women, and the majority of the membership being women, two men of privilege came forth to share narratives of vulnerability (This is not to imply vulnerability is inherently associated with women; it is to contrast a notable conference demographic with an unequal distribution of authorization of the men). There is an element of metonymy at work as a growing sentiment was endorsed that "the staff are fine and working" in the wake of the disclosures. It could be equally stated that the "white men in leadership with privileged dimensions of identity are fine enough to share aspects of themselves related to the conference work"—but that's a bit cumbersome. It was as if identifying the repository function of the two authorities wouldn't draw much of the collective in its wake, and therefore it was under-attended to.

The "hybrid vigor/hybrid nigger" parapraxis is almost the opposite. It contrasts, in content, some of the white male privilege of the previous dynamic. However, unlike the above, no staff want to be directly associated with the literal comment but almost all staff had a fairly idiosyncratic association to the comment. In that sense it had an element of synecdoche to it—the term "nigger" is so over-arching and defining as a repugnant and vile slur that it was hard for the staff to view it or play with it in the "conference-in-the-mind"—as was a primary task of ISE event. If synecdoche is a "substitute for representation," the staff failed to query what was being represented for the conference or conference subgroups in this term.

Lastly, both dynamics lacked the perspective of irony. Double or surplus meanings were not applied in either case sufficiently. The disclosures served as something like a safety valve, righting certain staff dynamics. When they happened and the result was mostly positive, little more exploration was done regarding them. Certainly listening for or thinking about the unintended messages or results of the disclosures did not happen in real time. Nor was the unintended audience perspective taken. It was as if the communications had reached the intended audience and that seemed like enough. The parapraxis, on the other hand, was destabilizing in its nature. It left groups in confusion and paralysis and individuals with very personal associations. It was not dealt with like other conference phenomena, it was not applied to the conference-in-the mind, viewed as symbolic of something important that resonated with the group mentality, or listened for as a comment meant for a different set of ears or potentially different context. Play with the comment was replaced with either quarantining it via avoidance or using it like a projective instrument (what do you think of when I say [blank]?) to further interpersonal processing.

To a degree, both events were accepted with a degree of literalism, which was at odds with exploring them metaphorically. The first situation, acting like an intervention of sorts, and providing work relief to two groups, was met with gratitude and accepted. The second dynamic, acting like an IED (as if the unconscious is not still activated by this, I first used wrote the term "IUD" here when writing this ...) on the roadside, was met with a fight/flight defense and was rejected as a potential learning.

# CHAPTER EIGHT

# Trauma, the group, and remembering with the body

*Clive Hazell*

It is the aim of this section to connect thinking about the group-as-a-whole to some of the latest thinking on trauma. This, we believe, inevitably leads to connections to the body in the group since trauma is a biopsychosocial phenomenon.

In the book, *What Happens When You Touch the Body* (2011), Hazell and Perez argue that body workers often activate repressed traumatic memories in their line of work. Often, the body worker does not explore the source of the feeling with the client but simply allows for the expression and sharing of the feelings and memories as they surface. The following gives a fairly common experience.

Many people who work with the body report experiences like the following. They are palpating a muscle, or asking a patient to perform a certain action when, out of the blue, the patient has a powerful emotional reaction. They might start to cry, or become angry, for example. The patient themselves might be puzzled and frightened by their response. Often the body worker is also taken aback. The following case vignette gives an example of this.

## Case vignette

Andrew is a healthcare worker in his mid-forties. He is married and has two children. He comes to Max, a massage therapist, complaining of plantar fasciitis. It is so bad that he cannot walk barefoot and has had to stop his exercise regimen. He is contemplating surgery. After two sessions with Max the pain has abated and he has postponed the surgery. He continues the weekly treatment for four months and shows small gains. He complains that he thinks he has "restless leg syndrome." Max is unsure of this and notes an inward rotation of the left leg, the same side as the plantar fasciitis, and starts to work with the tibialis. Andrew starts getting irritated. Max senses an opportunity and says, "If you are willing we can just see where this takes us. Stay in touch with those feelings. There isn't much I haven't seen." Andrew trusts Max enough to give it a try and stays with the body-work and the feelings. Andrew's leg starts to shake a lot and Andrew, who was usually quite quiet, growls in rage and then lets out a roar. His left leg flops around and then he slams it onto the table, after which his whole body goes limp. Max ends the treatment with a relaxation massage. The next day Andrew calls to report that the pain has gone completely and that he was able to start exercising again. Max notes to himself that it is as if the plantar fasciitis contained a lot of pent up rage. Interestingly, the source of this rage and the meaning of the outburst on the treatment table was never addressed. Max's relief continued unabated.

## What is happening here?

This common experience can be explained as follows. The patient was traumatized emotionally by something in his past. He has, for the most part, placed that trauma and the memory of it, in the repressed part of his unconscious mind. However, there are strong isomorphisms (parallels) between the body and emotional experience. Thus the musculature that was involved in the trauma has become involved in the unconscious memory of the bad experience. When the body worker activates that muscle in a certain way, it also activates the unconscious memory and all the connected thoughts and feelings. The repression weakens and the feelings flood to the surface, sometimes along with the memories of the trauma, sometimes not. It is as if, when we work with the body we are working directly with the mind and its mechanisms of defense.

The human body has many languages. When most people think of the language of the body they think of gestures and bodily positions. Birdwhistell (1975) writes of this in *Kinesics and Context*. Another language of the body is less "fluid" and more structural in nature. This line of thought argues that the characteristic forms of the body, its shape, posture, energy distribution, express the character of the individual. When we decode the language of the body in this way we may see the person's personality, her history and issues, often unconscious issues. The major exponents of this approach are Lowen (1972, 2003, 2005) and Reich (1980b).

Our body structure is affected by many different factors: genetics, accidents, illnesses, diet, culture, personal choice, and psychosocial trauma are items that would certainly be on the beginning list of forces that shape us, shape us not only emotionally, but physically. All of these interact and mix together to give us the body we have today.

Following a similar line of reasoning, we here posit that the Tavistock group often acts upon members in a similar way, that the group-as-a-whole experience creates a context which is hospitable to the re-experiencing of trauma. This means that the group will frequently be the venue for physiological manifestations of that trauma. Following Van de Kolk (2015), Levine (2010), Reich (1980a), Lowen (2012), and Janice Fisher (video) we believe that the working through of trauma of necessity involves the reworking of one's physicality. The Tavistock group, with its profound provisions of psychological safety will often be the context for just such a reworking. How this might occur is suggested, in part when we examine a simplified model of trauma.

## Model of trauma

On the next page is a diagrammatic representation of a model of trauma we find useful.

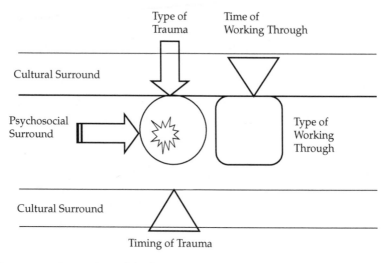

Figure 20.  General model of trauma.

## Key to model

This model is an extremely simplified version of psychosocial trauma, but it does alert the practitioner to key elements. What follows is an explanation of each of the elements in the model.

### The trauma

As we will soon see, trauma can vary along many dimensions. It can come from different sources, human or non-human. It can be sudden or gradual, expected or unexpected. It can be acute or chronic. It can involve physical or psychological violence or both. It can come from those we trust or strangers. All of these variables and more will determine the intensity and seriousness of the trauma.

### The person

The individual who experiences the trauma can vary widely along many dimensions. They might be very resilient or more vulnerable. They could be outgoing and extroverted, or shy and introverted. They may have a history of serious previous traumas or not. They might be suffering from depression before the trauma occurs or be in good spirits.

All of these variables and more will affect the impact of the trauma on the person.

## The timing

Traumas that occur earlier in life are usually, other things being equal more serious in their consequences than those that occur later, when people are usually better prepared to protect themselves and get help. Also we need to consider the developmental stage of the person at the time of the trauma. What psychosocial tasks were they working on that might have been derailed by the trauma, perhaps causing secondary problems?

## The immediate psychosocial surround

Trauma can be ameliorated or worsened by the family or social networks or community one inhabits. Some of these environments can be extremely helpful in coping with and working through trauma in that they provide help, guidance, and support. In other cases this support is not available and the impact of the trauma is greater.

## Cultural factors

Certain cultural factors can operate to help individuals cope with trauma. In some cultures it is customary to rely on others for assistance, while in others people are more likely to have to deal with trauma on their own. Sometimes religion plays a vital role in helping people cope with trauma.

## The working through

Working through means the extent to which the individual "talks through" the trauma with someone else who listens and cares. This might be a professional counselor. Generally speaking the closer this is done to the trauma, the more effective it is. Early working through of a trauma will lessen its effect (van der Kolk, 2015).

By thinking of the trauma their clients have been through in these terms, helping professionals of all kinds will be better able to assess the depth and seriousness of the trauma. For example, if a trauma was sudden, unexpected, was early in life, involved being let down by trusted others, occurred in an unsupportive social matrix and was never worked through, then the results will tend to be on the more serious end of the spectrum. Professionals should also be aware that because individuals tend frequently to deny the impact of trauma and that "symptoms" can emerge many months, sometimes years after the trauma, people frequently do not associate their symptoms to the trauma that may have happened years ago.

The Tavistock group figures into this model in the three psychosocial elements in the model. First, it provides a psychosocial surround which, although it is not specifically designed or purposed to deal with trauma, does, in its working form (that is when it is, in Bion's sense, a *sophisticated* group) in fact, serve as an excellent context for just such work. Thus, individuals who have been containing unworked trauma for some time may, upon finding themselves in a functioning Tavistock group, bring that traumatic material to the situation, sometimes in an organized, well prepared way, sometimes in a more disorganized "symptomatic" fashion. The same can be said for the element of culture. The Tavistock group will create a different micro-culture. In the case of larger groups, a number of micro-cultures will be created. Again, it is possible that this new cultural experience will be more supportive of reworking the trauma.

Third, a Tavistock group, when it is functioning well and examining primitive defense mechanisms operates at times like a dialysis machine for the kidneys for the psyches of the members (Hazell, 2005). This very process supports the working through, the metabolism of trauma.

Peter Levine (video, 2010) demonstrates how, with a somatically based approach he helped a veteran who had been exposed to two almost simultaneous IED's (Improvised Explosive Devices) while on patrol in Afghanistan. One of the crucial symptoms of the soldier's PTSD was a tic wherein his head would uncontrollably twitch at a frequency of about fifteen times a minute. Levine is able, in working with the soldier to reduce the tic frequency to nil in five one-hour sessions, demonstrating the effectiveness of bodily based psychotherapy for such symptom clusters. The tic was understood as a frozen behavioral response to the two explosions, first that of orienting towards the explosion and then of turning away self protectively. Since there were two explosions in rapid succession this was repeated. Although the upper centers of the brain knew that the event had passed, the body was still re-enacting the trauma as if it was still occurring, resulting in a tic. Levine works with the soldier in a step-by-step fashion unlocking the neuro-muscular circuits so that the tic dissolves.

I recall a group to which I was consulting several years before I viewed this taped series of therapy sessions where one of the members was, in fact a veteran and indeed did have a tic very similar to the one seen on the Levine tape. At that time my model of tics was not as elaborate as it became after studying body-based approaches to trauma therapy so this veteran's tic was left as a prominent phenomenon in the group, but yet a phenomenon that was not commented upon by any of the members or by the consultant.

This begs the question, "What would I do with this experience today?" Insofar as the consultant's task is to speak to the unspoken in the group and the very obvious fact that one of the members has a tic but no one is commenting upon it, one is drawn to the idea that it might be on task to consult to this fact. However, to comment directly upon it, especially since there is only one person with a visible tic in the room, is to place one individual very much in the hot seat. They will become the center of attention. Countering this, one might recall the very high frequency of tic-like behaviors in the general population, a fact remarked upon by Sacks (1998) in the chapter on "Ticcy Ray." In addition, it is reasonable to surmise, given the prominence of the tic, that it is already very much on people's minds.

What might a consultation look like if it integrated these perspectives and concerns? One might hope that the group might provide a "bridge," that is, some sort of comment that enables the consultant to connect the observation of the tic with some other element in the life of the group. Such a phenomenon is present in individual work where a patient might suggest that they are ready to examine the transference by saying, for example, in passing, "My father always used to wear ties like that." Such a comment can open the way to wondering if there might be other similarities and differences. Similarly, in this group, someone might help the consultant by talking about startle responses, things that made them jump, loss of bodily control. They might even make a transferential derivative comment on doctors who seem to be blind to the obvious symptoms of their patients, almost chiding the consultant for not acknowledging that someone nearby had a problem.

Given such assistance as this from the group, the consultant might be able to weave together a consultation like:

> "The group is ignoring the startle reactions in the group and is concerned that the consultant does not seem to notice or respond to these. The group is a stressful place and members are manifesting this stress and strain in different ways, sometimes bodily, sometimes verbal. These responses are perhaps linked with previous startling events."

Looking back on this group with the unacknowledged trauma that I think was locked up in the soldier's neck, face, eyes, and shoulder girdle, I wish I could have come up with something like that consultation. Perhaps it would have enabled him to decompress some of the psychosomatic, socio-somatic pressure he was under. Perhaps it would have enabled some reduction in his sense of isolation. Perhaps it would have enabled some work on the trauma in the group as a whole, both in the here and now and in the past.

The example above is of an "unmade consultation." I find it very helpful as I debrief a group to ask myself and my co-consultants, "What were our unmade consultations?" What are some ideas that seem to sit with us now, that we think have some validity but that we never shared with the group? What is the "unfinished business"? These often serve as a guide, or as some form of preparation for the next group. It is as if these consultations are sitting in the ante-room, perhaps in the preconscious of the group mentality awaiting the time of their invitation into the group. It is perhaps in the realm of what Bion (1978) is writing about when "preconception" meets with "conception" and results in a "concept"—something one can actually think with. Apparently some of these unmade consultations remain for a long time.

This sense of failure, I believe, is part and parcel of working with trauma. Trauma is "unspeakable." It is "mindless." And yet the group is a place where speech takes place. Consultants offer words. But these words will fail to capture the nature of trauma that is "beyond words." Modern literature, such as we find in Kafka (1926a, 1926b) or Blanchot (1998) or in the stream of consciousness of Septimus Warren Smith in *Mrs. Dalloway* or of the individuals in *The Waves* (Woolf, 1990, 1978), might "bend language" enough to capture the essence of the terror or anguish, but consultants might be hard pressed to come up with such achievements. Even were they to succeed there will perhaps always be a remnant of unspeakability, of incommunicability.

As another example of unconsulted-to trauma I recall a difficult group where the sparks started to fly even before the end of the first session. It was a student group of twelve individuals, seven white, three African American. The group had had several hours of lecture and discussion on group dynamics and was comprised of graduate students in psychology. One member, female and white, about half an hour into the first session turned to one of the African American women and stated that she was afraid of her, because she seemed angry. In doing this, it seemed that she was following some guidelines of confrontation in an "encounter" group style. The reaction of the black female member was of rage, anger at being singled out, at being misperceived, and at being treated unfairly. The white woman was very upset and became tearful at the angry response, apologizing and insisting that she did not mean to cause such pain. This seemed to have no effect on the offended woman whatsoever. She responded by asserting that the white woman's tears were fake and that she would continue to feel angry; her anger was not the cause of the other's discomfort and she was in no way responsible for it.

This situation continued for the next ten weeks, with this couple being the focus of much of the group's attention. Every now and then others would attempt to repair the relationship or introduce other topics but this dyad of "angry black woman" and "hurt, guilty, and sad white woman" formed the leitmotif of the group.

Unfortunately, I had not, at the time of this group, read Hopper (2003) who points out that trauma in groups manifests in the forms of "aggregation," where the members become rather like a sack of billiard balls—assembled in the same space but essentially sealed off from any but the most superficial contact—or "massification," where members fuse together—where boundaries are dissolved and difference negated and members become "one" (These two adaptations, by the way, are remarkably close to Tustin's (1972) depiction of two types of autism). Had I read Hopper, I might have come up with this consultation:

"The group has selected two members to bounce off of each other repeatedly like two billiard balls, touching surfaces, but never making anything but the most fleeting and superficial contact. This performance is an attempt by the group to represent something traumatic, either in the here and now or from its past."

Another group shows a similar pattern, with a slightly different outcome, namely an individual who is containing a severe trauma who is exerting a powerful influence on the group for an extended period of time without this trauma being consulted to. This group consisted of a dozen students assembled in a training group format that met over a year for some thirty sessions of one and a quarter hours. One member, a white male, ex-policeman in his early thirties occupied a good deal of the group's energies by taking up the role of "anti-work leader." This took the form of arguments with others in the groups about the nature of mental illness, the place of personal choice in behavior and the existence of the unconscious mind. In simplified form, his position was that people should take responsibility for their behavior, learn about the consequences of their actions and stop behaving in irrational, erratic, and unethical ways. This set of ideas was distasteful to the humanists and psychodynamically oriented others in the group and a debate that became quite acrimonious would ensue. It was powered, in addition by a good amount of suppressed anger on the part of the key person—the ex-policeman. For reasons that were not entirely clear this changed quite abruptly in the last session when the ex-policeman announced that he had something to share and then embarked on a chilling narrative of an episode of extreme brutality he had been involved in whilst he was serving in the police force. He shared that this experience had informed his actions and beliefs ever since and had probably affected his behavior in the group. The group was stunned by this admission and also very moved by it. A few members managed to make consoling and understanding comments but, too soon it seemed, the group ended forever.

Again this intrusion of trauma into the group seems to take the form of an individual adopting the defense of super-isolation, akin to the "myth of individuality" that manifested in an ideology of hyper individualism that is an example of what Hopper (2003) calls "aggregation." Again, this was not consulted to, but in this case the dynamics of the group lead to the trauma being shared as a "doorknob issue," right at the very end of the group, leaving the group with unmetabolized affect, thoughts, and fantasies, but with some inkling, perhaps of the origin of the disturbance. Once again, we have an unmade consultation.

Perhaps, if there had been time or sufficient awareness in the consultant (Hazell) a comment like the following might have been apposite:

> "The group has just heard a very distressing narrative. Previously this story was contained in one individual. Now it is contained in the group. The group is now attempting to find ways of coping with this episode. Perhaps this task is made more difficult by the existence of other disturbing narratives in the group and the fact that the group is coming to an end, which is also disturbing. The group is re-experiencing the overwhelm state associated with trauma."

As we examine these examples of trauma in the group, we may see that each involves the experience of alterity. In each case a member or subgroup introduces something which is other-than-the-group in some form. Trauma is always alteric (Hazell, 2009). Recognizing this struggle with alterity and all that this can involve (Hazell, 2009) can assist consultants in formulating helpful consultations. We might also hypothesize that a significant number of other issues in groups that involve otherness—issues having to do with gender, race, age, religion, and so on, are encoded ways of attempting to address trauma.

When we consider that trauma is transmitted through social networks via secondary and tertiary trauma and that it extends through time via intergenerational trauma we are lead to the conclusion that humans are swimming in an ocean of trauma, trauma weighing down upon us from perhaps the last ten generations of life on Earth and trauma feeding into us through our social networks of several hundreds of people, each with their own networks and multi-generational networks. Thus, when individuals assemble in a group and a "group mentality" starts to form (a sort of mini collective unconscious) this will contain a sampling of this trauma. The bulk of this will usually be repressed and the group will operate on a manifest level quite unaware of what lies in the group mentality but at times the group dynamics and stressors will lead to the surfacing of some of this material. One useful way of thinking about this set of phenomena is through the speculative theory of "imaginary groups" (Hazell, 2003). Rather like geological forms, one may imagine layerings and criss-crossings of repressed groups, composed of split of parts of individual minds, residing in the group mentality. From time to time and place to place, just as one might see, for example an ancient Pennsylvanian limestone of 300 million years of age emerging through the 10,000-year-old boulder clay of Northern Illinois, so might an ancient trauma of generations ago emerge in the here and now of a group, in the form of a subgroup conflict or in the behavior of an individual. Frequently, if one does not approach these phenomena with this explanatory template, the individual or subgroup is pathologized and re-traumatized and the untoward symptomatology continues and worsens.

An example of this comes from the staff of a conference where one male, a Jew, shared with a German female colleague that he could never visit either Germany or Austria, since he had lost so many of his relatives in the Holocaust. The German lady seemed hurt and some-what puzzled by this and sought an explanation. The man began his explanation of his feelings, but before he could get very far, the man in between them said, "I feel very sad ..." and broke down sobbing, out of the blue. This man, an Englishman, went on through his tears to recount fragments of memories from his childhood in post-war England, his terror and deep-felt sense of enormous, wordless trag-edy and human suffering. The rest of the group was very consoling and the group seemed to recover its sense of task, but the experience was a powerful and mysterious one. It is an experience that can be well understood with the model of secondary, tertiary, and intergenera-tional trauma outlined above. After this event several others who had witnessed the scene shared that the event had great meaning for them because it sparked similar memories for them. One individual recalled gunshots and explosions of a civil war going on around him while he was a child in Latin America. Another, an American-born Jew, found it helpful in organizing some of his thoughts and feelings about the trauma his parents, grandparents, and great-grandparents had gone through in Europe.

At first blush, the admission of such explanatory templates seems counter to the premise of a Tavistock group, which is a "here and now" event. The bringing in to the here and now of events from history and that enter into through the group via social networks, seems as though it could be a defensive flight from the task. However, all consultations are both synchronic and diachronic. They attempt to refer to a cross section of the group and yet, they inevitably involve an historical com-ponent insofar as they will involve some data from the past, even if it was just a minute or so ago. In addition, if we assume the unconscious knows not time, place, or person, or at least not in the same way that the conscious mind knows them, these eruptions are here and now events that the group is under some strain to cope with as much as it is at odds as to how it might cope with the present or the future.

The three examples just examined are all instances where the consultant did not provide a consultation at the time and this is consistent with much recent thinking on the nature of trauma. Not only does trauma inhabit the realm of the "unspeakable" in every-day speech, there is neurological evidence to underpin this notion for when an individual is experiencing a trauma or is recalling a trauma, the hypothalamic-linguistic-forebrain circuitry in the brain is "shut down" and the amygdala-right-brain-limbic system is acti-vated (Chapman, 2014; van der Kolk, 2015). Given this, it is no won-der that the group and the consultant should be dumbstruck when a traumatic experience or recollection enters the room. However, it is perhaps more likely that, given this and other understandings of trauma, consultants may be more able to open up the linguistic chan-nels in their brains and offer some helpful comments. This is probably more likely to occur in the context of ongoing groups where consult-ants have more opportunity for reflection, supervision, and consulta-tion and the ability to come back at a later time to offer a consultation that includes references to the trauma in the group and its attempts to come to terms with it.

By offering the opportunity to talk about the trauma, we are on old pathways. The "talking cure" of Breuer and Freud (1885) can now be seen to have a neurological underpinning (Chapman, 2014). By taking the "unspeakable," the "unthinkable," and the "indescribable" and actually transmuting it into a coding system (usually spoken language) we activate a cascade of events that aid in the metabolism of trauma. For example, the trauma becomes something that is shared, in a group and this reduces the alienation and isolation that is part of the PTSD syndrome. In addition, the translation of the traumatic experience into a language offers a sense of controllability. It is as if the trauma is contained in a narrative and the person moves from being someone who is "possessed by a trauma" to someone "who has had a traumatic experience." Furthermore, the linguistic centers of the brain are more likely to connect with the frontal lobes which are better able to come up with plans for the future, unlocking the grip of the past on the person (Chapman, 2014; van der Kolk, 2015).

The assertion, "What is refused in the symbolic re-emerges in the Real" (Lacan, 1997, p. 13) applies par excellence to trauma. The "real" is traumatic and, if left undiscussed, that is, if left in the register of the real and not dealt with in the register of the "symbolic," will emerge as an event or as a symptom in the group. By offering a consultation to the trauma, the consultant is opening the way to dialogue, unfreezing the rigid templates bestowed by trauma. Trauma then moves from being undiscussable to discussable, to use Argyris and Schon's (1995) felicitous terms. This aids in the metabolism of trauma. It also aids, in multiple ways the development of group cohesion and the sense of community.

# CHAPTER NINE

# The body and the group

*Clive Hazell*

inkages between the body of the individual and group dynamics
have been part of psychological thinking since the work of
Cannon on *Voodoo Death* (1942) and the work of Selye (1978) on
stress. In this mode of understanding the body is related to the group via
perception, the hypothalamus, the sympathetic, and parasympathetic
nervous systems. Since the human is a social animal whose well-being
relies upon positive engagement with a supportive social network, dis-
ruptions in this network will activate the well-known stress cycle in
the human body. The field of psychoneuroimmunology (Daruna, 2004)
elaborates these impacts into the immune system and other subsystems
of the human body that regulate physical health. This way of thinking
about the relationship of the group to the body of the individual has
important implications in terms of the health of the individual and of
society where social relationships can be shown to have direct meas-
ureable impacts on physical health. In addition the relatively new field
of interpersonal neuropsychology (Leiberman, 2013) examines and
establishes important connections between physiological processes and
interpersonal and social interactions.

But there is another pathway through which the body may
be influenced by the group. This one may label the metaphoric,

metonymic or symbolic pathway. This pathway interacts with the autonomic nervous system insofar as it may amplify or attenuate this system or in turn be amplified and attenuated by it. However, it can be seen to operate on an entirely different set of codes, codes that are linguistic, that are symbolic as opposed to the "signals" or the semiotic triggers we find in the autonomic nervous system and its adjuncts.

Through this pathway, the phenomena of the body can be understood as "symptoms." As such the Lacanian "Borromean knot" again comes to our assistance. With its three overlapping sets of the symbolic, the imaginary, and the real we may clarify this circuit. The "Real" of the body is symbolized and saturated with imaginary elaborations. These symbolizations and imaginings become socially constructed reality and in their turn affect the body.

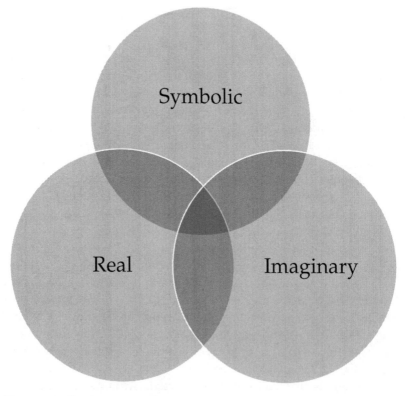

Figure 21. The Borromean knot.

That which is repressed returns in the real (Lacan, 2007). Thus, if the group represses, in its discourse, certain feelings, thoughts, and fantasies, these will return and be manifested in the "real" of the body. These manifestations could be in the form of phenomena that are diagnosed as illnesses by medical professionals or they might manifest in behaviors that are seen as part of the quirkiness of every-day life.

As an example of the latter category we provide the following: It is day one of a "Tavistock" group with graduate students. In many ways, it is typical. There is a long anxious silence as the consultant enters the room. Someone asks where the consultant comes from, but there is no answer. Someone else asks the consultant if they are doing what they are supposed to do but again, no answer is forthcoming. In many ways the group is typical of the "dependency" assumption posited by Bion (1961). The group seems to get more and more flustered, more and more confused. Somehow this confusion is not given full voice because, after all, it is a group of graduate students who should, "know better." At about two thirds of the way through the group a female member says, "I am going to need some help here!" The group turns her way and sees that somehow she has managed to entwine her feet in the book rack under her chair and, since they are stuck at a seemingly impossible angle, she cannot move or extricate herself. In a mixture of anxiety and laughter, several of the group gather around her and spend several minutes attempting to free her from the trap in which she has become ensnared. They finally succeed. Despite the goldmine of possible interpretations that this event evokes, nothing is mentioned of it and the group moves on to other topics; vacations, restaurants, classes to avoid. Eventually the consultant offers that the confusion of the group, unvoiced, had found its expression in the body of one of its members.

In this example the repressed confusion and associated ideas of entrapment found their expression in the "real" of the female repository's body, expressed in this instance in her gestures and contor-tions. At other times the repressed in the group may manifest at a more organic level. It is a commonplace for a consultant to offer the consulta-tion that, "The piss is being exported from the room." When a member leaves the group to urinate, especially if there is supporting evidence with strong associations to "piss" (such as anger or overflow) and its multiple overtones and undertones.

At other times the bodily phenomena can be much more serious in nature as reported in Hazell and Perez (2011). Individuals may develop illnesses that are diagnosed and treated by medical professionals and that have their origin in unconscious, repressed group dynamics. The case of M in Hazell and Perez (2011), who had to take "all the shit" in his organization and developed ulcerative colitis and other chronic intestinal illnesses, serves as a good example of these types of phenomena where the usual hypothalamic-adrenal pathways are activated but also, in addition there is activation of the metaphoric/metonymic pathways under discussion here. These cases of what we call "sociosomatic illness" are we believe, common, under-recognized and extremely costly. We are very close here to a reformulation, if not a rewording of Reich's ideas regarding the emotional plague (1980).

## There are multiple pathways connecting the body to the group

The body is affected via the socially constructed "realties" of the body—commonly accepted ideas about how the body should look, operate, and behave—ideas of what the "average" or normal body does, ideas of how the body should age, ideas of how and when children should have control over certain bodily functions, ideas about the body as it relates to gender, ideas about how the body may reflect social class, privilege, culture ideology, location in historical time and place. All of the "isms" affect the body and are expressed through it—sexism, racism, ethnocentrism, classism, and ageism, to name but a few. Examples of this type of society-body interaction are plentiful. Witness the oft-cited correspondence between anorexia and the culturally purveyed images of how women of certain categories "should" look.

The body is affected by the unconscious "programmings" developed through the life-course of the individual, their locations in their society and their familial and individual history. The body may be used to serve as a monument to an event in the history of the individual or even in the history of that individual's family, culture or class. In this category we would place the metaphorization of trauma, along with the autonomic adaptations and the ensuing cascade of effects that result from trauma to the individual, be it acute or chronic. These responses are covered widely in the literature on the body-based psychotherapies (Lowen, 1972, 2003, 2005, 2012; Reich, 1980a, 1980b). These responses that are so readily available to the individual as a characterological expression of their traumatic history may set that individual up as a repository for such somatic expressions in the group. Thus, an individual who expresses the emotional suffocation of their childhood in the form of sociosomatic asthma attacks when the group is attempting, largely unsuccessfully, to cope with feelings that make the members feel suffocated. Unable to express the emotion in words, the individual will find themselves reaching for an asthma inhaler. The consultant, at this point may find it helpful to use introspection and empathy to make contact with the suffocated thought, feeling or phantasy and make an attempt at giving it verbal expression, perhaps pointing out how the group is using one of its members (the asthma-sufferer) as a container for their seemingly unbearable affect. Often, in such cases, we have found that the asthma can represent unwept tears, as if the lungs are crying inwardly instead of the eyes crying outwardly. This is not to suggest that all asthma attacks can be explained thus. Asthma can result from allergies and other physical causes. However we concur with Minuchin (1978) that there are "psychosomatic families." We also suggest that there are psychosomatic, or, as we prefer, sociosomatic groups and communities.

The body is in direct contact with the unconscious mind of the individual as exemplified in the case of Jung's controversial diagnosis of a physical condition in a young girl solely through hearing a dream. Jung, in a public lecture is told of a dream experienced by a young girl and asked to come up with an analysis (Jung, 1970). Upon hearing of the dream (which was about an animal in a pool of toxic water) Jung recommends that the girl see a doctor. It later turns out that the girl was in the early stages of a cerebro-spinal fluid disease and, as Jung had surmised, the animal represented the brain and the toxic pool the unhealthy cerebro-spinal fluid.

Extending on this idea, we may hypothesize that the "group mentality," the unconscious of the group, is also, at its deepest levels in reciprocal contact with the bodies in that group and that the two may inform each other. Thus, a social dream or any manifestation of the group unconscious may represent underlying physical conditions in the bodies of the group members. In addition, the bodily expressions of the group members may serve as indicators of unconscious dynamics operating in the group.

There are numerous potential examples of these phenomena. While there is "real" fatigue, there is also "imaginary" or "symbolic" fatigue. The chronic fatigue that may manifest in groups could be a metaphorization of a deep, unspeakable fatigue in the group, a fatigue that might result from an expenditure of effort that has not been adequately recognized in the symbolic register or it might result from the fatigue of erecting defenses (often reaction formation which is a very energy-consuming defense mechanism) against forbidden desires. Just as the individual can only stand on one leg for so long and before they eventually collapse, so the psyche can only hold back "primitive" impulses from consciousness for so long, before deep fatigue sets in. If this fatigue is not acknowledged in conventional linguistic forms, then it will emerge in the body. What is repressed in the symbolic emerges in the real.

The same line of "sociosomatic" explanation might also apply to some cases of fibromyalgia, although clearly, there are a litany of other possibilities. With fibromyalgia the explanatory narrative chain has more to do with the individual introjecting a "bad other experience." The introject, in the style of Fairbairn (1952) takes up active residence in the unconscious and then expresses itself in symptoms. Sometimes these symptoms are behavioral. Sometimes they are somatic. With fibromyalgia the "bad other experience" finds expression in the body, as pain, often diffuse, inchoate pain. The test of this explanation would involve talking about the "bad other experience" in the manner prescribed by Janet (1889), Breuer and Freud (2000/1885), and by the modern trauma theorist (van der Kolk, 2015). This ventilation of the experience in a very titrated way, in a very safe environment should result in the alleviation of the fibromyalgia. As in the previously described case, individuals with fibromyalgia if it approximates this explanatory sequence, will, in a group, be "set up" to express physically that which is going on in the group but is not being spoken about, especially when it has to do with negative introjects. If such ideas are roughly congruent, they can be of very high value to the group and especially to the individuals who unwittingly are acting as repositories for unexpressed ideas, feelings, and thoughts in the group. Such individuals are prone to act as a sort of "weather vane" for these types of issues. Perhaps Jung would identify them as "intuitive/feeling" types, very sensitive to the emotions of those around them. Perhaps neuropsychologists would find that they come equipped with more mirror neurons (Baron-Cohen, 2012) and are more susceptible to feeling the feelings of others as if they are their own.

In addition, pre-existing conditions of group members may be utilized as expressions of underlying unconscious situations in the group. For example, in a large community meeting, one member had an extremely debilitating illness that seriously affected her ability to speak, to enunciate. This resulted in her uttering highly impassioned, but barely comprehensible speeches. The group accepted this uncomplainingly and without ever asking for clarification. (The consultant was often reminded, during these episodes, of Lucky's speech in *Waiting for Godot* (Beckett, 1982).) While this incomprehensible, impassioned speech was part and parcel of the effects of her devastating illness on her body and while her powerful affect laden expressions were communicative of her suffering and her anguish, they were also an expression of the incommunicable pain and suffering that existed in the group which was comprised of twenty-five individuals in a long term care facility, all of whom carried diagnoses of "severe mental illness," all of whom suffered from extreme ostracism and loneliness and had experienced unspeakable traumas.

Sometimes, this boundary requires extraordinary care in its management. Levine (2010) in an extraordinary video, demonstrates the alleviation of a tic that was a major presenting symptom of an Iraq War veteran who had been exposed to the explosion of two Improvised Explosive Devices (IED) in very rapid succession. By working in a "bottom-up" sequence, that is, through the use of body-based interventions, he is able to facilitate the release of the grip of the tic within five sessions.

While Levine's case is in a one-on-one situation, we have worked with groups where individuals in the group manifested similar symptoms, such as psychogenic tics, symptoms that in all likelihood resulted from exposure to trauma. Such events require very careful consideration and high precision of interventions and wording. Why? First because any interpretation of this behavior that relies too heavily on the group-as-a-whole premise that all behavior is on behalf of the group has the potential effect of undermining the validity of the individual's trauma while also exposing a person who has probably been traumatized to becoming the focus of attention, to having their traumatic history publicized and potentially to becoming flooded with traumatic re-experiencing in an un or anti-therapeutic, untitrated manner and in a context that is ill-suited to cope with it. On the other hand, groups will often, as exemplified in the previous case, utilize such symptomatic expressions to make manifest unconscious dynamic processes. In addition, there is usually a high level of reluctance in groups to discuss openly these symptoms; usually driven by conventional politeness, or not wishing to cause pain, people will not comment on such phenomena as a tic or a bodily manifestation in one of its members even when it is very obvious and demanding of attention.

Bion also sits on our shoulder, with his edict that we should consult without desire, memory or understanding. If we start timing our interventions so that they are attuned to the coping skills of the group and its members, are we not "managing" the group, and as such are we not filled with goals, purposes, desires for it and them? Have we moved from the role of consultant to the role of facilitator? Have we moved from the discourse of the analyst to the discourse of the university or master, or perhaps hysteric? Have we moved from cell II8 of the Hill interaction matrix? Have we been captured? Interesting problems indeed. Further, could it not be that all of these musings are but a counter-transferential reaction to the phenomena at hand? As such, it is a situation filled with desire, desire to protect from re-exposure to trauma, desire for control.

It is perhaps this last question that offers us a clue, for there are several ways of working with countertransference and perhaps one of these would offer a way out of the dilemma. One way is proffered by Ferenczi (1995) who, in a difficult, stuck case, removes the impasse he has met with in a patient by letting the patient analyze him for a few sessions. Perhaps one way of dealing with this stressful situation would be for the consultant to make a consultation that acknowledges their own inner dynamics, concerns, anxieties, and desires, thus rendering them part of the field of forces operant in the group. As with transference interpretations, which Freud tells us will be "invited" by the client, who will offer an avenue, as if building half of a bridge from their side of the river, ready and waiting for the therapist to reach out to them with their half of the bridge, so with countertransference interpretations. The group will offer a sign or signal, a green light, a clue or a hint, that they are ready for such a comment. In turn, the consultant, far from feeling filled with pressures such that they feel they "have" to say what they are about to say, will feel relatively free from "desire, memory and understanding" as they offer the interpretation, which might go something like this:

"This consultant is experiencing a good deal of anxiety and conflict currently. He thinks he is not alone in this. One group member has a very distinctive physical manifestation. While politeness and concern for this person's comfort and well-being militate against bringing it to the group's attention, the fact that the group has not mentioned it, and the fact that the physical manifestation seems linked with what is going on in the group is placing this individual in the position of being used by the group, albeit unwittingly, to express thoughts feelings and phantasies that it feels are undiscussable."

Interestingly enough, in response to such a consultation, which does not identify the individual clearly, but leaves it open for the group to decide just who or what is being spoken about, the group will frequently pick several other people, all of whom have valid reasons for thinking it is they at whom the consultation is aimed. This usually turns out fine. It is often as if the group is using some practice run-ups to the more intensely charged phenomena involved in the individual about whom the consultation was crafted.

It is also important to note that symptoms of PTSD often manifest in a multiplicity of bodily symptoms such as tics, pains, digestive problems, and working with the body is in all likelihood an effective way of treating PTSD (van der Kolk, 2015). There is thus an important linkage between this section and the previous section on trauma in the group.

To focus on the body in the group is to return to Freudian psychoanalysis. Freud's theory is intensely embodied insofar as it is sexual and founded upon desire. Each of the stages of psychosexual development involves a cathexis or decathexis of regions of the body. Furthermore these bodily cathexes occur in a social context, a point Freud emphasized frequently (1912–1913, 1921) Freud thus provides explanatory templates for many phenomena that involve bodily expression in the group. Castration anxiety is frequently in evidence in groups, in the form of jokes, references to castration stories in the news, in disguised forms where members will talk of being "cut off" or beheaded or "hacked off." At other times castration anxiety will manifest itself in a massive desexualization of the group, where there is a sort of "sexual numbing" as if to deny the presence of the genitals. These anxieties seem to be emphasized in the presence of a male consultant (leader/chieftain) who in the group mentality, in a manner similar to that outlined by Freud, threatens any sexual competition with death or castration.

Connected with this, it is also not at all uncommon for the group to symbolically offer up one of the members for the consultant to "marry" or "enjoy." This is perhaps being done to get the consultant to veer from their task of consulting, to capture them or perhaps to stop them from attacking. Often times the member who is selected for this offering is suited by virtue of their personality for this task, usually by being attractive or seductive or by having a personal history where such seduction was necessary or functional. As Reich (1980a) and Lowen (2012) argue, there is an isomorphism between the body and the character. The character goes to informing the role one plays in a group, it goes to establishing the predisposition one has for certain repository functions. Thus the bodily structure and the disposition of its energies and its flows can be read by the consultant to inform them as to the forms of usage of individual members in the group.

Existence in a group is closely interwoven with the issues of separation and individuation. Arguably in the individual, there is a wish to become part of the group and a wish for differentiation from it. The group thus provides a challenging venue for individuals to manifest and perhaps to work with their own issues of separation and individuation. Mahler (1975) provides a cogent model of this process as it occurs in the infant and toddler during the first three years of life. Of particular interest is the extent to which the body plays a role in this. In fact, "Motility is the paradigm for independent development." "Movement establishes bodily boundaries." "Being able to move the torso ... is the midwife to 'hatching'" (Mahler, 1975) Mahler's theory is saturated with references to the body. It is little wonder then that groups, which provide such a potent stimulus for separation individuation issues should be a place where such bodily phenomena are so apparent.

Examples of such phenomena might include the member who insists on sitting on the floor or who moves their chair outside of the circle, thus differentiating themselves, and by extension the group from the "mother"—the group, the consultant, the institution. Sometimes members will suggest "group hugs" or mutual physical exploration through offering massages. The group hugs are reminiscent of Mahler's symbiotic stage while the massages perhaps are linked with the curiosity of the other found in the differentiation sub phase of Mahler's theory. In inter-group events, the anchoring will frequently be at later stages of

Mahler's theory. As members leave their home group to explore other groups and places, there is a motile recapitulation (or inhibition) of the practicing and rapprochement sub-phases.

## Munchausen in the group

Munchausen's syndrome by proxy or as it is currently called, "factitious disorder by proxy", is usually thought of as a dyadic phenomenon, where someone, usually a parent, is certain that another, often their child, has an illness and then takes them to various medical specialists for diagnosis and treatment. Even though the tests come back as negative, they persist in the delusional belief that the other is ill. They gain no material benefit from the imagined illness of the other—no disability payments or court settlements—the payoff appears to be entirely psychosocial. Often enough, and unfortunately a healthcare professional will be found who will provide treatment for the illness. Then various types of iatrogenic issues can emerge and these can be used as further justification for yet more treatment and so the dyad starts and continues its career of "patient" and, often enough, "long suffering caretaker or partner." While this syndrome is thought of as a phenomenon that occurs in dyads, it is quite common in families (as described in Hazell & Perez, 2011) and groups. In these contexts it will often manifest in the form of the "identified patient" making an attempt to get better, or even having a period of "symptom reduction" only to find that the group in which they are enmeshed attempts to undermine or sabotage their progress. Thus we might see the son, who has had the identity of "the sick one" since early childhood make attempts to get healthy in their young adulthood, only to have parents and siblings claim that they are actually going crazy or getting worse, often calling the counselor to warn them of the harmful effects of the "patient" losing weight, or improving their diet, or starting an exercise program. While fairly common in families, this dynamic can also occur in groups where the unconscious dynamics can feed off of and into the "symptoms" of the scapegoated individual.

For example, the group, might reach a collusive agreement with an obese female in such a way that her level of depression and inactivity can be relied upon to put a damper on certain types of ideas flowering in the group—ideas pertaining to assertion, individuation, sexuality, and mobility, for example. This would be perhaps consistent with Reich's (1980b) and Lowen's (2012) notion that the "masochistic" character structure is often associated with such features. However, if the identified individual in the group started to derive therapeutic benefit from the group and started to make attempts to move out of the "group masochist" role and activate different aspects of their personality, we could perhaps expect resistance from the other group members, as if to say, "NO. Stop that exercise and diet and movement you say you are starting. For if you continue changing your body, your character will change and you will no longer be available for us to use in this group in the same way. We need you here in your immobile, obese form to act as an anchor, a sort of deadweight to our own potential for movement, for differentiation." The body is so connected with issues of shame. Perhaps the very experience of shame can be defined as, "The loss of control of the body in front of others." This painful connection makes such issues very difficult for most people to broach. While this shame brings growth and sharing to a standstill, it also acts as a very strong seal on the group's defenses.

Lacan argues that the unconscious is structured like a language. We agree with the utility of such an assertion. However, we think that the term "language" has been interpreted too narrowly. There are multiple languages, multiple "codes." Among these codes are the languages of the body. The plural is used because as stated at the outset of this section, there are multiple pathways through which the realities of the world are expressed in the body. We have, in this section, touched on several: the hypothalamic-adrenal system and its codes, the language of the body as it is expressed in movement and gesture, the ways in which experience is encoded and communicated through bodily structure and the manner in which primary process thinking at the level of the individual and the group may express itself in the body.

The language in the group will often enough use bodily metaphors and these too may be used by the consultant as data bearing upon the group-as-a-whole. Members may speak of not having a leg to stand on. This may relate to issues of independence, of taking a stand, of feeling grounded and so on. There may be talk of headaches of various sorts—blinding, splitting, numbing—and these may refer to psychological conditions in the group. Perhaps members will find certain things in the group "hard to swallow" and some may be visited by feelings of nausea. These allusions may refer to psychic material that has been introjected and that does not agree with the hosts.

A key to the consultant becoming aware of the body in the group is that they are in touch with their own bodies. We highly recommend that group consultants participate in some activities that heighten their awareness of their own bodies—yoga, body-based psychotherapy, dance, exercise etc.—to facilitate this. The consultant may then scan their own body as they engage in the process of consulting and use it as another stream of data regarding the group.

For example, a consultant may find that they are finding it very hard to be "in their body" in a session. This phenomenon of dissociation is described by Guntrip (1992), Laing (1965), Lowen (2005), and Winnicott (1965), as associated with a schizoidal response to trauma, as if the person "jumps out of their skin" or is "beside themselves" with terror. This numbing process is quite common, we believe, and often enough the group will locate such a psychophysical defense in a vulnerable member in response to stress. If the consultant themselves is not able to track the comings and goings of their own bodily dynamics they will miss these vital aspects of group life. The body is a vehicle for the expression of unconscious group dynamics.

# CHAPTER TEN

# The large group, community, and therapeutic potential

*Clive Hazell*

## Introduction

In what follows we will describe some of the many ideas regarding large groups and problems encountered when attempting to use the large group or a community meeting as a therapeutic tool. We will argue that many of those preconceptions are unnecessarily negative and have led to large groups being under-utilized especially as a therapeutic modality. We will then describe and develop a novel theory of community. This will lead to a set of ideas on the important functions of community as defined herein. We integrate this with Edelson's theory of social systems (1970). We then outline the components of community based upon the preceding arguments. We argue that the community function as we define it is of vital importance in any socio-therapeutic effort and in the psychological well-being of the individual. We end the section by describing practical ways in which the community function can be enabled, facilitated, and supported. Throughout, we shift back and forth from the terms "large group" and "community." "Large group" refers to the number of individuals present in the group. Usually a group starts to be considered "large" when it exceeds twelve in number of members, "median" when it reaches about forty-five and

187

very large when it approaches about 120 members. "Community," refers to a function that is either absent or present, to a greater or lesser extent in a group. A further definition of that function is, in part, the purpose of this section.

## Common preconceptions regarding large groups

Since the earliest days of thinking and writing about the large group, its immense power has been recognized (Freud, 1921; Kreeger, 1975; LeBon, 2002). For the most part this power has been seen as negative. Indeed one could make a strong argument that humans are not meant to be in large groups, that it is likely that for most of human history we were only exposed to small groups. The list of negative impacts of large groups is a long one.

It is often assumed that large groups tend to:

- Cause deindividuation: The overwhelming power of the large group weakens individual ego boundaries and creates a merger between the individual and the group. This is usually seen as undesirable because although it may provide transient feelings of omnipotence and fused well-being, it weakens the sense of individual responsibility and can result in mob-like behavior.
- Foster dependent idealization of the leader: The regressed merger-state facilitated by the large group in addition brings about a quest in group members for a parental figure who has magical properties. This is the state described by Freud (1921) and Le Bon (2002). In this condition the large group becomes all too manipulable, since part of this regressive identification involves a suppression of more evolved critical thinking faculties.
- Weaken object relatedness: Insofar as face-to-face personal contact becomes difficult as a group gets above a dozen or so in number, the interpersonal relatedness in the group declines, depersonalization increases as do all of the social ills associated with depersonalization. Being depersonalized usually makes people feel anxious, as they are treated as if they do not exist or as if they are a thing or a category and this adds to the terrific burden of functioning in a large group.
- Weaken the superego: The conscience of the individual is often yoked to internalized personalized object relations and as these are weakened in the large group so the moral sense is softened. In addition,

there is likely to occur the facilitation effect and the phenomena associated with diffusion of responsibility cited in several social psychology studies (Menzies-Lyth, 1960).

- Promote mob behavior: History is replete with examples of large groups run amok: soccer hooligans, angry crowds after disasters or unpopular court decisions or assassinations. These can be explained by the list of phenomena elucidated here.

- Induce psychotic-like primary process thinking: A group is often a hard place to think in anyway, and that becomes more difficult if the group is large and leaderless. Primary process thinking or sensorimotor and preoperational thinking can easily predominate in a large unstructured group, leading it to make decisions, that when viewed in the light of formal operations (Piaget, 1969) do not make much sense.

- Induce splitting: In addition, the regression that can occur in large groups can take on a Kleinian inflection (1975) and we can see experiences, people, categories, objects in general being self-protectively split into good and bad groupings. This leads to black and white, binary, for us or against us, extremist cognitive styles and this can have very deleterious effects, especially if the inhabitants of the group are already under duress and prone to this psychological defense mechanism.

- Induce psychological fragmentation: The large group, and perhaps any group most of the time does not provide a reflection of the self that is cohesive and coherent. In addition, the use of projective identification in the large group setting results in the psychological situation of unconsciously having many parts of oneself scattered throughout the group. This results in a sense of fragmentation or anxieties of incohesion. This can be very distressing and may bring about some or all of the defensive maneuvers mentioned here.

- Create a sense of helplessness and frustration: Life in almost any group can become frustrating. Simply picking a place to eat with several people can be quite a chore. With a large group, these issues multiply and result in feelings of helplessness and depression. Again, if the members are feeling depressed and powerless to start with, it is often assumed the large group is not the thing to which they should be exposed.

- Cause subgroups: Often these will take the form of cliques or gangs to form as a defense against the anxiety of a large group. Quite commonly, people, upon entering the large group look for someone or something to hold on to as a protection against these tendencies. Sometimes these others are held on to for dear life. This desperation, coupled with splitting and projective identification can result in a divisive social atmosphere. Once a few "shots have been fired" these splits can be difficult to undo.

There thus is a widespread assumption that in many ways humans are not designed to operate in large groups. While this might be the case, there are countervailing hypotheses that follow from the ideas of Agamben (1993), Blanchot (1988) and Nancy (1991) that seem to lead to the conclusion that there is in humans a drive for community. This drive may be as powerful as any of the other drives posited by psychodynamic thinkers and, if compromised, thwarted or distorted by trauma, would result in negative outcomes ranging from the neurotic through to psychotic.

We thus are placed in a familiar situation when things are viewed from a psychodynamic perspective. On the one hand we may have a drive which if not satisfied in some manner that leads to deleterious results ranging from mildly neurotic to psychotic. The drive is inexorable. On the other hand the realization of the drive is fraught with difficulties and pitfalls, false turns, and anguish. We are, in the words of Bion, in a position where we are trying to make the best of a bad situation. If there is a drive for community, if this is one of the manifestations of desire and if the large group presents the difficulties outlined at the outset, what possible solutions are there for community living? That this problem is in desperate need of solution is quite easily demonstrated. Nancy argues that the outcropping of Nazism (and thus I would argue, by extension all forms of what Erikson would call "totalism" (1993)) was a tortured quest of individuals for a sense of community, a psychotic-like solution to the dilemma just posited.

The value placed on community varies from culture to culture. The beginning anthropologist encounters the "communitarian–individualism" dimension early on. It is also quite likely that capitalism, with its emphasis on rapid deployment of labor and skills, along with its competition and emphasis on the individual erodes, if not obliterates, the sense of community and belonging.

Fortunately, humans do have language and the capacity to develop techniques and technologies to cope with novel social and environmental situations. This is not easy, especially in the case of social situations like large groups, but it seems that it has to be done. Like it or not, we inhabit large groups and while they can at times be catastrophic in their consequences, we also derive great benefits from them. They are like large powerful engines that have great power for good and terrible things. In addition the frustration of the urge to be a part of a community results in serious problems and dangers.

For the reasons cited above and perhaps because of an underestimation of the importance of community-belonging to humans, the use of a large group as a therapeutic medium has been quite limited. Those groups that do seem to involve assembling in large groups typically do not involve the examination of group dynamics in the here and now (we would hypothesize because of at least an assumption about some of the above dynamics). Those large groups that do attempt psychotherapy are often quite structured and frequently involve the influence of a charismatic leader, programmatic psycho-education and uniform desired end states for the participants.

What we seek to explore in this chapter is the possibility that while many of the concerns enumerated above regarding large groups are true, they do not necessarily imply that a large group cannot be a very fruitful medium for therapeutic change. The group is a high energy system. A large group is a very high energy system. Tapping into this energy for biopsychosocial change for the better would seem to be a possibility upon which would be unwise to prematurely foreclose.

Having outlined some of the problems in conducting large group meetings and having suggested that there is a drive for community membership which calls for satisfaction, we now proceed to outline a theory of community.

## Theory of community

Inspired by Nancy (1991) we hypothesize three overlapping sets of concerns in a group; political, management, community. The political has to do with the routinization of power relations and the distribution of authority in decision-making. Managerial has to do with the actual operational processes carried out within the political structure. What then, is community? Much writing on community seems to work on the assumption that these two sets, namely, political and managerial provide a sufficient explanatory base for community. A moment's reflection shows this cannot be so because one can easily come up with political and managerial units that do not have this sense of community. Nancy, in citing Bataille (1991), argues that this very lack of community has led nostalgic longings for community, longings which are either left unrealized or that sometimes emerge with catastrophic results in what might be called hyper communities, such as gangs, cults or Nazism. There is thus something impossible "inoperable" about the community. How can we cope, intellectually and practically with this powerful, yet so difficult-to-manage, force? The yearning for community does not seem to go away, and if ignored it has negative results. History is also replete with stories of communities gone haywire. In addition, the very establishment of a community seems to stand in opposition to the exigencies of politics and management.

Perhaps these often antagonistic forces can be represented as a tensional model. In this model we see three sets of concerns; managerial, having to do with operational and pragmatic issues, political, having to do with the processes and procedures for decision-making and especially the power and authority to make and implement decisions, and community which has to do with the strivings of individuals to be part of a group, a group ranging in size from median through to large. Each of these domains operates according to different rule-sets. Each has in its own way, different criteria for "truth." Each sector must function reasonably well if the social system is to run reasonably painlessly and each sector requires work. The nature of the work done in each sector varies considerably. These differences cause tensions to arise in the social system since there are different concerns amongst the subgroups that emerge to carry out these functions. For example the managerial function requires attention to the operational pragmatics, both day-to-day and strategic, of the running of the social system. This function is akin to the ego of the individual. It is reality oriented and adaptive. It corresponds to the "adaptive" category in Edelson's model (1970). The political set is concerned with the distribution of power and authority and the processes and procedures for making decisions. Pragmatics and adaptation to reality enter this domain from the other two but it is more affected by other less "rational" concerns that might emanate from, say, culture, ethics, tradition, and religion. These two sectors interact and in most conventional understandings of social systems this is as far as it goes, there are a set of concerns about reality and how to adapt to it and a set of concerns over who has the power to implement policies.

The word "community" will be used often enough but attempts to raise community spirit are approached usually through managerial and political means. This model posits that that is hopelessly inadequate and that the sense of community is built from its very own origin, obeying its own set of rules and codes. When the community has "spoken" in its own language, this speech informs the other two domains of management and political; it informs the other domains of what is "brewing" in the community, what might be emerging in the collectivity that needs attention and what is the community's perception of the actions of the political and managerial spheres.

Thus the social system can be regarded as a "troika" of Management (M), Political (P) and Community (C) concerns. Much of what happens in communities can be understood by observing and interpreting the nature of the relationships between these three components. The three spheres of MPC are reminiscent of Lacan's "Borromean knot" (2007) and, like this knot, if any one of three is broken, the whole thing falls to pieces. Different signs and symptoms emerge depending on which of the three subsystems is compromised. This simple model has thus become predictive. If any one of the subsystems fails to function, the entire social system will founder. If the political system fails, we have a failed state. If the managerial system fails, we have a system that is going out of business. If the community system fails ... ah! This is where not enough thinking has been done. The conventional answer would be that people simply do not feel good. They feel lonely, alienated, cut off, anomic, directionless. What this model predicts is that if the community system fails, there will be a "social earthquake"—rebellion, revolutions of certain types, protest movements, profound and mysterious psychosocial, socio-somatic disorders.

Optimally the three subsystems will progress with minor frictions emerging between them which will be addressed, often with anxiety, and adjusted to in a set of small increments. Each of the three MPC subsystems informs and "makes demands" upon the others. Shifts occur in each that require adjustment in the other two subsystems. The analogy might be when two tectonic plates slide along each other a millimeter at a time resulting in barely detectable tremors. However, if the plates do not slide for a century, then enormous pressures build and when the adjustment does take place and the plates move several meters all at once, terrible damage occurs, with much loss of life and property. Similarly, we frequently see managerial and political systems alter quickly (often potentiated by technological changes) and relatively little attention paid to community. Severe tensions develop between the subsystems and the social system becomes extremely turbulent, even chaotic or "vortical" (Emery & Trist, 1965).

In addition, each subsystem is filled with internal tensions. There are ideological splits in the political sphere. There are differences in the managerial group and the very concept of "community", as we shall argue, is founded upon a paradoxical inclusion of the unique individual within the totality of the community. This is, in and of itself, tensional, or as Nancy (1991) and Blanchot (1988) would say, respectively, "inoperable" and "unavowable." Usually, social tensions are analyzed at the level of these tensions that exist at the level of the subsystems. In addition, we would argue there should be an analysis of inter-systemic tensions.

Each of the MPC subsystems requires a "space" to conduct its business. Management has teams and organizational meetings. Politics has rallies, conventions, debates, and discussions. When we come to community, however, we find a gap. Certainly there are activities that are labeled as belonging to this domain but we would argue they hardly ever meet our criteria for valid community activity. There is thus a woeful and deleterious lack of "spaces" where the discourse of the community may take place, where it may be articulated and potentially be registered by the political and managerial subsystems. This space, broadly defined, will be similar to the dialogical space described by de Mare (2011). Philosophically it will embody the conversational space delineated by Rorty (2000, 2009). Examples of such spaces would include the Tavistock large group experience, social dreaming groups (Lawrence, 2003), and listening posts (Gould, 2006).

This model is not a utopian one for we recognize that the socio-technical system (McGinn, 1990) is very rapid and highly unpredictable (Ellul, 1967; Emery & Trist, 1965). Thus the MPC does not always have time to adjust, but the lack of "space for community discourse" is so glaring that we predict a little could go a long way.

Having argued that there is a risky lack of community spaces and community discourse of a type that would help improve managerial and political functions, we now go on to sketch out a definition and theory of community. This will be followed by suggestions as to how such spaces and discourses might be established.

We argue that the sense of community emerges like true self of Winnicott (1965). In this, the individual engages in a floating,

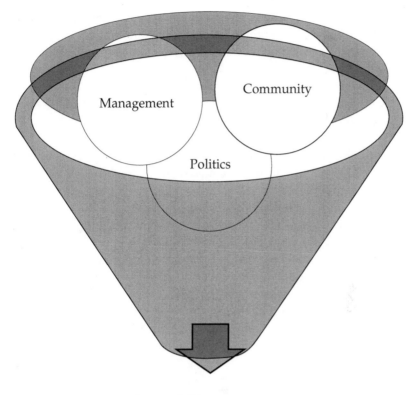

## Social Dynamics

Figure 22. The three spheres of community, management, and politics, interacting in the flux of the chora.

unintegrated state (not disintegrated), a state that we think is very close to what Khan (1996) calls "lying fallow" or Bion terms "reverie." It involves free-floating attention. Out of this floating state emerges an impulse and around this impulse ideas, thoughts, and actions coalesce. These impulses (Winnicott calls them "id impulses") are experienced as real by the subject since they are not responses to impingements from the environment. It is responses to such environmental impingements that result in the formation of something of a false self. Something spontaneous emerges throughout the floating. The desire for community can thus be seen as the desire for the spontaneous gesture in the context of a large group. This gesture is in tensional relation to, is at odds with, the demands of politics and management, yet it is deeply longed-for and, if heeded, can inform politics and management so as to render them more meaningful and more tied to desires. The spontaneous gesture is usually inconvenient (perhaps like falling in love). If, however, these gestures are not heeded they build up rather like tectonic pressures in the earth's crust and a paroxysmal release ensues.

Many cultural forms seem to express the drive to community as posited here. They take on different forms and seem to meet the need for community to varying extents. For example, "happenings" of the late nineteen-sixties, "spontaneous" demonstrations, town hall meetings, flash mobs, and popular music concerts seem to embody some of the experience of community.

Several organized attempts have been made to utilize the sense of community in the pursuit of mental health, for example, Maxwell Jones (1968, 1976) and Edelson (1970). This conceptualization of the community in no way supersedes either of these. It functions more as an added dimension, an important one, to consider when embarking on sociotherapy or ultimately, we would argue, any form of "management," in the fullest sense, of a social system. In what follows, we will examine how the system being posited here might interact with that of Edelson.

## Integration of Edelson's theory and theory of community

Edelson, following Parsons, (1971) posits four elements or functions that comprise a social system: motivation, consummation, integration, and adaptation.

### Motivation

This function corresponds to Freud's "ego ideal" (1927). It has to do with the "mobilization and commitment to values" (Edelson, 1970). In everyday language, the ego ideal gives us something to live up to, something to aspire to. It is the root of ambition insofar as there is ideally an optimal tension between the ego (the situation at hand) and the ego ideal (the situation as it ought to be according to the ego ideal). This would be manifested typically in the social system's statements of mission, in its ideals, in its narratives of its origin, in the exemplars it honors to symbolize cherished values and ideals. Such activities inspire, give hope, and boost morale in that they give people something to live up to, perhaps to live and work for.

## Integration

This function corresponds to the superego of Freud (1927). It thus operates as a "conscience" for the social system, organization or group. It is involved in "the selection among alternatives of shared norms." (Edelson, 1970, pp. 3–5). This function is typified by system activities that have to do with how people are supposed to behave. It would thus involve codes of conduct, both formal and informal, human resource functions like hiring and firing would be involved and the ethics of the group's internal and external functioning would be monitored and regulated.

## Consummation

This function has to do with the attainment of ends and corresponds with the Id of Freud (1927). It is typified in social systems by celebrations, graduations, award ceremonies, parties, and rituals having to with successfully meeting goals. It can frequently bear the marks of primary process or magical thinking. These functions offer the satisfactions of goal attainment and successful completion of tasks.

## Adaptation

This has to with the functions in the organization that are involved in assessing the current situation internal and external to the system and coming up with action plans to adapt to these situations. This function corresponds to Freud's ego (1927) and is typified in organizations with functions that have to do with planning, assessment of threats and opportunities, marketing research, and the development of action plans. Strategic planning, operational planning, project management, and activities that have to do with assessing strengths, weaknesses, opportunities, and threats (SWOT analysis) are also involved, as are the manifold protocols for decision-making in organizations.

We will now examine each of these functions to show how a social system will not function well if any one of these is overlooked or fails.

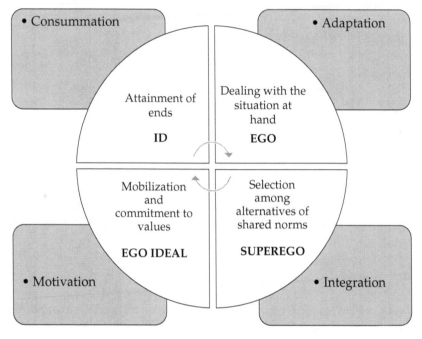

Figure 23. Edelson's four organizational functions.

## Failure in the motivation sub-system

Chasseguet-Smirgel (1985) gives an excellent account of the catastrophic consequences of the collapsing of the ideal tension that should exist in the individual between the ego and the ego ideal. This tension is calibrated, in her theory at the onset of the oedipal crisis. Trauma at this stage can result in a merging of the ego (things as they are) with the ego ideal (things as they ought to be). This results in a magical over-valuation of the self where one believes oneself to have already effortlessly arrived at one's ideal state. This dynamism provides an explanation, for Chasseguet-Smirgel, of the dynamism of narcissism. Lacan (1997) seems to use similar ideas when he speaks of the fusion of the ego with the ego ideal creating the ideal ego. This ideal ego can be, in his thinking, quite delusional and he mobilizes this theory in his explanation of the psychoses.

We can find examples of these types of social systems. Typically they will be social systems that have suffered considerable narcissistic damage, perhaps through defeat, humiliation or the desecration and damaging of sustaining culture, myth, and narrative.

In addition, following Kernberg's insights (1994) on the influence of leaders with personality disorders we may find that organizations headed by narcissistic personalities will be vulnerable to failure in the motivational system of this sort.

Another way in which failure in the motivational sub-system may show is in the phenomenon of demoralization. In this case the tension between ego and ego ideal is not coped with by a regression to a fusion of the two, but by a depressive, perhaps even passive aggressive giving up on ideals. Here individuals in the social system have just given up, even though they are showing up, they are "phoning it in." They are not putting their heart into it. Again this can result from severe damage to the cultural heritage of the society or it can emerge in authoritarian cultures which create a sense of "learned helplessness" (Seligman, 1992) in its denizens. Examples of this are plentiful. This corresponds to the type of alienation Marx refers to in his early works, the type of alienated labor that has to do with work not being a fulfilling vehicle for self-realization (Marx, 1965).

Attempts to remediate such failures often miss the point entirely since they frequently will emerge from the "integration" sub-system, that is, they emerge as "moral" pleas for doing one's duty. It is our observation that a more "Kohutian" approach works better in reactivating a failed motivational system (Kohut, 1971, 1977), that is, an approach that involves the provision of the three self-object needs of empathy, twinning, and idealization combined with merger—listening, provision of emotional contact, and the availability of idealizable objects with whom one may identify.

## Failure in the adaptation sub-system

Failures in this sub-system are perhaps the easiest to identify and diagnose since there is usually the focus of most organizations and institutions. However these sub-systems do fail at quite a high rate for an array of reasons. Systemic trauma can be one such cause. Disasters, both natural and of human origin can overtake social systems with such rapidity that the coping mechanisms are flooded and the reality sense is compromised. Floods, epidemics, rapid climate change, disasters borne by warfare can all bring about severe regressions in this sub-system and we see large masses of people resort to primitive defense mechanisms—magical thinking, denial, delusion. When groups panic and seem to shut out perceptions of reality, when they fail, for example, to see the way out of a burning theater but trample each other to death, or when a military unit instead of retreating in an organized manner simply turns and runs and is routed—these provide examples of these types of failures in the adaptive sub-system.

Other failures are more subtle and complex. In such failures we see an undermining through various pathways, of the systems reality function. For example, knowledge of global warming and its likelihood has been readily available since the mid 1960s and yet it is only in 2014 that it and some of its harmful consequences is finally somewhat accepted. Whether or not this delay in perceiving reality is so great that we will be unable to adapt effectively to the changes wrought by a warming planet we will discover in the coming decades. The reasons for the failure in this adaptive function are manifold: it is beyond our usual horizons of understanding, there are too many vested interests in not believing it to be true, believing it might cause us to change our religious, philosophical or existential outlook, and so on. At times social systems repress or, worse, deny the existence of incontrovertible data that creates discomfort. And, as in repression or denial in the individual, while the data is not acknowledged consciously, it is acknowledged in some register and is ultimately symbolized in a symptom. Any textbook on decision-making (E. F. Harrison, 1998) is replete with examples of such failures in adaptational subsystems. We also find many further examples in the literature that examines socio-technical systems and their breakdowns (Hirschorn, 1990; McGinn, 1990).

The incidence of such failures in the adaptational sub-system can be reduced if the social system builds in structures and processes aimed at anticipating a wide array of potential internal and external environmental conditions and developing contingency plans. This sometimes involves the system bearing some anxiety and might be met with some resistance from more "nostalgic" elements in the organization or from other sectors of the system that are for one reason or another, vulnerable and stressed. Ideas about upcoming change can also be gathered from community meetings if they are conducted in the way we are forwarding here, as in the nature of "listening posts" (Gould, 2006) or, say, as "social dreaming events" (Lawrence, 2003).

## Failure in the consummation sub-system

Failures in this sub-system will show in a sense of depression and hopelessness; at times in an ongoing sense of misery. This sub-system has to do with celebrations of successes. It has to do with a happy feeling of having reached a goal or passed an important milestone. Graduation ceremonies, celebrations of all kinds would fall into this category. The phenomenon of the *mardi gras* is a joyous event aimed at balancing the self-denial of lent. Similarly, individuals can be seen to oscillate between depression and manic states as the superego holds on tight and then releases the drives of the id. Just as an individual can regulate themselves along the dimension of mania and depression in such a way that their adaptation is harmed, so an institution or any social system can dysregulate itself and develop functional problems. "All work and no play makes Jack a dull boy" can fit for organizations as well individuals. Perhaps the regression involved in the consummation sub-system can be functional a *"reculer pour mieux sauter,"* a regression in the service of the ego. The celebrations of the consummation sub-system help regulate moods and strengthen the adaptive and other sub-systems. The grandfather of a friend of mine had a saying, "Always keep a good bottle of wine on hand because you never know when you will have to celebrate." This family had an intact consummation sub-system, ready to have a joyous occasion at the success of one of its members. The consummation system has a role in supporting hope in the social system.

In addition, what is celebrated is of importance in securing the values of the social system. A graduation emphasizes academic achievement, a wedding anniversary celebrates commitment and love, a victory celebration might celebrate teamwork and so on.

The consummation sub-system, like all the other sub-systems, can fail by being excessively activated as well as by being absent. Sometimes social systems will use "circuses" to distract its members from pressing concerns in the other domains. A company whose sales are falling may avoid contemplating this dire fact by celebrating other less meaningful benchmarks. The consummation sub-system is linked, we recall, with the id of Freud and is thus prone to magical ideation and wish-fulfilling thinking. It is a pleasant, heady brew, but one can have too much of a good thing.

## Failure in the integration sub-system

The integration sub-system corresponds to the superego of Freud so when we see failures in this sub-system, we will see the familiar issues we see when the superego undergoes transformations in the individual. In some cases there will be a lack of oversight, little or no monitoring or regulation or such patchy and inconsistent monitoring that there is a high frequency of impulsive behavior that shows very little concern of the community or others. There is a distinct lack of socio-centric thinking and behavior. The organization runs a very high risk of running into problems with community standards, laws, and ethics. Often the "human resources" department has responsibility for ensuring the functioning of the integration sub-system. This will show up in adherence to codes of conduct, industry standards, and laws regarding hiring, firing, promotion, and disciplinary procedures.

At times the integration sub-system can be unnecessarily severe, as in authoritarian systems dominated by paranoid ideation or Bion's "fight–flight" basic assumption (Bion, 1961). Authority in social systems should be calibrated in such a way that there is sufficient authority to carry out the tasks of the system. If there is more authority than is necessary, then the system is authoritarian. If there is less authority than necessary then the system's functions will start to fail.

Edelson, in his definition of this sub-system, uses the term "selection" of guiding norms and this is important, for selection will necessarily involve some discussion and thought. A functional social system will thus involve conversations about the guiding norms, evaluation of alternatives and some open process of selection and hierarchization of those norms such that they enhance system functioning. To the extent that these are not available, the system will falter and perhaps fail.

## The role of community in the maintenance of the four sub-systems

We may now "cross-hatch" the three sub-systems of Nancy (1991) and the four sub-systems of Edelson. Doing so reveals the functionality of the community function in social systems. We argue that this function is usually overlooked but is of very high importance. The table below serves to illustrate this cross-hatching.

|  | Motivation | Integration | Adaptation | Consummation |
|---|---|---|---|---|
| Politics | A | B | C | D |
| Management | E | F | G | H |
| Community | I | J | K | L |

Figure 24. Edelson/Nancy grid.

We thus see that political activity, behaviors having to do with the distribution of power and the disposition of decisions can be aimed at motivation, integration, adaptation, and consummation activities. These would be included in cells A, B, C, and D. Managerial activities, behaviors aimed at coping with the pragmatic requirements, the logistics and the operations of the motivational, integrative, adaptive, and consummatory sub-systems are included in cells E, F, G, and H. Finally, community activities can be directed towards motivation, integration, adaptation, and consummation. These are covered in cells I, J, K, and L.

It does not take much effort to come up with examples of activities in cells A through H, namely activities that are political and managerial and have to do with Edelson's four domains. The table below gives snapshot examples of something that might occupy each of these cells.

| A | "Ask not what your country can do for you, but what you can do for your country." <br> "We should take pride in our work!" |
|---|---|
| B | "A new law or rule is passed by the governing bodies." <br> "We must establish an oversight committee!" |
| C | "Our children must learn more science!" <br> "Our leaders have their heads in the sand!" |
| D | "I move we celebrate this important day." <br> "Mission accomplished!" |
| E | "We will be introducing a new bonus scheme." <br> "This person is someone we should emulate." |
| F | "We are introducing a new code of conduct." <br> "We should all behave professionally." |
| G | "Our research points us in this new direction." <br> "Our funding sources seem to be in for a change." |
| H | "There will be a party this Friday afternoon to celebrate having met this sales benchmark." <br> "We have worked hard, achieved much, and deserve a rest." |

However, when we attempt to come up with behavioral items, statements or activities that would fit in cells I through L, one does not encounter many common examples. We believe that this is because the community dimension of social systems is typically ignored. Worse, what we find is that activities that are typically called "community" are usually managerial or political and thus not only ignore the community dimension but also purvey the idea that the needs for community are being met when they are not. The result: widespread dysfunction of social systems, malaise, and dissatisfaction arising from the lack of integration of the political, managerial, and community spheres.

We believe that this absence is in part due to the "unavowable" (Nancy, 1991), "inoperable" (Blanchot, 1988) "future" (Agamben, 1993) inchoate nature of community. De Mare (2011) seems to uphold this opinion in his definition of community as a state of dialogical flux. While we agree with these opinions we also believe that certain key phenomena in the experience of community can be described. Following is an attempt to delineate eight elements of community. The vibrant presence of these elements indicates the presence of the experience of community, and this experience can be used to inform the political and managerial spheres just as it will reflect them.

## Components of community

In most thinking and writing about community, it seems there is a focus on managerial (getting things done) and political (making decisions about how decisions will be made). Bataille (1991), Blanchot (1988), and Nancy (1991) point out that this overlooks the most vital aspect of the sense of community. It is a sense that is neither managerial/ pragmatic nor political-authoritative-legitimative although it overlaps with and affects both these domains. Upon what is it founded? It is difficult to point to the data in this domain since it is in Blanchot's words "unavowable"; in Nancy's language, "inoperable," and in Agamben's, "coming." Because of this is it is analogous to Winnicott's "transitional space," an area of illusion. It is in the domain of the imaginary, where one does not ask, "Is this real? Is this a symbol?" However the transitional space is of terrific importance in domains of meaning, richness, and well-being. It is the space from which culture, in the broadest sense of the word, emerges. It is the domain of the emergence of spontaneity and the true self. It can easily be crowded out but the managerial, the political, the real, and the symbolic, but at great personal and social cost. While the community is unavowable and inoperable, there are some markers, some hints at its constitution. Here are some that the above authors suggest:

Love
Death
Literature
Ritual
Myth
Sacred Spaces
Being
Identity

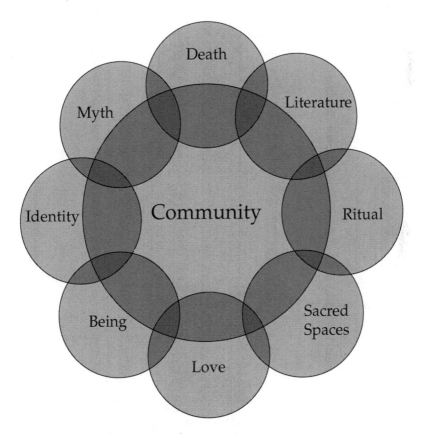

Figure 25. Particular aspects of community.

## Love

Love is unspeakable. In some respects it is absurd to write of love. But it must be spoken of. Love has its origins in an era of the unspeakable—infancy—in the relationship of mother and baby. This love then radiates outwards and suffuses the social realm. One of its destinations is the community. In technical parlance, the libido expands and has as its aim the world of the people. Erikson (1993) speaks of this occurring in the generativity–stagnation stage, alerting us to the fact that not all have such highly energized libidos and that the pathway is fraught with complexities, complexes, and paradoxes. Love holds the world together. It holds the community together as it holds the world of inner objects together. Perhaps the one mirrors the other. Longing for a coherent, cohesive, continuous, and lively self, we also long for a cohesive, continuous, coherent, and lively community.

This very desire itself is fraught with conflict. The community organizes itself around love. It might be stated as a love for one another, but it usually is symbolized and encoded in displacements and condensations. These will take the form of any of the items on the list above (love for a sacred space, for a book, for one who is dead, and so on) or it may organize itself around a myth of love—a loving couple, the love of a god for a place, person or people. The binding power of love will be captured and mythicized to hold the community. If the myth dies, is killed, shrouded over or debunked there will be a terrible disorienting period and a quest for re-mythicization. Myths will be brought forward as candidates for future community-building (often with parallel efforts in the realms of the political and managerial). This is a vulnerable period, as are all periods when a deep human drive has insufficient targets and outlets. Sometimes myths are cooked up in the attempt at re-mythicization, but these are only stopgaps. They do not meet the deep needs for love as spontaneous. It comes out of the blue. It is often "inconvenient." Romeo falls in love with the wrong girl from the wrong family. It needs fallow ground, a sort of emptiness in which to develop and this is hard to find when there is a panic at the loss of the sense of community, of the sense of what was. Sometimes there will be a return to the old myths in the hope that the gods did not really die. Again these turn out to come up empty-handed. Nostalgia, pleasurable at first, is in the last analysis, only an entertainment, only a way of killing time while waiting for the true love, the true sustaining myth.

## Death

Blanchot (1988) argues that communities are intertwined with the phenomenon of death. Death is only experienced in the community and communities seem to coalesce around a death. The first element in this assertion is bound up with Blanchot's ideas that the individual cannot experience their own death. It is only experienced by the other or by a number of others who are then tied together by this experience in a community of those who have experienced the death of an individual. To varying degrees, this death is mythicized or narrated at the very least and this comes to form the fabric of a community. We have experienced this in large groups where one of the members dies and the group takes on a funereal tone as members share their experiences of the departed. The departed and the group's experience and memories of them then serve as a binding force. This binding force is undergirded by love, for arguably, if there was no love (or love's corollary, hate) for the departed then there would be no attention paid to them and consequently no remarking of their passing away.

Freud's *Totem and Taboo* (1912–1913) introduces this idea. The death of the father establishes a fraternity. Religions are frequently founded around the death of the master, the messenger or one of the adherents. Ecstasies of passion pour forth around these memorializations, myths, rituals, and narratives.

## Literature

Blanchot (1988) posits that literature is above all a community activity. This function extends far beyond the obvious fact that when something is written and published in some form, this publication creates a communicative network of readers, a pool of commonality in a group.

Viewed from a group-as-a-whole perspective the literature (especially if it is "spontaneous" in the sense forwarded by Adorno (2001)) expresses that which is on the mind of the group mentality. It is an expression of a "social dream" which contains all the meaning for the group that the "individual dream" might contain for the individual. In this way, author is communitarian and the literature is performing a community oriented task insofar as she is expressing the dominant, albeit unconscious, concerns of the community. Just as the individual dream may contain references to traumatic experiences, so the literature of a community can articulate trauma that operates for the group-as-a-whole.

We hypothesize that at certain points in the recovery from trauma, literature, broadly conceived, becomes especially important in facilitating the process. For example, one client became almost obsessed with reading memoirs of individuals who had overcome traumatic childhoods, reading several books of this sort for many months on end. Another takes up journaling, including detailed descriptions of flashbacks of their childhood abuse. Yet another brings in to every session a sheaf of his writings for me to read while another, a teenager, shares a short story she has written. We hypothesize that the function of these goes beyond those that are commonly listed, namely, as a form of catharsis, as a means of sharing or having others witness their experience, as data that can be analyzed in a manner similar to the interpretation of dreams and as a means of encoding linguistically that which has heretofore been encoded in the non-linguistic (in the narrow sense) centers of the brain.

The function that these literary activities serve beyond those just mentioned is communal. In this we are borrowing ideas from Blanchot (1988). These dual hypotheses, namely, that literature is of essential service in the working through of trauma and that literature is a lynch-pin in the establishment of community, combined with the fact that traumatized individuals usually feel an intense sense of alienation, of ostracism of exclusion from the community, leads us to some potentially useful ideas regarding helping individuals who have suffered trauma in the context of a large group or community.

## Ritual

The ritual serves as a binder for communities. One of the ways it binds and links is that it serves as a complex symbol for many of the conflicting passions of coming together, of social living, of the realities of life, desire, and death. Freud (1928) argues that religion is akin to a massive institutionalized obsessional neurosis. Religion is replete with rituals, as is the behavior of an obsessional personality. These symptoms work rather like dreams or multilayered codes, encrypting the multiple conflicting experiences of the individual or the group or community. Winnicott astutely reminds us that when we call out "God save the King," in ritual form we are both wishing for the preservation of the

King's life and making a plea that the King should be safe from our own murderous wishes. The ritual operates beautifully on the manifest and the latent level, calming our nerves, enabling us to function, laden with meaning, should we care to examine it. The ritual, in a way is a solution to one of life's conundrums. This solution is frozen into a set, a fixed sequence, a collection of objects, performances, and behaviors arranged in space and time in a predetermined manner. This frozen solution then is set free from the original problem, much like a symptom is in an individual and the original conflict or problem is repressed (forgotten and then forgotten that it has been forgotten). And the ritual stands free from its original support. Free yet endowed with powerful meaning for woe betide anyone who should challenge or alter it or question it for this would threaten the return of the repressed and all its attendant anxiety. The group, the community, as well as the individual, would be re-traumatized. Often the group is not yet ready to deal with the re-visitation of the original conflict and the offender is dealt with summarily.

Thus, when a group unites around a ritual it is uniting around a neurotic core, around an unspeakable, unavowable conflict, desire or event (perhaps a trauma) that as in any good neurosis must be known and not known at the same time. The ritual provides the solution. This is shaky ground indeed for the formation of a community, as shaky a ground as it is for an individual or a group. It is a house built on sand and it requires nerves of steel to acknowledge this vulnerability of the community based as it is on a compromise formation, while also recognizing the necessity for some basis, some starting point (Lacan might say, some *"point du capiton"*) for the beginning of community life.

As with all of the other eight elements of community life, there is radical interpenetration. Myths require rituals. Literature includes rituals. Death is marked by rituals and so on. Thus the compromise formation penetrates all of community life. The neurotic stopgap is all around and everywhere. We are very close to joining here with Rorty (2000, 2009) who argues for an irony and a conversation that is perhaps akin to Bion's "binocular vision" in our interpretation of community.

## Myth

Communities are built around myths. Sometimes it is a founding myth, having to do with the origin of our people. Often it is ill-advised to call these myths for they are so foundational that they are taken for the real and the word "myth" implies some contingency, as if the narrative is constructed, as if it could have been otherwise. In the USA, for example, one is likely to encounter some ire if one posits that the narrative of the "founding fathers" is or functions even in part as, a myth. In these instances the myth functions much in the same way as a personal narrative that protects the individual from psychological pain. A client might enter therapy with the narrative that their parents were wonderful. Six months later that same client is discussing the extensive abuse they suffered at the hands of these selfsame parents. They experience great pain and complex difficult emotions as the narrative is exchanged and modified. Myths interact with memory. One myth blocks one set of recollections while encouraging others.

So once again we find, at the heart of the community, a dilemma. On the one hand a myth is dearly needed in order to bind the community together, form a narrative, to organize memory, experience, and hope. On the other hand, this myth serves to repress and block other memories, to negate, even before they are articulated, certain ideas, emotions, and wishes. In short the myth binds and organizes and represses and enables. Saturated with paradox and antinomy, it is unavoidable, unavowable, and inoperable. How is one to cope with this? Perhaps again, the answer is in taking up a position with binocular vision, irony. It is this irony, this openness to alternative meanings that undoes delusion, the fervent commitment to a narrative and one's role in that narrative. Irony states, "Perhaps it could be otherwise." Again, irony can go too far. The irony that is a stereotyped element of the "hipster" subculture itself serves as a self-protective myth, preventing too deep and too risky a commitment to something. The joys of commitment are thus foregone. We now find ourselves back in the horns of a dilemma, a dilemma nicely put by Perry (1981) the dilemma of commitment to that which is temporary. For anything to happen, there has to be some type of commitment. But everything is temporary thus one is certain to lose something precious if one makes a commitment. As Rank (1954) states it, we owe life a death, some of us attempt to forestall or even cheat death by not living. Perry lays out a developmental scheme where we see individuals coming to different resolutions of this dilemma at different levels of complexity. Perhaps the same schema could be applied to communities. This community; to be or not to be?

## Sacred spaces

Communities organize around sacred spaces. Nancy (1991) expands on this idea. Sometimes these spaces are wholly sacred and recognized as such by an organized religion—the wailing wall, the Ka'aba stone, the holy mount. Sometimes they are a mixture of sacred and secular—the Lincoln memorial, battle sites, Buckingham Palace. Sometimes they are natural phenomena imbued to a greater or lesser extent with the presence of the gods—Glastonbury Tor, el Capitan, Ayers Rock, the Thames. Sometimes they are quite low key and small in scale, performing the function of the encounter with the sacred on an everyday basis for a village—the swimming *cenote* for a small hamlet in rural Mexico, the brook where children swim outside an English village, the tree referred to by Haile Gebrsellassie in his autobiographical movie, *Endurance* (1999). Sometimes they are man-made and entirely adventitious— Lambeau Field, Big Ben, the Royal Albert Hall, Wrigley field. We visit these and are often surprised at the numinous, larger-than-life nature of these—the sense of history, or connection of community. Again, these "adventitious" "sacred" places can be quite small in scale and local in their binding effect—a bar used by a few blocks-worth of city residents, a farm used as a retreat for a local company, a summer camp used by a group of several hundred children and teens, a bunch of plastic flowers at the site of a fatal accident. These sites take on a larger than life quality that speaks to their role as a binder of communities. The sense of the sacred that adheres to these spaces and places speaks to the possible connection between community and the religious. These thoughts help explain why certain places take on extra meaning for certain groups and why their destruction or compromise results in such furor. It is not simply a matter of the old ways dying, for often these conflicts are interpreted as part of the grand narrative of the enlightenment, of science, which would nullify the special meaning of a place. Euclid tells us that all points are equal and even non-existent, and the advance of scientistic capitalism crushes magical tribalism. It is also a matter of a basic drive for community being thwarted and this thwarting results, as it would with any other drive (sex, food, love) with anxiety and hostile resistance. This re-formulation is perhaps useful insofar as it points the way to possible solutions, solutions which enable change while respecting this deep human urge for community, an urge which is met, in large part through the recognition and visitation of sacred spaces, sacred spaces that serve not only for expression of the religious, but (and perhaps more importantly) also for the expression and realization of the drive to community.

## Being

Being is at a deeper level than identity. In the realm of identity we are in the domain of roles and social constructions. The concept of being holds the possibility of a self-sense beyond this clearly social domain. And yet, especially when we consider Levinas (1969, 2005) and the early child developmental theories of Stern (2000) and Kohut (1971, 1977) and perhaps most importantly Winnicott (1965) we find that this realm is intensely social. For Winnicott it is the holding environment of the mother that provides the basis for the sense of going-on-being, that wonderful secure sense that one is, one has been and one will continue to be. We link this with Stern's self-sense of continuity (Stern, 2000) and it is related strongly to the secure healthy narcissism posited by Kohut. It is also connected to the concept of "ontological security" as deployed by Laing (1965). Although Lacan would have it that this reflected self is a manifestation of the falsifying function of the ego, the stabilization of this reflected image, "false" though it may be lends much comfort in the stormy seas of existence. The metaphor of the reflecting mirror is prevalent throughout these thinkers. The subject looks into the face of the other and in this gaze and its return establishes a sense of being. The content of the gaze will determine the specifics and details of the qualities of this being, but the substrate of being is essential for the latter to emerge.

The community is, once again a paradoxical place. As a reflecting mirror for the subject it has enormous power. As Connor (in Nancy, 1991, p. xxxvii) states, "Only a being-in-common can make possible a being-separated." The community can reflect back a "being affirming" beam to the subject or it can emanate nothingness. The individual can be seen or invisible, can be a somebody or a nothing. Again the community can enable the emergence of being by providing a holding environment, an environment that does not impinge upon the individual but enables for a free-floating "unintegrated state" a biopsychosocial condition of looseness that allows for the expression of the true self. On the other hand, the community might impinge upon the subject in such a way that it has to erect defenses against these incursions and fend off attacks and

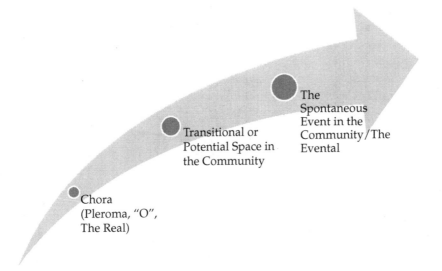

Figure 26. The flow from the chora through the transitional space to the spontaneous event in the community.

interferences, all this resulting in the emergence of a false self. This is related to the *chora* notion and community described by Kristeva (1984)—the indeterminate space, not managerial, not political, that allows for the emergence of the spontaneous semiotic and of the true self.

Figure 26 is an attempt to visualize the relationship of the chora, as formulated by Kristeva (1984), to the phenomena of being and the community. The chora is, for Kristeva, a pre-linguistic stage of child development, roughly approximating conceptually the symbiotic phase of Mahler (1975). Kristeva hypothesizes that the community can be seen as related to a group chora and that, given the opportunity, this chora will bubble up into the community discourse. For her, poetry is one of the major avenues for this to occur. We posit that the creation of potential spaces (Winnicott, 1965) in communities will enable just such translations from the chora into the conversation of the community. This movement from the pre-linguistic chora to the verbal (what Kristeva calls the "thetic phase") is significant not only in that it shifts experience into the linguistic coded form with which a community may come to terms, but also in that it is associated with the process of separation/individuation, with the assertion of the separation of subject from the object, with the process of coming into being, in this case, a coming into being not only in the presence of the mother, but also in the presence of the community. The term "coming into being" has significant resonances with Allport's work on the topic (1955).

In the diagram, we note that the chora is roughly equivalent to the "O" of Bion (1978) and the "pleroma" of Gnosticism and as attributed to Jung (Hoeller, 2012).

The translation of the chora into the transitional space of the community discourse can result in the "spontaneous gesture" (Winnicott, 1965) in a community setting. In other words, the creation of such emergent spaces enables the efflorescence of the "true self" (Winnicott, 1965) in public. In so doing, it creates the possibility for the articulation of the true self with the community. In this a step towards the lessening of the fundamental alienation of the human being from society is taken. The individual may begin to see the community as a medium through which his truest self may be realized. This establishes the potential for deep-seated feelings of gratitude in the individual for the possibilities for self-realization afforded by his community.

We also note that the spontaneous gesture in the community setting counts as an *event*. The spontaneous is out of the usual run-of-the-mill occurrences. As such it becomes a marker of something important having happened and serves as a reference point for the community. In this, we believe we are close to the thinking of Badiou (2013). We may place events into two categories. First there is the event of Badiou (2013) which is close to the concept of the event as it is being constructed here—spontaneous, puzzling, deeply significant, and perhaps inconvenient for the truth it bears from the pre-linguistic chora, or group mentality. The second type of event is a pseudo-event, a happening that has been planned for one reason or another. Adorno (2001) makes a similar discrimination between cultural phenomena that are spontaneous and of deep interpretive value and those that are products of the culture industry and are interpretable as defenses, manipulations, and attempts at oppression, indoctrination. These operate as the *psi barrier* of Bion's theory of thinking. We argue that those working with groups and especially large groups would benefit from an ability to perceive the difference between these two types of group performance.

*Identity*

We conceptualize identity as a surficial deposit overlaying being. It interacts with being in very significant ways and it interacts with the

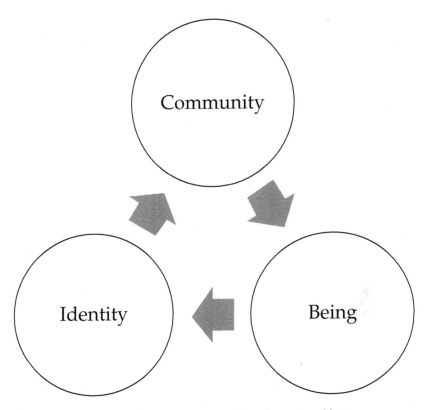

Figure 27. Interaction between community, identity, and being.

social surround. It therefore is sandwiched on the one side by being and on the other by community at all levels of definition. In addition, the previous section attempted to establish that being is determined, to a significant degree, by community. We thus have a familiar triad/cycle.

One's being, in its coherence, continuity, and cohesiveness is affected and affects community. A stable community that allows for the emergence of the spontaneous in being and that provides ample opportunities for "lying fallow" will create in its members a flowing yet stable being—a deep sense of "ontological security." In the reverse flow, a community that has, in its membership, persons who occupy influential roles who are secure in their being will have, as a result of their contributions structures and processes that facilitate the establishment of "going on being."

In a community where there is a high level of "ontological security," there will be a vibrant "flexicurity" (i.e., a flexible security) of roles. This means there will be an experienced stability and consistency of roles in the presence of dynamic role flux. Role flux is essential as the sense of being shifts and as the adaptive tasks of the community change. Again, in reverse flow, this stability and flexibility of roles will feed being and facilitate the development in the community of structures that enable the emergence of being.

Communities vary widely in the array of roles they provide to participants and in the ease with which members may enter and exit certain roles. In reverse fashion, the roles played in a community shape that community, sometimes mildly, moderately or at times and usually less functionally in a monopolistic manner.

We trust we have conveyed some of the complexity of the community enterprise, how serious it is and yet what subtlety of thought, feeling, and vision is required to negotiate it. However, it is rendered even more complex by the fact that is difficult for a variety of reasons, to think in public. We now will address some of these difficulties.

## Thinking in public

It is notoriously difficult, to think in a large group. In large part, this can be understood as emanating from the dynamics listed at the outset of this section. For example, powerful forces of splitting, projective identification, regression, attacks on linking (Bion, 1959) and scapegoating, just to mention a few dynamics, can hobble any attempt at thinking. In addition, thinking in public may evoke spoiling envy in sectors of the audience that can add fuel to the fire that can be so destructive of thinking. The human costs resulting from this difficulty of thinking in public are enormous. We can see this exemplified when a politician or leader "dares" to think about something in public, before acting or making a decision. All sorts of anxieties are stirred up and she is often attacked for being "weak" or "indecisive." I would argue that these are defenses against deeper anxieties. It is difficult to think in public, and the larger the public, the more difficult it becomes. And yet, it is so important to be able to do so, to be able to create formats where thinking in public is possible. This section will present Bion's theory of thinking and argue that it, connected with the foregoing ideas has something to offer in assisting us to think in public, especially in large groups and that this might aid in the development of the community, no matter how "inoperable," unavowable," "impossible," or "coming" it may be.

Bion's grid (1978) provides us with a theory of thinking. Stated simply, thinking commences as "bits" and these bits are connected by a linking function, the alpha function. The linking of pieces of thought continues with increasing complexity, with thoughts emerging from the "marriage" of conception and preconception (which in this context does not mean "prejudice" but the capacity for thinking a thought prior to its actually being thought, before it is "entertained"). Finally there is a theory which may be expressed in an algebraic form. The process is not always smooth. There is a "psi" function in column two that opposes this conjunction of pieces that resists linking. Curiosity, the pursuit of truth is fraught with risks, as Bion points out in his interpretation of the Oedipus myth (1978).

Bion's theory of thinking can be applied with some utility to the topic at hand. How may we think in public? Free-floating thinking can occur in an analytic or therapeutic setting. It may also occur in group-analytic settings. Less commonly is it encountered in a community meeting. Often when it occurs in a large group it is met with some shock, shocks enumerated at the outset of this paper. However, with a slight shift of perspective, it might be that the community as "O" could be a very valuable contributor to life in large groups and institutions.

Following Nancy (1991) we have argued that "community" should be differentiated from that which is "managerial" and "political." I would also argue that there is a flow of information between these three domains. Examining institutions it is apparent that the political and managerial dominate the scene and that even when there is an attempt at "community involvement" it is a thinly veiled attempt at management or politics. The community experience, as it is defined here is remarkably absent. This is quite consonant with the naïve materialist, empiricist (in the narrow sense of the word), scientistic bent of much modern business-driven, culture. Where is the conversation, and all it implies, invoking the deeper meanings of the term "conversation" forwarded by Rorty (2000, 2009) and De Mare (2011).

Absent from this, the political and managerial roll on, uninformed by community and its stirrings. When this occurs, the seeds of protest have been sown. "Community" becomes an unacknowledged underdog. At first it becomes "symptomatic," perhaps in anomie, demoralization, and socio-somatic illness and after a while the protest becomes more manifest. Perhaps at this time there is a managerial or political response, or perhaps, as Nancy (1991) seems to suggest, the drive for community overwhelms the political and managerial and there is a paroxysm, usually one with enormous social cost, such as the Nazi uprising of the twentieth century or, more recently, the real estate boom and bust or the "Arab Spring" of the early twenty-first century.

Referring to Bion's grid (see page 117), his theory of thinking, we may provide two examples of how it may be used as a "map" to help us chart the various forms of "thinking in public" we may witness in groups, especially large groups.

An easy place to start is cell A6, or as we like to call it, "the acting out cell." Cell A6 is at the intersection of "action" and "beta elements." We note that cells A3, 4, and 5 are blank, indicating no "notation," "attention," or "inquiry" has taken place. Something popped up, was interceded by the psi barrier and then an action was taken upon this alpha element, all in a manner like the reflex arc of Freud's early model (Gedo & Goldberg, 1976). No reflection or curiosity is manifested as the individual or the group "does something." This something might be as seemingly harmless as closing the door, or mounting a raid on their neighbors. Thinking, in such a group will be extremely difficult. There may even be the development of a "negative K" culture as described by Hazell (2003).

Cell E4, E5, and F4, F5 represent a kind of thinking that might be typified as more "analytic" in nature for in these spaces, the intersection of curiosity, attention, conception, and concept occur. Phenomenally this will show as individuals having new ideas, putting thoughts together in new and different ways and gaining insight. In addition, they are perhaps capable of bearing the anxiety of this mental situation and warding off the "attacks against linking" (Bion, 1959). We note that a precursor to this is a state of reverie which enables the condition of "preconception" (Row D) to emerge. This corresponds, in our thinking to the potential space that can be provided in certain types of groups, both large and small. This emergence, however rests upon the establishment of a certain type of culture, the type we find in the sophisticated group of Bion or of the "koinonia" of De Mare (2011).

## Enabling the emergence of community

Complex as the phenomena related to the enabling of community are, it is still possible and, we would argue, of vital importance. Following are some examples to help concretize procedures that allow for the emergence of community and to allow that which flows from it to inform the managerial and political spheres.

A guiding principle throughout these examples is captured in the use of the word "emergence." Winnicott informs us that the false self is that aspect of the self that emerges in response to impingements from the environment. We believe the same applies to community. While it is vital to manage the experience and set its boundaries and task, these should not impinge upon the group in such a way as to cause the group to have to fend off impingements. In other words, there should be a time of "lying fallow" in the group to enable the emergence of what is on the mind of the community at a deeper level, at the level of the chora, or the group mentality. In addition vehicles are provided, in each of these examples to make some sense of that which emerges, to think in public, to get curious and, perhaps, to take action.

Bion's experiments at Northfield, allowed for the emergence of interest groups (T. Harrison, 2000). The structure Bion describes as being part of his Northfield experiment which, fascinatingly enough, was set up to help soldiers work through what we would nowadays call PTSD, involved individuals posting interest groups that would then meet and develop activities based on the interest. Apparently it was successful and was modified by later practitioners.

Bion's approach is similar to the "open space" structure (Gould, 2006, Harrison, O., 2008) that we have used as part of a community retreat weekends. In these a large group would assemble and individuals would announce a desire to meet with others who shared their passion, interest or curiosity in a certain domain. Examples might include dance, leadership, ethnicity, nature walks, ultimate Frisbee. The groups would then meet in assigned spaces and times, and then would meet again in the large group for debriefing. Important in both of these is the allowance of a time for reflection upon what is deeply interesting to the individual who then takes the chance of announcing this in a large group in some format.

We find a similar format in the opening event of the "institutional/inter-group event" and most Tavistock conferences (Colman & Geller, 1985). Here the large group is informed that they may regroup in small groups in assigned spaces based upon interests. In addition these groups will interact with each other and with staff to examine the intra and inter-group dynamics that emerge from such formations. Throughout the focus is on examining covert processes.

Group formats that have emerged from the Tavistock tradition also enable the emergence of community. Notable among these are the "social dreaming" contexts described by Lawrence (2003) and the listening posts established to attune members of communities to issues that they confront (Gould, 2006). To this list we would also add the approach of Seikkula and Arnkil (2006) who, in their utilization of "dialogical meetings in social networks," demonstrate that severe mental illness may be circumvented through the integration of the individual into their communities. In doing this they manage to radically reduce the reliance on the long-term use of medications that is so common in the United States.

In addition, similar structures can be seen operating in some open education settings where, for example, the children might meet as a group at the start of the day and individuals and subgroups would announce their interests for say the morning, for example, making a play, caring for the animals, reading or measurement activities. Then arrangements would be made to manage these groups operating simultaneously in the room for the morning with a debriefing at the end.

The open classroom, leads us conceptually to John Dewey and the central focus the term "interest" has in his educational philosophy (Dewey, 1997). It also sparks associations to his definition of freedom, as the capacity of the individual to frame purposes and carry them into effect (Dewey, 1998, pp. 302–314). The purposes should clearly belong to the individual, to their true self, not their false self, and this circles us back to Winnicott.

Building community involves the creation of a "floating analytic space" in the organization or political unit and having this flow into the other two sets. Thus, in the examples above, the initial large group meeting serves as a vehicle for the emergence of the spontaneous interest and its articulation with the community. This "bottom-up" approach stands in contrast to much community building effort that attempts a "top down" approach, often prescribing activities or ideological notions that would impose "community" rather than letting it emerge.

Emery and Trist (1965), in positing that organizations inhabit a chaotic environment, lead us to the idea that institutions and other groups need, in order to begin to successfully adapt to this context, to enable conversational spaces like the ones we describe here thus creating a discourse parallel to and informing of the managerial and political discourse in organizations.

Czochara, Semmelhack, and Hazell (2016) describe a group conducted in the Tavistock tradition that involved seventeen to twenty-five individuals all of whom were diagnosed with severe mental illness. The group met monthly for well over a year and participants were questioned as to their experience towards the group and their attitudes towards it. Large groups are not usually recommended for individuals with severe diagnoses, especially if the group involves the examination of unconscious dynamics. The results, which showed an entirely positive response, are therefore surprising. However, if we accept some of the notions presented in this section, such findings make sense. The free-floating attention, the "dialogue" (to use De Mare's felicitous term) (De Mare, 2011) enabled individuals to link with a community with all of its complexity and dynamism. Far from being ego-destructive, this experience was ego-enhancing for the participants and continues to be so at the time of writing. This experiment suggests that elements of the Tavistock approach are useful, if introduced and managed correctly in facilitating the sense of community.

The study cited above (Czochara, Semmelhack, & Hazell, 2016) seemed to show that the Tavistock style median group helps evolve the sense of community in ways very akin to the dynamics described by De Mare (2011). The group engaged in a dialogue or a discourse in which multiple perspectives were brought to bear on the understanding of the group in the here and now. In this we saw many parallels with Bakhtin's ideas (1982) on the novel as a dynamic exchange of multiple voices, clamoring in their attempts to offer ideas on what is going on in the world. The groups felt like creativity in the making. At times they would veer towards problem-solving, or political vying (the political and managerial aspects of groups) but the tonic note was always the here and now and the unending dialectic of the dialogue of the group.

All of the elements of community listed earlier in this section were present in this group. The group very frequently would have moments of "sacredness" as a member might break into a hymn, or a prayer, or when an individual wished to share a religious chant he had learned. Since the group included several old members, death of a member was not uncommon and this death became a vital part of the group's process and had, predictably, a powerful binding force on the group. The group would often participate in the staging of plays and musicals. These always carried deep meaning for the members and these would be discussed at length in the group. Thus literature, ritual, and myth became lively threads that wove through the fabric of the group.

For all of its liveliness, the group was not a "forced" environment. There would be periods of "fallowness" and out of these people would share something quite spontaneously. In these moments it seemed as though the group provided a transitional space which enabled members to be become unintegrated in public and to share with their community whatever came to mind. Winnicott argues that this is extremely beneficial since it enables the individual to get in touch with deep impulses and organize themselves around these, thus giving a deep sense of aliveness and meaning to the lucky individual. We believe we witnessed this multiple times in this large group. Individuals frequently expressed gratitude for the group meetings and we hypothesize that the gratitude was for the facilitation of the experience of spontaneity in a community that could welcome and support it.

Such experiences of spontaneity, involving the activation of treasured parts of the self are very close to what Marx (1965) is writing about in his early concept of alienation. Unalienated work, according to Marx is work that enables the individual to realize his or her true nature and to connect with others through their work. Unalienated labor is work that springs from the "true self," of Winnicott (1965). The experience of community in the sense being described here thus might help participants to articulate their "true selves" with the society around them, with the median or large community group as a "nursery" for hatching and developing these ideas and actions.

# CHAPTER ELEVEN

# Fears and wishes on partnering and working as a team

*Clive Hazell and Mark Kiel*

T his section is an exploration of the dynamics of our work together. This book is a product of a pairing, a pair attempting to come to grips with some problems in group dynamics. We both strongly believe that it takes a group to understand a group and therefore endorse group projects aimed at this important task. Perhaps an examination of some of the processes involved in our collaboration might be helpful to others endeavoring to pursue similar projects.

The section is structured as an open forum.

## Clive Hazell

I think it will be helpful to think through the fears and wishes of our work together by following loosely the FABART template.

An important feature of our pairing is our age difference. I am sixty-seven at the time of writing. Dr. Kiel (Mark) is forty-two. I first met Mark as a student some twenty years ago when I was teaching at the Illinois School of Professional Psychology. This combination of age difference and authority difference at the outset of our relationship contributes to fantasies on my part. Over the years, Mark has increased in authority and has, at various times had authority over me as a conference leader or as the leader of extended group weekends held under the auspices of the school. It was my perception that these shifts in authority were accomplished with relatively little anxiety or acting out. To some extent this may have resulted from my being extra careful to play the role of what I considered to be a good mentor, namely one that is heartened when the mentee outstrips the mentor. This satisfaction of seeing Mark "do well" and carry the much-valued torch of Tavistock knowledge and practice into the future far outstripped any diminution in role and status I may have experienced. In some ways I think I was prepared for this transition by my father and father figures I have had who were not narcissistically injured by my accomplishments. In addition, the culture of "British understatement" which discourages seeking the limelight offered assistance in this regard. My role as "immigrant" in the USA somewhat prepares me for the role of supporter as does my arrival into psychology via another discipline, geography.

We thus found our collaboration to proceed well, despite the differences in generations and authority. Our collaboration was relatively sealed off from others, being only publicly announced at a group relations conference when the book was some three-quarters written. Thus the issues of envy and shame over the pairing, that Kernberg (1994) so nicely delineates were avoided. To what extent this was a defensive maneuver has yet to be seen.

Towards the end of the project external circumstances made it very easy for me to work on the book and made it very difficult for Mark. This difference did feed into my fantasies. I have a history of partners, friends, colleagues, and father figures "breaking down" under pressure. Several of my close friends suffered what were then called "nervous breakdowns" when facing final exams of various sorts. PTSD flashbacks have claimed the careers of several colleagues causing them to be hospitalized just as the point of success was reached. Thus Mark's slowness in responding to my emails as the final deadline approached stirred up some powerful and painful emotions that I felt I had to manage on my own. This handling it on my own, in addition, was part and parcel of the origin. These "breakdowns" of predominantly male partners and authority figures were also felt to be undiscussable, it seemed, bearing, as they did, such potent affects of shame, guilt, and anger. The shame seemed to be about the agonizing process of losing control in public. The guilt involved letting others down and, on my part, of being a survivor, still able, more or less, to function. The anger is deeper and has to do with being left alone to finish the job, of losing a friend, colleague or father figure. It is deeper since it is in conflict with the feelings of affection one has and with the wish not to kick someone while they are down. The coping mechanisms I developed for these feelings were to examine them, spell them out, look for their causes and, as I did in the past, almost obsessively focus on the task, resolving to myself that if worst came to worst I could finish on my own. These adaptations were accompanied by a mild depressive affect.

I hasten to emphasize that all the foregoing is my fantasy. Mark gave no evidence whatsoever of having any breakdown. He was just very busy and slow to respond to my emails. This was enough to stimulate my reactions.

Another fantasy involved in our collaboration is narcissistically driven. It is a narcissism combined with an oedipally tinged rebellion. I imagine this book to be a measured challenge to the status quo of Tavistock routine. Even the title includes the term, "beyond the frame." As such it is a questioning of the status quo. As we write this as a pair, the fantasy extends to us being two brothers teaming up to change the order of things. We do so in the politest of ways but perhaps are only able to do it as a couple, giving each other the courage to take a step forward, as it were, to stand up and be counted.

This pair has created a child—a "brainchild." As such we are perhaps subject to some of the fantasies and feelings linked to the basic assumption pairing group of Bion (1961). Basic assumption pairing seems to operate in groups as a sort of anti-depressant. The pair offers hope of deliverance—of a special child that will grow to redeem and aid its native group. I link with this fantasy insofar as I believe Tavistock ideas have a tremendous amount to offer the world, yet at times its ideas seem strangely beleaguered and ignored. This links with an anxiety lest these ideas die and this ties in with the importance of generativity in the "Tavistock movement," a concern that this set of ideas should continue. However, it will not continue if it becomes a rigid set of rituals. It must develop and to do this it must be an open system, becoming more complex as it integrates new ideas and broadens its horizons. However, this openness should probably not be indiscriminate such that the core identity of the Tavistock approach is compromised and its potency diminished.

The pair is thus placed in an ambiguous position being all at the same time a holder of hope, a harbinger of change and yet also representing a potentially debilitating alterity. I felt the pressure as Mark and I did this work to sustain a useful balance between these two possibilities; on the one hand bringing in news from outside, from "beyond the pale," but yet on the other hand not wanting to be too different, too oddball, too far out.

Boundaries, roles, and authority factored into our pairing. The boundaries around our task were quite clear. Mark and I had hardly any contact outside of our work together. Meetings over the book were about two hours in length. They were free-ranging discussions but always on task and did not extend into any informal realms beyond simply catching up on latest developments in our lives. It was rather like some friendships I have with people with whom I only play racquetball. We meet, talk briefly, play, talk briefly, and then part company. The relationship is warm, friendly, and open. It is episodic and task oriented. I find this pattern of relatedness common amongst my colleagues who work in the Tavistock tradition. It is as if there is carefulness regarding staying on task. This carefulness does not feel overly defensive; perhaps it is just a protectiveness of the task fueled by a sharp awareness of how a rational task can get overtaken by irrational forces if one does pay close attention to FABART.

As to the collaboration, there were clear boundaries implied in who wrote which chapters and thus who had authority and authorship. However, it was not a situation of "parallel play." We read each other's material and in meetings had free and far ranging discussions of the material. These meetings were extremely stimulating and encouraging of my creativity and even daring. This model of autonomy and exchange worked well for us, I believe.

I have published several books before. This is Mark's first. This placed me somewhat in the position of someone in the know. It gave me some authority. This gradient was not so significant in the early phases of the project, but, as the deadline approached I became aware of the tremendous amount of detail work in the last stages of production—things like editing, permissions, tables to be properly prepared, references verified. These always take me by surprise at how long they take, perhaps because once the book is "written" there is a tendency to think one is done. I wished to impart this urgency to Mark, but felt that this would disrupt our egalitarian arrangement and push me into the role of "nudge" and "micromanager." I was also aware that Mark was undergoing some stress in his work and that it was I who, that previous summer, had prepared and sent out the proposals to publishers thus setting the deadline for production. I adjusted to this by simply plugging along at my tasks and hoping for the best. I had seen Mark work under extreme pressure many times before. He had always acquitted himself admirably. There was good reason to think all would be well this time too.

One belongs to many groups at the same time. When I formed a pair with Mark in order to write this book, my membership in other groups was affected. Most of the time this passed by unnoticed but with one group it produced a strong reaction. This group was my family and especially the pairing with my wife. The time demands of this book increased significantly towards the last stages of writing and this took away from my intimate time with my wife. This lead to my having to be creative in finding times when writing would not eat into our time together. Despite this there was still tension in our relationship—a triangle with me, my wife, and "the book" at the apices. Towards the end I found myself looking forward to a time when it would all be done. However, in my heart of hearts, I knew there were several other books "in the pipeline" that I intended to write in the coming years.

## Mark Kiel

Perhaps it is cliché, obvious, or simply a lesson learned and re-learned, but from the inception of this book, parallels between the writing collaboration and consulting in a dyad or partnership struck me from the onset. To flesh out the learnings from such a parallel, from its earliest drafts, a chapter on partnership, collaboration, wishes and fears comparing and contrasting the writing partnership with consulting in a pair was a planned chapter. However, unlike all of the other chapters, little was discussed, planned or reconfigured on the topic. Rather, Clive and I noted our perceptions, phantasies, and processes of working on the project and wrote about them without sharing specifics until the book's first draft was due. My experiences clustered around the three basic phases of the project, the beginning, middle, and end.

The beginning: Since 1996, I have worked in one capacity or another with Clive Hazell. First as a student of his in graduate school, then as a junior staff member in group relations conferences, then as fellow faculty in the same graduate program, as a director of group relation events on which he served on staff, and as a coordinator in the Personal and

Professional Development program in which we both taught in and ran groups. As I was writing the first of the essays that would later become chapters, I began thinking this project would be much better if it were a collaboration. I immediately thought I would like to work on it with Clive. Yet, I continued working independently for much of the summer. After sharing one of the essays with a colleague and admitting I was not sure what to do with the collection of thoughts and theses, I said I was thinking about sharing the project with Clive and asking him to co-write with me on the effort in some way, shape or form. My colleague, knowing of my affection and respect for Clive, asked why I was hesitating in pitching the idea to him. I don't remember what I said in the moment, but I do remember the next few days. Each time I thought of the project I experienced an irrational insecurity. The scenarios all ended with Clive politely declining and me being left with a vague sense that my ideas and thoughts were not good enough. Preoccupied by this thought, one that was vastly different of then my actual past experiences with him, I emailed a draft of the first "meditations"—the book was originally designed as a set of very discrete explanations of specific group phenomena—along with some thoughts on the project to Clive. He readily responded that he was interested in the project and looked forward to working with me. Yet my anxiety and the dynamic around partnering were not on lost me.

Although I have run, led, and consulted to groups as an individual, these days I much prefer working in pairs, triads or in teams. Theoretically, I, like others, contend it takes a group to understand a group. In some ways, working with a consulting partner or consulting team is like other relational dynamics (perhaps you were aware of how the anxiety I recounted at the beginning of this section could have sounded like the fears of asking someone on a date, to become a friend, or to ask for help), but in a number of ways the dynamics of consulting and working in a team in a Tavistock learning group are unique. Consider: Groups, by their nature, are conducted, in a sense, in public. A collection of people witness and participate in the endeavor. This applies to the members and the consultants. Groups, by their nature, require "teamwork"—or more technically, interdependent collaboration. This too applies to the members and the consultants. Yalom (2005) suggested there is only one "group issue"—trust—and it is revisited time and again at different levels, much like a spiral staircase, that is, "I trusted the group enough to do *that* ... but now do I trust us enough to do *this*." And (as you probably can anticipate), this group issue of trust goes for consultants too.

Perhaps, as this was the first book I was attempting, I made an ideal repository for these insecurities (although it is interesting that I had no such feelings as the book application and sample chapters were sent to publishers). And having the belief I needed Clive's help more than he would need mine certainly spiked feelings of dependence. That all said though, it mostly reminded me of consulting for the first time in pairs and on large group teams—I often have the experience that no matter how much preparation, joining or familiarizing I and others might do before a conference, the "rubber hits the road" when we entered into the "here and now" and we work together, watch each other's blind spots, and challenge shaky or under-supported hypotheses—or we don't. As I wrote earlier in the Gibbs' chapter, I was also keenly aware of the "Tavistock dilemma" for members and staff alike—the double, oftentimes maddening task of contributing to the group mentality and attempting to understand it at the same time. Clive and I had a very generative and supportive relationship running groups, conferences, and events together, but would that transfer to a collaboration that was "out of time" and had very different boundaries? We had no deadlines to start, there was no overt institutional authority, and the roles needed time to develop. All matters much more diffuse compared to the clarity and definition of working in conference.

When I take a figurative step back and look at what I wrote and thought about in this phase of the process, many parallels and derivatives are clear to me both personally and professionally. Personally, my hesitancy to depend on "older" men for open-ended or ongoing endeavors was activated. My self-assessment that my writing style is a bit of mystery to me—seemingly coming and going on a schedule I did not have access to was a concern. As was striking a balance between having ideas and commentary that was worth articulating and sharing with others, while leaving room for the unexpected, the contribution of the other or the group and being open to what I did not know I needed.

Professionally, these matters manifest in consulting tensions I think about a lot:

- Working in the mirror—To consult, one needs to hold a multiplicity of dynamics without being rigid or preconceiving the origins of dynamics prematurely. The reflections and projections are manifold: between members and consultants, between the members as well as between the consultants.

- Alone with others—While consulting I am often surprised by the contrast between how much I think I observe and how little data I may have access to. Although said by others more originally or succinctly, this is the toggling phenomena between the potential for intersubjectivity and the limitations of absolute subjectivity.
- Working in public—As mentioned, group work is something of a public, or at least shared act. The dynamics of shame, voyeurism, and exhibitionism, discord, and vulnerability can be magnified in a public setting. As too can be the dynamics of interdependence, trust, accomplishment, and authenticity.
- Surrender—A colleague of mine often says to be a "groupie" means needing to have a "considerable capacity for risk-taking"—I think, in part, meaning the vicissitudes of group life, including the unexpected, creative, and genuine processes groups are known for are inherently harrowing at times. To work and live in these environments means surrendering the notion that these dynamics can be made certain, mechanical or anxiety-free.

The middle: The middle of the project was a joy for me. For about two years Clive and I met about every four months to review our work and plot the next step. The concept for the book changed and took a new shape, ideas and concepts were rearranged, added to, and discarded. It was enjoyable as we refined long contemplated pet theories, discovered new ground and gave each other feedback—sometimes swapping sections or chapters as it felt productive. There was a timeless quality to this stage as no external or artificial demands impinged on us. We both had multiple jobs, life changes, and other commitments, so we worked on the project as we were able to or so moved to and let it progress at what seemed an organic pace. The process was expansive and both of us commented at different times that end points would need to be considered thoughtfully as the complex nature of the project, coupled with the enjoyment of the process, could overtake the primary task of the writing and publishing the work product. We were working on publishing a book that someone may find useful or informative, not simply finding a reason to relate, collaborate or be engaged in a vacuum!

Writing and rereading the paragraph above reminded me a number of things. It reminds me of the stage of love that sometimes happens to people after they have met and have hit it off and before they leave the cocoon of the relationship that is all about them and has nothing yet to do with the outside world. Other associations included Kohut's concept of "twinship" (Kohut, 1971, 1977) as I recall the time. I thought that despite our differences a strong theme of similarity emerged in this stage. Although it was never a relationship that had much room for personal disclosures or free time spent together, we began person-ally checking in/updating each other about our lives more than at any other time in the process. Some of our life changes paralleled each other in process, if not in content, and our differences in ages (always more pronounced to me) and culture (seemingly less so) seemed minimized. Finally, this stage reminded me of the type of group process and cohe-sion that members feel after the hard work of risk-taking happens. Often this is characterized by a work stance that is beneficial and pro-ductive and which is achieved only after genuine effort and honesty has been put forth. In the Kleinian (1975) sense, the work in the mid-dle of the project brought up associations to feelings of gratitude and devotion that gather after poignant, depressive anxieties are worked through.

Again, when I take a figurative step back and look at what I wrote and thought about in this phase of the process, the parallels and deriva-tives intersect between the personal and the professional. Personally, a long-standing wish to have an "unfettered" creative process was activated for me. Between the demands of graduate school, starting an interesting if not demanding professional life, and being an all-around particular and demanding sort of person with my own priorities, hav-ing something "out of time," moved by interest and passion—not deadlines—was idealized. So too was the wish to freely share some-thing special with a collaborator who I trusted. (Not incidentally, it was during this time of work that I got engaged and married!). Near the end of this time, Clive and I worked together in a group relations confer-ence. Although we were on separate teams on a very large staff, we did get some opportunities to interact and work together and I remember the phantasy of a "secret code" between us as once or twice in pass-ing we referenced a concept from the book as an event or interaction regarding the conference experienced was being processed. This con-jured longings for a "chum" as Sullivan writes about (1953) at different times in my life that was never quite realized.

As a Tavistock consultant this part of the process and my reactions to it focused me on dynamics of:

- BA: pairing: On one hand, pairing is oftentimes necessary to the start of groups. They provide a sense of safety to the pair, afford an avenue for discourse to begin and often represent the first subgroups forming in the collective. Yet, even focused, dedicated, and rational pairs have a defensive quality, even if full-scale BA: pairing is not a group-wide defense. A common but sometimes under-attended dynamic to these instances include an over-cathecting of the pair that prevents a shift from a working pair or working group to that of a sophisticated pair or sophisticated work stance for the group.

  The two most common dynamics of this "stalling" include:
- Twinship as a distortion and defense: As Kohut (1971, 1977) suggests, twinship is a natural and necessary stage to build ego, investigate primary narcissisms as well as more general narcissistic needs. This can be true in groups, but can also be true of groups. Either in formal BA: pairing, more discrete repository functioning, or in the case of Clive and I, it can serve as a defense against widening the scope of interpretation, perspective, and activities that is required for a shift to a more sophisticated dynamic.
- Phantasies of utopia and the meeting of sentient needs: After hard work, groups need "breathers." They also need to integrate the new ways of relatedness that come from understanding previous irrational and BA functioning. Yet, there is a time after having been "in the fox hole" with each other and making it through the demands and stressors that a sentiment of "we have made it to the other side" emerges. This blurs the motive between enjoying the work of the group and the appreciation of the group work that continues to further its primary task.

To further this last point, I have recognized while consulting, I have the tendency to interpret or identify that dynamic quickly and tend to urge the group in some manner not to "sit on their laurels" too long. I note this, because in large part, this was not something I attended to in this collaborative process. Quite the contrary, as Clive hinted and encouraged a shift out of the pairing/utopia/sentient needs dynamics, I was slow and resistant to his suggestions, in retrospect, not quite ready to say goodbye to the idealized time as I saw it.

End: Not surprisingly, the end phase to this project has been fairly difficult for me. In my mind, the change in phases was triggered as Clive took the initiative in assembling the applications and sample chapters for submission. Although I had taken point on submitting chapters for presentation at conferences, this task was, in hindsight, a necessary "nudge" out of our business as usual routine. Although there were pragmatic reasons for a change in work style for me at this time (I changed jobs, moved, and needed to serve as an interim leader during a colleague's illness) my production of work slowed in pace and amount, as did the meetings and contact between Clive and I. I wrote four-fifths of three different chapters and experienced writer's block as to how to finish them. As I slowed, Clive sped up. I had a series of reactions I kept to myself. The first was that having worked on the material for so long before sharing it, Clive was simply "catching up." Then as some time past and his work continued, I felt pangs of inadequacy. Clive had written and co-written so many books compared to me I assumed he knew how to "turn it on" when he needed to—something I was still learning. My final machination paralleled a dynamic I sometimes struggle with when consulting in a pair or team. Early in my career as a consultant at Tavistock conferences I was quick to make consultations, quick to build on colleagues' consultations, and would sometimes make a consultation for the simple sake of voicing my presence to colleagues (to a greater extent) and members (to a lesser extent) if I had been quiet, lost, or otherwise gridlocked for an extended period of time.

Over the years, I came to consider some of these tendencies, some of the time, as about my insecurities, my ego needs, and for my protection. Whereas I still think there are appropriate circumstances to consult in those fashions and for those reasons, these days I think I have less "tendencies" and am more apt to try to respond to the data and group as unique. I am more willing and able to check "my tendencies" at the door much in the vein of Bion's (1961) "… without memory desire or understanding …" stance. This is a long way of getting around to my third reaction to Clive's acceleration and my deceleration. I wondered if he and I had created a platform or a forum with this book that allowed Clive to thrive. The thoughts were, "he's crushing it, check your ego Mark, and enjoy witnessing someone in the zone do his thing." It was as if my job became giving him space to do his job.

(Note that this was written before I read his experience of this time and this dynamic).

Well, given the rich phantasy life shared above, again, many of the processes parallel consulting dynamics. In retrospect, many of the features from our joining and work phases remerged here at the "end stage," less digested, less considered, and from my point of view, under-articulated and under-interpreted. The insecurities of writing "my first book," and "being dependent" on Clive re-emerged in new guises. So too did my resistances and phantasies from the utopic middle phase, especially the BA: pairing and twinship dynamic—more overtly defensive and irrational than in their first manifestation. My comment above regarding how the pleasure, acceptance or complicity with the state of a working pair and how it can hinder the development of a sophisticated work stances rings particularly clearly for me.

I am also aware that as a consultant these matters manifest in consulting tensions as well:

- "There and Then" *vs.* "Here and Now": As someone trained in the Tavistock tradition, the overt focus on the "Here and Now" tends to draw my hermeneutic lens away from the "There and Then." Yet, the same tenets of the model draws me to the focus of psychosocial lawfulness, the sequence, the cause related to the effect. The shifting, including the non-linear shifting, between the two lenses is a discipline practiced but infrequently perfected.

Related to the above, and not surprisingly given some of the material in the existential chapter, I have both a personal and consultative tension regarding the ending of groups. On one end of the continuum I think the "here and now" should be mined for every last minute of life. On the other, the denial of ending, of death, including an absence of looking back somehow seems even more incomplete, less reality bound.

### Clive Hazell: reaction to Mark's thoughts on partnering

I was struck by several aspects of Mark's reactions to our partnership. First I recognize the hesitancy in asking another person to collaborate. I have felt similar concerns myself when wanting to work with others, especially when that other is an older male. This is, I think a very complex anxiety, perhaps driven by wishes and fears of partnering with a father figure who might accept or reject one's requests. Either acceptance or rejection is potentially fraught with strong emotions. Rejection implies the pain of loss while acceptance evokes possibilities of closeness and of growth. These can lead to new horizons, new challenges and this can stimulate anxiety in the form of the fear of the new.

From my side, I have always been very impressed with Erikson's (1965) notion of generativity and its assumption that the healthy middle-aged person will want to assist, mentor, sponsor, and collaborate with younger generations. This, I believe, along with Erikson, is a drive, akin to the several other drives psychologists posit, and should thus be built into institutional and communal life.

I was struck by Mark's allusion to stages in romantic relationships, when he refers to the "bubble" phase of our partnership, when we did not have to worry too much about the outside world and we felt free to brainstorm together during our meetings. I agree that there was a somewhat regressive tug to this playful phase of our partnership. It did feel like something of a "wake-up-call" to actually prepare the drafts for publishers and assemble mailing lists, that is, to attend to the realities of the outside world. I was aware that this regressive tug was such that I had to use force of will, almost akin to a reaction formation, to make it start to happen.

Pursuing the "stages of a relationship" model suggested by Mark, I found that the final stages of the writing process, where we actually sent the final draft off to the publishers presented strains of a subtle nature. I found myself feeling rather like an "empty-nester," when the children, now adolescents, have gone off to college. What would I do with the free time I now had? I could return to those I had temporarily abandoned, my wife, and reinstate more intimate time. I found that she herself had adapted by joining a book club and by taking on more patients. In addition I found myself taking longer walks with my dog, and, while on those walks, planning the next book or books.

I am used to writing books and used to them selling but a few copies. I therefore have tamed, at least consciously, some of the narcissistic concerns and strivings related to the writing and publishing process. At this writing, Mark and I have not decided on issues such as whose name goes first or whether or not chapters should be labeled with our names. I think these concerns are eclipsed by the deep sense of gratitude I have for the working relationship with Mark and the opportunity it has afforded me to think things through.

Bion (1978) posits that there are three types of relationships; symbiotic, parasitic, and commensal. *Commensal* is rather like the parallel play one observes in children or in strangers working side by side and not collaborating. *Parasitic* is a relationship where one organism is a host and the other a parasite, resulting in the destruction of both parties. *Symbiosis* is a relationship where both parties grow and benefit each other. Samuel Beckett (who was an analysand of Bion's), when asked what *Waiting for Godot* was all about, replied that it was all about symbiosis. In the very best sense of the word, my working relationship to Mark was, like that of Vladimir and Estragon in Beckett's play, a productive, functional, modulated symbiosis.

## Mark Kiel: reaction to Clive's thoughts on partnering

I too was struck by several aspects of Clive's reactions to our partnership. Clive commented on his generativity and the focus on being a "good mentor." This comment made me reflect on how I did not renegotiate my role with Clive (both internally as well as with him) enough on the onset of the project. It was as if our history, previous work together, and personal affections were enough. In a sense they were—I think we produced something of value—but in a sense it could have been a bit easier and efficient on my part. I don't think I identified my drive to be a "good protégé" and "good partner" directly enough. Clive had been so generous over the years with my training and maturation and general fellowship I really wanted to give something back to him, and as I wrote above, I think it added a pressure that resulted in the opposite for a time.

Clive also spoke of Erikson's lifespan model and it made me reflect on a quote that has been in my head for the duration of the book project. Jung referred to age forty as "the noon of life" (Jung, 1966, p. 74)—the meridian between the first and second halves of life (Austrian, 2013). The book was started roughly when I was thirty-eight and is finished as I turn forty-two. As I have referenced, this was also a stage of my life when I got married and changed some aspects of my career. Whereas I initially associated the quote with literal turning forty, it resonates with me now as more associated with period of time and with another quote by Jung (1966, p. 75) about this phase, "The transition from morning to afternoon means a revaluation of the earlier values."

Two re-evaluations in particular come to mind. The first was leaving the graduate program I had taught over the past ten years and where I practiced much of group consulting in various classes and experiential learning events. I felt a need to practice Tavistock learning groups elsewhere, in other formats and to pursue diverse venues for this type of work and thinking (including this book, more conference work, and different teaching platforms). The second re-evaluation was more subtle but it included the vague goal of doing less of "what I was supposed to do" and more of "what I wanted to do" professionally. This was something I perceived Clive had done a few years previously and admired. In that sense, this book project was a tangible representation of that shift.

The last association has to do with Clive's comments about the "breakdowns" of others being "undiscussable." For me "my babies" were undiscussable. Literally, I am due to have my first child within one month of the submission of the manuscript. This is a great joy to me, one that I did not think were "in the cards" for me as my life progressed, but something that fills me with incredible amounts of joy, humility, and poignancy. The book and the child being due so close to each other have fused in my mind heralding this new chapter in life. The previously "undiscussable" part was that as timelines with my family, career, and other opportunities changed and altered my availability to work on the book, I did not want to signal that the work on the book was any less important, to the point of a pseudo-denial. "Pseudo" in so far the work on the book never stopped, but "denial" in the sense I struggled to directly comment on the demands and changes in real time to better orient Clive to the shifts and changes in my availability.

I think it is also important to identify one more dynamic. This book is the last of several professional goals I had put forth to myself over the past five years. And much like Clive's reference to the empty nest, I found myself asking what is next? However, whilst asking myself that, I have also found myself making some new commitments and exploring new possibilities I previously thought unlikely or foreclosed. And that has been the most consistent experience I have had with Clive. Time spent, work done, and connections made with him have opened personal and professional horizons in an organic, but also very powerful and life-changing way. I consider myself very lucky and immensely privileged for this.

## End note

Whereas this section is presented through points of views that are intrapsychic and interpersonal as much as from a group-as-a-whole paradigm, we hope that the implications and applications for utilizing FABART, and the work and perspective that accompany it, is evident. FABART is an important toolset in Tavistock work, but the anagram— for all its utility—can be difficult to present in all its potential complexity. We hope this chapter affords the reader the opportunity to glimpse some of this "process" in slightly different, but hopefully relatable fashion.

# Why Tavistock groups are well-suited to the learning task

## Graduate students

The utility of the Tavistock experience as a training method has been written about by Ganzerain (1989) and Semmelhack, Ende, and Hazell (2013). Several training programs have the participation in a Tavistock conference as a focal element in their educational program (footnote, Northwestern, Argosy and Teachers College). The writings above focus on the usefulness of the Tavistock experience in helping practitioners become aware of transference/countertransference issues, the dynamisms of projective identification and the related process of scapegoating or repository and the encounter with primary process thinking and primitive emotional states. The argument is that the Tavistock experience can provide practitioners with an educational exposure to these phenomena in a safe environment where there is adequate emotional and cognitive holding to be able to make use of them and potentially transfer them to other clinical settings. At the time of going to press, we are unaware of any empirical studies to demonstrate the potential validity of these assertions. This section, while it does not seek to provide such empirical findings (which would be more than welcome) does aim to provide a description of several other ways beyond those covered in the above-mentioned writings in which experience of a Tavistock group might be a good educational tool for psychological practitioners.

## FABART

We use the acronym, "FABART" when providing introductory didactic material to students about to experience the Tavistock approach. The letters stand for the following concepts:

Fantasies
Affect
Boundaries
Authority
Roles
Tasks

We encourage students to use this as a sort of a checklist when assessing group-as-a-whole phenomena. The concepts are described in some detail as applied to family dynamics in Hazell (2006) but following is a brief synopsis.

"Fantasies" refers to the imaginings, both conscious and unconscious, that might be present in the group. Thus the group might have the fantasy that the consultant is a mad professor carrying out some weird social science experiment on them or they might imagine that they are being secretly filmed. Bion's basic assumptions fit in this category, insofar as the group might have the fantasy that the consultant is a shepherd leading and protecting her flock, or that another group is out to attack them, or that they contain in their members, a magical couple that will deliver them from evil.

Affect refers to the feelings in the group. These might be mild or intense, energized or dull, persistent or fleeting. They may be acknowledged or unnoticed. There may be a predominance of certain feelings and a notable absence of others. For example, the feelings of anger and boredom might be quite common, but the feelings of tenderness and concern might be absent.

"Boundaries" refers to the multiple boundaries experienced in a group setting. It has to do with membership in the group. Who is in, who is out? An important boundary exists between the consultants and the membership. This is a formal boundary, but the group may have established an informal boundary amongst its members, say, between the males and females, the old and the young, rich and poor, black and white and so on. There is an important boundary between what is private to oneself and what is public in the group. How is this managed?

"Roles" refers to the roles being played in the group. Some of these will be formal roles, such as consultant, member or student. Others will be informal, such as the group "cheerleader" or the group "nurse" or "den mother." Sometimes members will be familiar with these roles and play them with relative ease. At others members might find themselves pushed into unfamiliar roles in the group or into roles that are not consistent with their conception of their personality.

"Authority" for some is the prime focus of the Tavistock tradition— the examination of authority in groups. We are of the opinion that it is an integral part of group life and one that interacts importantly with all the other phases mentioned here. It refers to power in the group—who has it? How is it established and maintained? What are the legitimizing processes? What are the attitudes towards authority and its corollary, followership? In what ways are authority related to task? Is the system authoritarian? What functions do the patterns of authority serve? Who sets the rules in the group? Are these rules discussable? Do they serve the task?

"Task" refers to the work that the group is engaging in to realize its goals. There will be a stated task, hidden agendas, and unconscious agendas. These are usually in some degree of conflict. The relationship to the stated task usually is ambivalent and this accounts for much of the reason why groups so frequently do not reach their goals, or, at best, do not reach them on time. Tavistock groups usually have a single task, namely, examining the group dynamics in the here and now. Sometimes there are add-on features to this task but this situation is much simpler than in most groups where there are usually multiple complex tasks, often at odds with one another.

A straightforward scanning of this list when one is in a social situation usually yields an insight or an idea as to its functioning and one's role in that system. One quickly sees the systemic nature of the group, how authority, for example, relates to boundary, role, affect, task, and fantasy. Everything in a system relates to everything else.

One also very quickly escapes from the "numbing sense of reality" and from the "myth of individuality" that pervades so much psychology. One can using a form of "binocular vision" arrive at different explanations for behavior in seeing that it is driven not only by intrapsychic forces but also by these very powerful social dynamics.

These awarenesses are of vital use to the professional psychologist even if they do not work with groups. The FABART checklist will provide useful insights into the dyadic counseling situation and will, importantly, help counselors spell out for their clients some of the social dynamics they encounter in their workplaces, communities, families, and other institutions that might be giving them difficulty. Such insight can be of great use, we believe to the clinical psychologist or counselor.

Often, in our discussions of the Tavistock approach with other psychologists, it is contrasted with the person-centered approach. This juxtaposition is based on the tendency of the Tavistock consultant to offer interpretations that address unconscious dynamics in the group-as-a-whole while the person-centered approach offers comments aimed at the individual that are either part of the person's conscious experiencing or not very far from their awareness. Both approaches, however, rely on the use of empathy. In the case of the Tavistock consultant this empathy is aimed at the group-as-a-whole and at individual members of the group since the latter will be assumed to contain feelings that are significant indicators of what is going on the entire group. The person-centered approach focuses on empathic responses to the individual absent the idea that this phenomenology may have isomorphisms with the group-as-a-whole. The Tavistock or group-as-a-whole approach thus offers trainees an opportunity to exercise binocular vision in a number of ways. They become trained in the twin views of the group through manifest and latent content—the discourse of the group and its potential for hidden meanings. They also become trained in the twin views of the group as an assemblage of unique individual responses and as a manifestation of a complex, ever-shifting "group mentality." The employment of such a flexible array of explanatory templates is, we believe enormously beneficial to students of mental health since it adds to the precision of their insights. The empathic attunement is thus expanded to include not only individuals but also groups and institutions. Such "horizon broadening" impacts are close to the idea of the expansion of the "hermeneutic function" described by Hazell (2003).

An important element of group-as-a-whole theory is that systems are nested. The individual, the therapeutic dyad, the group, the treatment team all exist in a psychosocial context and have exchanges across their boundaries that influence them. Training in the Tavistock tradition helps students become acutely aware of these processes that involve such dynamics as organizational mirroring, identification and all the items on the FABART checklist. These features can create health-promoting or psycho-toxic environments. Such processes are described in relation to medical practices in Hazell and Perez (2011). Frequently these dynamics are unnoticed and can impede the therapeutic process or even have anti-therapeutic effects. Tavistock training, especially if there is a component that involves the application of that which is learned to other contexts can have very beneficial impacts on these contextual factors in institutions aimed at promoting mental health.

The group-as-a-whole approach is an interdisciplinary one and this, we believe is one of its strengths. It is quite possible, when operating in a "Tavistock environment" to deploy concepts from neighboring disciplines such as political science, sociology, anthropology, management, organizational psychology, history, physiology, philosophy in its many facets and theology. This we believe is a healthy moment, since it is horizon-broadening and encourages creativity in the understanding of human predicaments. In perusing the literature, in an impressionistic way we conclude that psychology as a discipline has been recruited by the above-mentioned disciplines far more than has been the other way around. This has established psychology as something of a closed system to its terrible detriment. Closed systems do not grow well and tend towards entropy, disorganization, and randomness. The Tavistock approach, as an open system, counters this unfortunate tendency.

Major developments seem to be occurring in the fields of interpersonal neuropsychology that show that the social interactions we have with others have powerful influences on our mental health (Chapman, 2014; Leiberman, 2013; van der Kolk, 2015), not to mention our physical health (Daruna, 2004). The Tavistock approach which focuses so intensely on social contextual factors is perfectly aligned with these discoveries. The student who is well trained in the group-as-a-whole approach will be ready to link up with the latest findings regarding the impact of social interactions on neurohormones, psychological well-being, and psychoneuroimmunology.

One way of characterizing maturity in the human being is the capacity to think and feel at the same time. It is also perhaps the quality found in an effective leader, one who is in emotional contact with the group and yet is able, at the same time, to think about what is going on and what needs to be done. The Tavistock experience can be an excellent medium for developing this capacity in anyone. It is an especially vital quality for any would-be psychotherapist or counselor. In a Tavistock group, the passions can run high as unconscious ideation is brought to the surface. At the same time the intellect is robustly engaged. The dictum seems to be, "Let us have these feelings and let us also examine them, not just as they occur in the individual, but also in the group-as-a-whole." Exposure to this culture seems to be of inestimable value to the trainee counselor who will be working with individuals, families, groups, and institutions suffering extreme passions with which they needs must resonate but about which they must also think.

# Notes on an uncertain future

We hope it is apparent that both traditional Tavistock theory and practice as well as the extrapolations and augmentations posited in this book capture our passion, belief, and utility for the paradigm. The concepts collectively at the center of the model—projective identification, group-as-a-whole analysis, repository functioning, and social defenses—serve as a Swiss Army knife or multi-tool that is indispensable for our work as psychologists, for our functioning as people and are necessary for our understanding of the groups, cultures, and societies we find ourselves part of. Rarely does a psychotherapy session, class, meeting at work or family get together go by without dimensions of the model coming to the aid of understanding interactions, either mundane or extraordinary. The model guides us as people, professionals, and citizens trying to make sense of the world around us.

This all said, it would be disingenuous to not speak of pessimism. At a time where Tavistock theory and application could be more relevant than ever, the world at large and the psychology profession specifically, appear less and less interested and motivated to utilize the Tavistock tool set.

Consider the geo-political landscape. Upon publication, inter-group collaboration and interdependence is strained, be it the European Union and mass immigration, NATO and the unrest and civil war in Syria and the "Middle East" or the G8 and matters of global warming and "third world" economic aid and development. Matters of boundaries and territory are challenged via armed conflict and aggression, be it Russia's annexation of Crimea or China building islands to lay claim to contested waterways. Scapegoating and out-grouping at a massive scale is occurring, most notably in Europe with Muslims and in the U.S. with a long simmering race dynamic between largely white power structures and a largely black and marginalized aspect of the population. Literal colonization and appropriation of nations and resources in Africa and South America are replaced by economic and industrial colonization. Reliable leadership structures for many countries in the "Middle East" were dismantled by war and unrest, or never given the attention and resources to adequately develop—leaving lawlessness, struggling governments, civil war as well as rigid theocracies in the wake. In the U.S., the political landscape is as partisan and divided as it has been over the last forty years—easily identified as fuel by psycho-dramatic enactments rather than rational impetuses.

Also consider the post-industrial/virtual communication era much of the world is currently involved in and where social media and online representation and communication is the standard form of interaction in "Industrial Nations." From list-serves to online forums to social media communications, new forms of enactments, psycho-dramatic engagements and communications as well as distortions and misrepresentations are taking place. Attempts to do sophisticated work using these mechanisms and forums are uneven, often ineffective or at least cumbersome as often as not. This rich and evolving resource needs the degree of attention, investigation, and study other social systems have received.

Perhaps related to the matter above, in part, the phenomena of repository activation for extreme acts also litters the landscape. Whereas it would be naïve to consider the phenomena "new" (and equally naïve to under-consider other contributing factors), previously inoculated or safeguarded repositories are activated in incredibly damaging fashions. This includes the increase of mass shooters in the United States, the radicalization and activation of previously atypical recruiting targets to terrorist causes, the proliferation and increased participation in extremist groups and movements both in the "East" and "West" in political systems as well as without.

The examples could go on and on ...

Professionally, there are reasons for pessimism as well.

In the U.S., three major trends over the past fifty years have served to undermine the utility, application, and progress of psychosocial models like that of the Tavistock methodology:

First—the study and practice of group dynamics, especially by clinical psychologists, has slowly eroded since a high point in the 1970s (Leddick, 2011).

Second—the formal and informal redefinition of clinical psychology as "evidence based," anchored more and more by a "medical" model of disease and wellness and with a narrowing of focus to individuals' psychopathology (Wampold, 2001).

Third—the decreased participation of psychologists and psychosocial specialists from policy making and the larger social discussions (Jason, 2013).

We can't help but compare Kenneth and Mamie Clark's serving as expert witnesses in one of the cases included in *Brown vs. Board of Education* (1954), John Bowlby writing the *World Health Organization*'s report on the mental health of homeless children in post-war Europe (1951) or Donald Winnicott giving 600-plus talks on the BBC on child rearing practices to the APA's involvement with the U.S. Government as reported by David Hoffman and colleagues submitted *the Independent Review Relating to APA Ethics Guidelines, National Security Interrogations, and Torture* (2015).

To add to the profession-based pessimism, Group Relations in the U.S. specifically is mostly relegated to educational domains, as an instrument for training mental health professionals in specific programs or locations. The absence of a stronger applied arm (like the National Training Labs Institute or the Tavistock Institute) is limiting. And to a large degree it appears, consciously or not, that the U.S. "group relations community" has remained conflicted about changing this status quo—on one hand collectively rejecting too much innovation or change and on the other hand, using mechanisms of self–authorization to promote new initiatives without wide ranging institutional-authority or collective support.

Even the experience of submitting this book for publication was met with a discouraging sentiment as several publishers basically said the idea was great or worthy of publication but that there was little audience for the topic (… and then referred us to Karnac).

## Ending themes

In music, the coda traditionally gives a feeling of closure, usually by reminding the listener of the major themes and motifs in the work and by returning to the tonic chord, home base, as it were. This work does not lend itself to such a conventional ending. Musically, the parallel is in line with modern and postmodern pieces, such as Ives' "Unanswered Question" where, despite multiple responses to the offstage trumpets' questions, no definitive answer is arrived at by the flutes and we are left with a chorus of the ages, unending, unresolved.

There is, however, a unifying theme. It is that of the open system. Throughout this text and in its title, there has been a continual return to the theme of cross-fertilization of the basic ideas of the Tavistock approach with ideas from other paradigms. We hope that we have demonstrated that this hybridization can be done in such a way that useful fruit is borne forth and that the utility and vibrancy of the original tenets of the Tavistock tradition are maintained.

This coda also points forward. We believe that since this cross-fertilization has proven useful in these pages and elsewhere, such practice is worthy of continuation. Other paradigms exist that would be worthy of integration into the Tavistock model. The Jungian system, management theories, political science, spirituality, and decision-making theory, for example, would all seem to be good candidates for exploration and integration.

Such integrative activity is not a simple intellectual exercise aimed at improving and enriching the practice of Tavistock groups, for we believe that these times in the world are especially trying and dangerous. We see that precious little of the knowledge developed in the Tavistock tradition over the decades of its existence has been applied to the resolution of these pressing problems and crises. This is especially true at the level of the community, state, international relations, and the planet. We therefore believe that the further integration of the Tavistock approach with other related paradigms will help to show its relevance to a very wide array of situations while also spreading the word of its utility.

The Tavistock approach is challenging but its demands yield insight and knowledge that can be brought to bear in most productive ways upon problems and issues ranging in scale from the individual to the global. It is an under-utilized methodology. We hope that this text will in some way, however small, encourage the creative deployment and use of this valuable method.

# REFERENCES

Adorno, T. (1983). *The Authoritarian Personality*. New York, NY: W. W. Norton.

Adorno, T. (2001). *The Culture Industry: Selected Essays on Mass Culture*. London: Routledge.

Agamben, G. (1993). *The Coming Community*. Minneapolis: University of Minnesota Press.

Alford, C. (2002). *Whistleblowers: Broken Lives and Organizational Power*. London: Cornell University Press.

Allport, G. (1955). *Becoming, Basic Considerations for a Psychology of Personality*. New Haven, CT: Yale.

Argyris, C., & Schon, D. (1995). *Organizational Learning II: Theory, Method and Practice*. Upper Saddle River, NJ: FT Press.

Austin, J. (1953). How to talk—some simple ways. *Proceedings of the Aristotelian Society*, 53: 227–246.

Austrian, S. (2008). *Developmental Theories Through the Life Cycle*. New York, NY: Columbia University Press.

Baburoglu, O. (1988). Vortical environment the fifth in the Emery Trist levels of organizational environment. *Human Relations*, 41: 181–210.

Badiou, A. (2013). *Being and Event*. London: Bloomsbury Academic.

Bahktin, M. (1982). *The Dialogic Imagination: Four Essays*. Austin, TX: University of Texas Press.

251

Baron-Cohen, S. (2012). *The Science of Evil: On Empathy and the Origins of Cruelty*. New York, NY: Basic.

Bataille, G. (1991). *The Accursed Share: An Essay on General Economy, Vol 1: Consumption*. Cambridge, MA: Zone Books.

Becker, E. (1997). *The Denial of Death*, New York, NY: Free Press.

Beckett, S. (1982). *Waiting for Godot: A Tragicomedy in Two Acts*. New York, NY: Grove Press.

Berman, M. (1988). *All That is Solid Melts into Air: The Experience of Modernity*. New York, NY: Penguin.

Berne, E. (1996). *Games People Play: The Basic Handbook of Transactional Analysis*. New York, NY: Ballantine Books.

Bion, W. R. (1959). *Second Thoughts*. London: Heinemann.

Bion, W. R. (1961). *Experiences in Groups*. London: Tavistock.

Bion, W. R. (1978). *Seven Servants: Four Works*. New York, NY: Jason Aronson.

Bion, W. R. (1997). *Taming Wild Thoughts*. London: Karnac.

Birdwhistell, R. (1970). *Kinesics and Context*. Philadelphia, PA: University of Pennsylvania Press.

Blanchot, M. (1988). *The Unavowable Community*. Barrytown, NY: Station Hill Press.

Blanchot, M. (1998). *Death Sentence*. Barrytown, NY: Station Hill Press.

Bowlby, J. (1951). *Maternal Care and Mental Health: A Report Prepared on Behalf of the World Health Organization as a Contribution to the United Nations Programme for the Welfare of Homeless Children*. Geneva: World Health Organization.

Breuer, J., & Freud, S. (2000/1885). *Studies on Hysteria*. New York, NY: Basic. (Reissue edition).

Burke, K. (1945). *A Grammar of Motives*. London: University of California Press.

Cannon, W. B. (1942). Voodoo death. *American Anthropologist, 44*: 169–181.

Chapman, L. (2014). *Neurobiologically Informed Trauma Therapy with Children and Adolescents*. New York, NY: Norton.

Chase, D. (Dir.). (1997–2007). *The Sopranos*. USA: HBO Cable Network.

Chasseguet-Smirgel, J. (1985). *The Ego Ideal: A Psychoanalytic Essay on the Malady of the Ideal*. London: Free Association Books.

Clynes, M. (1989). *Sentics: The Touch of the Emotions*. New York, NY: Prism Press.

Colman, A., & Geller, W. (Eds.). (1985). Group *Relations Reader 2*. Washington, DC: A. K. Rice Institute.

Czochara, B., Semmelhack, D., & Hazell, C. (2016). "We need each other," adapting the Tavistock method for large group therapy for adults with severe mental illness. *International Journal of Psychosocial Rehabilitation, 20*:

Daruna, J. (2004). *Introduction to Psychoneuroimmunology*. Burlington, MA: Elsevier.

De Loach, S. (2009). The Institutional System Event (ISE): Design and Management. Unpublished Manuscript.

De Mare, P. (2011). *From Hate Through Dialogue to Culture in the Larger Group*. London: Karnac.

Derrida, J. (1982). *Margins of Philosophy*. Chicago, IL: University of Chicago Press.

Dewey, J. (1998). *The Essential Dewey*, Volume 2. Bloomington, IN: Indiana University Press.

Eagleton, T. (2008). *Literary Theory: An Introduction*. Minneapolis, MN: University of Minnesota Press.

Edelson, M. (1970). *Sociotherapy and Psychotherapy*. Chicago: University of Chicago Press.

Ellenberger, H. (1981). *The Discovery of the Unconscious*. New York, NY: Basic.

Ellul, J. (1967). *The Technological Society*. New York, NY: Vintage Books.

Emery, F., & Trist, E. (1965). The causal texture of organizational environments. *Human Relations, 18*: 21–32.

Empson, W. (1966). *Seven Types of Ambiguity*. New York, NY: New Directions.

Ende, L., Semmelhack, D., Hazell, C., Freeman, A., Barron, C. (2015). *The Interactive World of Severe Mental Illness: Case Histories of the U.S. Mental Health System*. New York, NY: Routledge.

Erikson, E. (1993). *Childhood and Society*. New York, NY: W. W. Norton.

Fairbairn, W. R. D. (1952). *Psychoanalytic Studies of the Personality*. London: Routledge.

Ferenczi, S. (1995). *The Clinical Diary of Sandor Ferenczi*. Cambridge, MA: Harvard University Press.

Fisher, J. *Body Oriented Trauma Therapy*, (video). Nevada City, CA: Cavalcade Productions Inc.

Foucault, M. (1980). *History of Sexuality, Volume 1*. New York, NY: Vintage.

Fowler, H. (1908). *The King's English*. Oxford: Clarendon Press

Fowler, H. (1926). *A Dictionary of Modern English*. Oxford: Oxford University Press.

Franzen, T. (2005). *Godel's Theorem, An Incomplete Guide to its Use and Abuse*. Wellesley, MA: A. K. Peters.

Freud, A. (1965). *Normality and Pathology in Childhood*. New York, NY: International Universities Press.

Freud, S. (1900). The interpretation of dreams. In: J. Strachey (Ed. and Trans.), *The Standard Edition of the Complete Psychological Works of Sigmund Freud*. London: Hogarth Press.

Freud, S. (1901). The psychopathology of everyday life. In: J. Strachey (Ed. and Trans.), *The Standard Edition of the Complete Psychological Works of Sigmund Freud* (Vol. 6). London: Hogarth Press.

Freud, S. (1905). Jokes and their relation to the unconscious. In: J. Strachey (Ed. and Trans.), *The Standard Edition of the Complete Psychological Works of Sigmund Freud* (Vol. 8). London: Hogarth Press.

Freud, S. (1911). Psychoanalytic notes on an autobiographical account of a case of paranoia (dementia paranoides). In: J. Strachey (Ed. and Trans.), *The Standard Edition of the Complete Psychological Works of Sigmund Freud* (Vol. 12). London: Hogarth Press.

Freud, S. (1912–1913). Totem and taboo. In: J. Strachey (Ed. and Trans.), *The Standard Edition of the Complete Psychological Works of Sigmund Freud* (Vol. 13). London: Hogarth Press.

Freud, S. (1916–1917). Introductory lectures on psychoanalysis. In: J. Strachey (Ed. and Trans.), *The Standard Edition of the Complete Psychological Works of Sigmund Freud* (Vol. 15–16). London: Hogarth Press.

Freud, S. (1921). Group psychology and the analysis of the ego. In: J. Strachey (Ed. and Trans.), *The Standard Edition of the Complete Psychological Works of Sigmund Freud* (Vol. 18). London: Hogarth Press.

Freud, S. (1927). The ego and the id. In: J. Strachey (Ed. and Trans.), *The Standard Edition of the Complete Psychological Works of Sigmund Freud* (Vol. 19). London: Hogarth Press.

Freud, S. (1928). The future of an illusion. In: J. Strachey (Ed. and Trans.), *The Standard Edition of the Complete Psychological Works of Sigmund Freud* (Vol. 21). London: Hogarth Press.

Fukuyama, F. F. (2006). *The End of History and the Last Man.* New York, NY: Free Press.

Ganzerain, R. (1989). *Object Relations Group Psychotherapy: Group as an Object, a Tool, and a Training Base.* New York, NY: Guilford Press.

Gedo, J., & Goldberg, A. (1976). *Models of the Mind.* Chicago and London: University of Chicago Press.

Gibb, J. (1964). Climate for trust formation. In: L. Bradford, J. Gibb, & K. Benne (eds.), *T-Group Theory* and the *Laboratory Method* (pp. 279–310). New York, NY: Wiley and Sons.

Gleick, J. (1987). *Chaos: Making a New Science.* New York, NY: Viking Publishing.

Gordon, W. (1969). *Synectics: The Development of Creative Capacity.* New York, NY: Collier-Macmillan.

Gould, L. (Ed.). (2006). *The Systems Psychodynamics of Organizations: Integrating the Group Relations Approach and Organizational Systems Perspective.* London: Karnac.

Grotstein, J. (1977). *Splitting and Projective Identification.* New York, NY: Jason Aronson.

Guntrip, H. (1992). *Schizoid Phenomena, Object Relations and the Self.* London, Karnac.

Harrison, E. F. (1998). *The Managerial Decision-Making Process.* Cincinnati, OH: South Western College Publishing.

Harrison, O. (2008). *Open Space Technology: A User's Guide, (3rd ed.).* Oakland, CA: Berret Kohler.

Harrison, T. (2000). *Bion, Rickman, Foulkes and the Northfield Experiments.* London: Jessica Kingsley Publishers.

Hazell, C. (1984). Experienced levels of emptiness and existential concern with different levels of emotional development and profile of values. *Psychological Reports, 55:* 967–976.

Hazell, C. (2003). *The Experience of Emptiness.* Bloomington, IN: Author House.

Hazell, C. (2005). *Imaginary Groups.* Bloomington, IN: AuthorHouse.

Hazell, C. (2006). *Family Systems Activity Book.* Bloomington, IN: AuthorHouse.

Hazell, C. (2009). *Alterity: The Experience of the Other.* Bloomington, IN: AuthorHouse.

Hazell, C., & Perez, R. (2011). *What Happens When You Touch the Body?: The Psychology of Body-Work.* Bloomington, IN: AuthorHouse.

Hegel, G. W. F. (1977). *The Phenomenology of Spirit.* Oxford: Oxford University Press.

Heidegger, M. (1988). *Hegel's Phenomenology of Spirit.* Bloomington and Indianapolis: Indiana University Press.

Heidegger, M. (2008). *Being and Time.* New York, NY: Harper Perennial.

Herman, J. (2015). *Trauma and Recovery.* New York, NY: Basic Books.

Hill, W. F. (1965). *Hill Interaction Matrix.* University of Southern California, Los Angeles, CA: Youth Study Center.

Hirschorn, L. (1990). *The Workplace Within.* Cambridge, MA: MIT Press.

Hoeller, S. (2012). *The Gnostic Jung and the Seven Sermons to the Dead.* Wheaton, IL: Quest Books.

Hoffman, D. H., Carter, D. J., Lopez, C. R.V., Benzmiller, H. L., Guo, A. X., Latifi, S. Y., & Craig, D. C. (2015). Report to the special committee of the board of directors of the American Psychological Association: Independent review relating to APA ethics guidelines, national security interrogations, and torture. Chicago, IL: Sidley Austin LLP.

Hofstede, G. (2010). *Cultures and Organizations.* New York, NY; McGraw-Hill.

Hopper, E. (2003). *Traumatic Experience in the Unconscious Life of Groups: The Fourth Basic Assumption: Incohesion: Aggregation/Massification or (ba) I:A/M.* London: Jessica Kingsley Publishers.

Janet, P. (1889/1973). *L'automatisme Psychologique: essai de psychologie experimentale sur les formes inferieures de l'activite humaine.* Paris: Felix Alcan, 1889. Societe Pierre Janet/Payot, 1973.

Jason, L. (2013). *Principles of Social Change.* Oxford: Oxford University Press.

Johnson, S. (2001). *Emergence: The Connected Lives of Ants, Brains, Software, Cities and Software.* New York, NY: Scribner.

Jones, M. (1968). *Beyond the Therapeutic Community.* London: Yale University Press.

Jones, M. (1976). *Maturation of the Therapeutic Community.* New York, NY: Human Sciences Press.

Joyce, J. (1999). *Finnegan's Wake.* New York, NY: Penguin Classics.

Jung, C. G. (1966). *Two Essays on Analytic Psychology.* New York, NY: Routledge.

Jung, C. G. (1970). *Analytical Psychology: Its Theory and Practice (The Tavistock Lectures).* London: Vintage.

Jung, C. G. (1977). *Mysterium Coniunctionis.* Princeton, NJ: Princeton University Press.

Kafka, F. (1926a). *Das Schloss.* Munchen: Kurt Wolff Verlag.

Kafka, F. (1926b). *Der Prozess.* Berlin: Verlag die Schmeide.

Keats, J. (1899). *The Complete Poetical Works and Letters of John Keats.* Cambridge Edition, Boston, MA: Houghton, Mifflin and Company.

Kernberg, O. (1994). *Internal World and External Reality.* New York, NY: Jason Aronson.

Khan, M. (1996). *The Privacy of the Self.* London: Karnac.

Kierkegaard, S. (1843a). *Fear and Trembling.* Princeton, NJ: Princeton University Press.

Kierkegaard, S. (1843b). Journals IV A 164.

Klein, M. (1975). *Envy and Gratitude and Other Works 1946–1963,* New York, NY: Free Press.

Koestler, A. (1967). *The Act of Creation, a Study of the Conscious and the Unconscious in Science and Art.* New York, NY: Dell.

Kohut, H. (1971). *The Analysis of the Self.* Chicago and London: University of Chicago Press.

Kohut, H. (1977). *The Restoration of the Self.* New York, NY: International Universities Press.

Kojeve, A. (1980). *Introduction to the Reading of Hegel: Lectures on the Phenomenology of Spirit, Ithaca.* New York, NY: Cornell University Press.

Kreeger, L. (Ed.). (1975). *The Large Group: Dynamics and Therapy.* London: Constable.

Kristeva, J. (1984). *Revolution in Poetic Language.* New York, NY: Columbia University Press.

Lacan, J. (1981). *The Four Fundamental Concepts of Psychoanalysis.* New York, NY: W. W. Norton.

Lacan, J. (1990). *Television: A Challenge to the Psychoanalytic Establishment.* New York, NY: Norton.

Lacan, J. (1991). *Seminar Two.* J. A. Miller (Trans.). New York, NY: W. W. Norton.

Lacan, J. (1997). *The Seminar of Jacques Lacan: The Psychoses.* New York, NY: W. W. Norton.

Lacan, J. (2007a). *The Seminar of Jacques Lacan: The Other Side of Psychoanalysis.* New York, NY: W. W. Norton.

Lacan, J. (2007b). *Ecrits: The First Complete Edition in English.* New York, NY: W. W. Norton.

Laing, R. D. (1965). *The Divided Self: An Existential Study in Sanity and Madness.* London: Penguin.

Langs, R. (1979). *The Listening Process.* New York, NY: Jason Aronson.

Lawrence, W. G. (2003). *Experiences in Social Dreaming.* London: Karnac.

LeBon, G. (2002). *The Crowd: A Study of the Popular Mind.* Mineola, NY: Dover Publications.

Lecky, P. (1969). *Self Consistency: A Theory of Personality.* New York, NY: Anchor Books.

Leddick, G. (2011). *Oxford Handbook of Group Counseling.* Oxford: Oxford University Press.

Levinas, E. (1969). *Totality and Infinity.* Pittsburgh, PA: Duquesne University Press.

Levinas, E. (2005). *Humanism of the Other.* Champaign, IL: University of Illinois Press.

Levine, P. *Resolving Trauma in Psychotherapy: A Somatic Approach* (video). Mill Valley, CA: Psychotherapy.net.

Levine, P. (2010). *In an Unspoken Voice: How the Body Releases Trauma and Restores Goodness.* Berkeley, CA: North Atlantic.

Lieberman, M. (2013). *Social: Why Our Brains are Wired to Connect.* New York, NY: Random House.

Lipgar, R., & Pines, M. (2002). *Building on Bion: Branches.* London: Jessica Kingsley Publishers.

Lorraine Schroeder, J. (2008). *The Four Lacanian Discourses Or Turning the Law Inside Out.* Abingdon, Oxon: Birkbeck Law Press.

Lowen, A. (1972). *Depression and the Body.* New York, NY: Penguin.

Lowen, A. (2003). *Fear of Life.* Alachua, FL: Bioenergetics Press.

Lowen, A. (2005). *Betrayal of the Body.* Alachua, FL: Bioenergetics Press.

Lowen, A. (2012). *The Language of the Body.* New York, NY: The Alexander Lowen Foundation.

Madigan, S. (2010). *Narrative Therapy*. Washington, DC: American Psychological Association.

Mahler, M. (1975). *The Psychological Birth of the Human Infant*. New York, NY: Basic.

Marcuse, H. (1991). *One Dimensional Man: Studies in Ideology of Advanced Industrial Society*. Boston, MA: Beacon Press.

Marx, K. (1965). (T. B. Bottomore & E. Fromm Eds.). *Marx's Concept of Man; Marx's Economic and Philosophic Manuscripts*. New York, NY: Frederick Ungar.

Maslow, A. (2013). *A Theory of Human Motivation*. Eastford, CT: Martino Fine Books.

McGinn, R. E. (1990). *Science, Technology and Society*. New York, NY: Pearson.

Menzies-Lyth, I. (1960). A case in the functioning of social systems as a defense against anxiety: a report of a study of a nursing service in a general hospital. *Human Relations, 13*: 95–121.

Meyers, N. (Dir.). (2000). *What Women Want*. Los Angeles, CA: Paramount Pictures.

Minuchin, S. (1978). *Psychosomatic Families: Anorexia Nervosa in Context*. Cambridge, MA: Harvard University Press.

Nancy, J.-L. (1991). *Inoperative Community*. Minneapolis, MN: University of Minnesota Press.

Obholzer, R., & Roberts, A. V. (1994). *The Unconscious at Work*. New York, NY: Routledge.

Parsons, T. (1971). *System of Modern Societies*. Upper Saddle River, NJ: Prentice Hall.

Perls, F. (1965). *Gestalt Therapy Verbatim*. Lafayette, CA: Real People Press.

Perls, F. (1973). *The Gestalt Approach and Eyewitness to Therapy*. New York, NY: Bantam.

Perry, W. (1981). Cognitive and ethical growth: the making of meaning. In: *Arthur W. Chickering and Associates, The Modern American College* (pp. 76–116). San Francisco: Jossey Bass.

Piaget, J., & Inhelder, B. (1969). *The Psychology of the Child*. New York, NY: Basic Books.

Polanyi, M. (1957). *The Great Transformation: The Political and Economic Origins of Our Time*. Boston, MA: Beacon Press.

Polanyi, M. (1974). *Personal Knowledge: Towards a Post-Critical Philosophy*. Chicago and London: University of Chicago Press.

Ramis, H. (Dir.). (2002). *Analyze That*. US: Village Roadshow Pictures, Warner Brothers.

Rank, O. (1954, 2014). *The Trauma of Birth*. London: Routledge.

Redl, F. (1967). *When We Deal With Children: Selected Writings*. New York, NY: Free Press.

Reich, W. (1980a). *The Mass Psychology of Fascism*. New York, NY: Farrar, Strauss and Giroux.

Reich, W. (1980b). *Character Analysis*. New York, NY: Farrar, Strauss and Giroux.

Rice, A. K. (2013). *Learning for Leadership*. London: Routledge.

Rorty, R. (2000). *Philosophy and Social Hope*. New York, NY: Penguin.

Rorty, R. (2009). *Philosophy and the Mirror of Nature*. Princeton, NJ: Princeton.

Rosenfeld, H. (1985). *Psychotic States: A Psychoanalytic Approach (Maresfield Library)*. London: Karnac.

Rosenfeld, H. (1987). *Impasse and Interpretation: Therapeutic and Antitherapeutic Factors in the Psychoanalytic Treatment of Psychotic, Borderline and Neurotic Patients (The New Library of Psychoanalysis)*. London: Routledge.

Sacks, O. (1998). *The Man Who Mistook His Wife For A Hat: And Other Clinical Tales*. New York, NY: Touchstone.

Sartre, J. P. (1993). *Being and Nothingness*. New York, NY: Washington Square Press.

Sartre, J. P. (2004). *Critique of Dialectical Reason*. London: Verso.

Seikkula, J., & Arnkil, T. (2006). *Dialogical Meetings in Social Networks*. London: Karnac.

Seligman, M. (1992). *Helplessness: On Depression, Development, and Death (Series of Books in Psychology)*. New York, NY: W. H. Freeman and Company.

Selye, H. (1978). *The Stress of Life*. New York, NY: McGraw Hill.

Semmelhack, D., Ende, L., & Hazell, C. (2013). *Group Therapy for Adults with Severe Mental Illness: Adapting the Tavistock Method*. New York, NY: Routledge.

Semmelhack, D., Ende, L., Hazell, C. G., & Freeman, A. (2015). *The Interactive World of Severe Mental Illness: Case Studies in the U.S. Mental Health System*. New York, NY: Routledge.

Seuss, Dr. (1954). *Horton Hears a Who*. New York, NY: Random House Books.

Shengold, L. (1991). *Soul Murder: The Effects of Childhood Abuse and Deprivation*. Yale University: Ballantine Books.

Stern, D. (2000). *The Interpersonal World of the Infant: A View From Psychoanalysis and Developmental Psychology*. New York, NY: Basic Books.

Sullivan, H. (1953). *The Interpersonal Theory of Psychiatry*. New York, NY: Norton Publishing.

Tillich, P. (1952). *The Courage to Be*. New Haven, CT: Yale.

Trist, E., & Bamforth, K. (1951). Some social and psychological consequences of the longwall method of coal getting. *Human Relations, 4*: 3–38.

Tuckman, B. (1965). Developmental sequence in small groups. *Psychological Bulletin, 63*: 384–399.

Tustin, F. (1972). *Autism and Childhood Psychoses*. London: Hogarth.

Unamuno, M. de (2015). *Tragic Sense of Life*. Mineola, NY: Macmillan and Company Ltd.

Van der Kolk, B. (2015). *The Body Keeps the Score*. New York, NY: Penguin.

Volkan, V. (2014). *Psychoanalysis, International Relations, and Diplomacy: A Sourcebook on Large-Group Psychology*. London: Karnac.

Wampold, B. (2001). *The Great Psychotherapy Debate*. Mahwah, New Jersey: Lawrence Earbaum Associates, Inc.

Watzlawick, P., Bavelas, J., & Jackson, D. (1967). *Pragmatics of Human Communication: A Study of Interactional Patterns, Pathologies, and Paradoxes*. New York, NY: W. W. Norton.

Wells, L. (1985). The group-as-a-whole perspective and its theoretical roots. In: A. D. Colman & M. H. Geller (Eds.), *Group Relations Reader 2* (pp. 109–126). Washington, DC: A. K. Rice Institute.

Winnicott, D. W. (1965). *The Maturational Processes and the Facilitating Environment*. New York, NY: International Universities Press.

Woodhead, L., & Greenspan, B. (Dir.). (1999). *Endurance*. Los Angeles, CA: Walt Disney Pictures.

Woolf, V. (1978). *The Waves*. Arlington Heights, IL: Harvest Books.

Woolf, V. (1990). *Mrs Dalloway*. New York, NY: Mariner Books.

Yalom, I., & Leszcz, M. (2005). *The Theory and Practice of Group Psychotherapy*. New York, NY: Basic Books.

Žižek, S. (1993). *Tarrying with the Negative: Kant, Hegel and the Critique of Ideology* (Post Contemporary Interventions). Durham, NC: Duke University Press.

Žižek, S. (2012). *Enjoy Your Symptom! Jacques Lacan In Hollywood and Out*. New York, NY: Routledge.

# INDEX